THE BODY HISPANIC

EMBLEMA. 64

Soy hic, & hæc, & hoc. Yo me declaro,
Soy varon, soy muger, soy vn tercero,
Que no es vno ni otro, ni está claro
Qual destas cosas sea. Soy terrero
De los q̃ como a mõstro horrẽdo y raro,
Me tienen por siniestro, y mal aguero.
Aduierta cada qual q̃ me ha mirado,
Que es otro yo, si viue afeminado.

Cũ

The bearded lady: an emblem of androgyny (see pp. 9 and 17). From
Sebastián de Covarrubias Orozco, *Emblemas morales* (Madrid, 1610). By
permission of the British Library.

The Body Hispanic

Gender and Sexuality
in Spanish and
Spanish American Literature

PAUL JULIAN SMITH

CLARENDON PRESS · OXFORD

Oxford University Press, Walton Street, Oxford OX2 6DP

Oxford New York Toronto
Delhi Bombay Calcutta Madras Karachi
Petaling Jaya Singapore Hong Kong Tokyo
Nairobi Dar es Salaam Cape Town
Melbourne Auckland

and associated companies in
Berlin Ibadan

Oxford is a trade mark of Oxford University Press

Published in the United States
by Oxford University Press, New York

© Paul Julian Smith 1989

First published 1989
First issued in paperback 1992

British Library Cataloguing in Publication Data
Smith, Paul Julian
The Body Hispanic: Gender and
Sexuality in Spanish and Spanish
American Literature
1. Spanish literature to 1988.
Special subjects. Sexuality. Critical
Studies
I. Title
860.9'353
ISBN 0-19-815874-2

Library of Congress Cataloging in Publication Data
Data available

Printed in Great Britain by
Book Craft (Bath) Ltd.
Midsomer Norton, Avon

PREFACE

THIS book is not a history of sexuality in Hispanic literature, but an attempt to introduce an awareness of the latest theoretical debates on sexuality into Hispanism. To that end it gives accounts of a number of different theories and relates them to readings of specific literary texts. Although there are links between chapters (both thematic and theoretical), each chapter is written in such a way that it may be read on its own, without knowledge of the others. Hence the broadly chronological order in which the literary texts are treated implies no historical narrative or teleological imperative. Likewise I have not attempted to smooth out any contradictions between the various theoretical positions which I adopt in turn. Indeed, it would be improper to do so in a book which seeks to promote difference and unsettle homogeneity.

Although Hispanists have not made any systematic application of theory to the question of sexuality, there have indeed been a number of empirical or polemical contributions by them to women's or gay studies.[1] In addition, Jean Franco is about to publish a study which reads Latin American women writers in the light of French feminists, such as Irigaray. Anne Elizabeth Jones has recently submitted a Ph.D. thesis 'Representation and Luis Britto García's *Rajatabla*' (Nottingham, 1988) which reveals a thoroughly assimilated knowledge of deconstruction, psychoanalysis, and theoretical feminism. Most of the theoretical texts to which I referred in the original French have now been translated into English and Spanish, and this will no doubt facilitate a broader awareness of their importance.

Over the last four years I have attended lectures and seminars (often at the Institute of Contemporary Arts, London) by a number of women working in the interrelated fields of feminism, psychoanalysis, film theory, and the visual arts: Michèle Barrett, Rosalind Coward, Elizabeth Cowie, Jane Gallop, Luce Irigaray, Cora Kaplan, Mary Kelly, Toril

[1] I would like to draw attention to the work of North American scholars such as Rupert C. Allen, Daniel Eisenberg, and James Mandrell in this context.

Moi, Naomi Segal, Morag Shiach, and Elizabeth Wright. Those who are not cited in the footnotes have no doubt left their trace in my text. I would also like to thank Dr Jonathan Romney for twelve years of discussions on literature, theory, and film. My greatest intellectual debt, however, is to the French department in Queen Mary College under the headship of Professor Malcolm Bowie, and in particular to Dr Margaret Whitford, specialist in feminist philosophy. My thanks are also due to members of the Spanish department during the period the book was written: Professor O. N. V. Glendinning, Miss L. E. Ingamells, and Dr I. Vázquez de Castro.[2]

Most of the literary texts treated here are ones I have taught in QMC (although students may not recognize my readings of them). Versions of much of the material in the book were read as lectures or seminars between 1984 and 1988 at the following institutions: Chapter 1, Darwin College and New Hall, Cambridge; St Peter's College, Oxford; Chapter 2, the French Research Seminars of QMC and Cambridge; the Annual Conference of the Association of Hispanists of Great Britain and Ireland (Leeds, 1985); Chapter 4, New Hall, Cambridge; Universities of Leeds, Nottingham, and St Andrews; Chapter 5, Institute of Latin American Studies and Westfield College, London; New Hall, Cambridge; Chapter 6, ILAS and QMC, London; Universities of Nottingham, Pittsburgh, and Columbia (New York City).

Early versions of Chapters 1 and 2 were published in *MLN* 102 (1987), 220–40, and *PMLA* 101 (1986), 82–94. I am grateful to the editors of these journals for permission to reproduce this material in revised and expanded form.

London, 1988   P.J.S.

---

[2] I would also like to thank the following Hispanists for bibliographical help: Jean Franco, Stephen Hart, William Rowe, and Geraldine Scanlon.

CONTENTS

ABBREVIATIONS

The following abbreviations have been used both in the footnotes and the bibliography:

AG	*Anales galdosianos*
ALEC	*Anales de la literatura española contemporánea*
BHS	*Bulletin of Hispanic Studies*
CQ	*Critical Quarterly*
FMLS	*Forum for Modern Language Studies*
GLR	*García Lorca Review*
HR	*Hispanic Review*
IL	*Ideologies and Literature*
LATR	*Latin American Theatre Review*
LTP	*Literature Teaching Politics*
MLR	*Modern Language Review*
NRFH	*Nueva revista de filología hispánica*
OLR	*Oxford Literary Review*
PMLA	*Publications of the Modern Language Association of America*
RI	*Revista iberoamericana*
RN	*Romance Notes*
RQ	*Romance Quarterly*
RR	*Romanic Review*
RS	*Romance Studies*
SS	*Studi secenteschi*
TLS	*Times Literary Supplement*
TP	*Textual Practice*
TQ	*Tel Quel*

Neutrumque et utrumque
  CΟVΑRRUBIΑS, *citing* ΟVID

El hombre invisible
  NΕRUDΑ

Le sexe sans la loi et le pouvoir sans le roi
  FΟUCΑULT

For E., again

INTRODUCTION:
READING THE BODY

THE questions of gender and sexuality are amongst the most important facing the contemporary critic. Yet there has been almost no work attempting to analyse Spanish and Spanish American literature in the light of modern theories of sexuality.[1] The aim of this book is twofold: to provide an introduction to the varied and complex treatments of sexuality since Freud; and to read a representative selection of major texts from different areas of Hispanic studies in the light of these treatments.

This introduction will give a brief account of six theories, their relation to Freud, and their significance for critical practice. The six chapters which follow fall into three sections: Renaissance, modern peninsular, and Spanish American. Chapters 1 and 2 offer readings of two women writers in the light of French theoretical feminism, and of texts by Góngora in relation to Barthes's conception of gender and narrative. Chapters 3 and 4 give a Lacanian reading of desire in the nineteenth-century novel and a Foucaldian interpretation of power and pleasure in Lorca's drama. Chapters 5 and 6 include Marxian readings of nature and politics in Latin American poetry and a postmodern approach to the Latin American novel. The Conclusion argues that in spite of the diversity of texts and theories treated, there are three broad areas of coherence or coincidence: the problematic status of woman in a male culture; the possibility of resistance to an

---

[1] Some recent work on Spanish women writers does appeal to theory. *Reading for Difference: Feminist Perspectives on Women Novelists of Contemporary Spain*, special issue of *Anales de la literatura española contemporánea*, 12. 1–2 (1987), contains theory-based articles by Elizabeth J. Ordóñez and Elena Gascón Vera. The guest editor for the volume is Mirella Servodidio and the special editorial board consists of Linda Gould Levine, Gloria Waldman, and Marcia L. Welles. See also Janet N. Gold, 'Reading the Love Myth: Tusquets with the Help of Barthes', *HR* 55 (1987), 337–46. Luso-Brazilian studies may be ahead of Hispanic studies in this area. See e.g. Marta Peixoto's excellent 'The Absent Body: Female Signature and Poetic Convention in Cecília Meireles', *BHS* 65 (1988), 87–100.

authority always already in place; the dual role of the body as material and theoretical protagonist in that resistance.

Traditional criticism is disembodied. That is, it adopts a transcendental viewpoint from which the critical object beneath it is submitted to 'objective' analysis. In a previous book I have attacked this humanist approach, which is dependent on the myth of 'Man' as founding father of the text.[2] The role of the body as a critical term is to undermine this façade of neutrality, to call attention to the (nominal) erasure of the critic's own position. But if the bodily approach is hostile to objectivity and rationality, this need not lead to random subjectivism. An attention to the body will stress the multiplicity of factors which determine the place from which I speak and, indeed, the manner in which I am heard by others. Like the structuralism of the 1960s, then, bodily criticism is suspicious of those who appeal to Nature as validating principle and to the individual as transcendent subject. But where structuralism assumes the existence of autonomous linguistic structures and scientific methods, bodily criticism stresses the materiality of discourse and the positionality of the speaker. Following the example of feminist theory, it would involve both a re-evaluation of the question of experience (because there can be no scientific assessment of the world) and a calling into question of that experience (because there can be no unmediated access to the world). This is a problem hinted at by Jane Gallop when she speaks of 'the bodily enigma': if the body is that which precedes interpretation, then it will inevitably precipitate an endless theorizing, a continuing attempt to draw into visibility that which determines the very limits of our perspective.[3]

The question of the body, then, is linked to the question of theory. I take it for granted that to adopt a thematic approach (the supposedly empirical analysis of 'content') is inappropriate where sexuality is concerned. In this particular case it would lead either to a scrapbook of Hispanic erotica or to the vindication of some reassuringly stable 'Latin' temperament. Thus I am concerned less with the specificity of Spanish or

---

[2] *Writing in the Margin: Spanish Literature of the Golden Age* (Oxford, 1988).
[3] 'The Bodily Enigma', paper read in London, 1987; to form part of a forthcoming book *Thinking through the Body*.

Latin American 'experience' of sex, as with the enabling conditions of sexual difference itself. The role of theory is to investigate those conditions and not simply reproduce them in the guise of manifest content. In the realms of gender studies content analysis goes hand in hand with the search for 'positive images': the literary text is to be judged against a set of pre-existing standards against which it is invariably found wanting. To take an example, it seems unhelpful simply to dismiss male writers who exhibit signs of sexism, but far more productive to examine those 'negative images' for the contradictions they bear within them, to reveal that any such content is an ideological construct. Indeed, some of the most recent feminist criticism has attempted to 'deconstruct' sexual identity itself, to unsettle the classic metaphysical opposition that is gender difference.[4]

Such a practice is as applicable to men as it is to women. The glossy programme for the production of Lorca's *El público* (first performed in 1987) carries a full-page advertisement for the well-known department store Galerías Preciados.[5] The main caption reads: 'Protagonista: el hombre', and the copy continues: 'Man is the protagonist in *Galerías*. His lifestyle is reflected in his way of dressing. Today's man gets the most out of his free time.' As is so often the case, such messages are more complex than they might first appear. There is the irony (lost to the sponsor) that such an advertisement should appear in the programme for a work in which man is indeed

[4] See Chris Weedon, *Feminist Practice and Post-Structuralist Theory* (Oxford, 1987); and Morwenna Griffiths and Margaret Whitford (eds.), *Feminist Perspectives in Philosophy* (London, 1988). For gender in relation to literary and cultural studies see *Sexual Difference*, special issue of *OLR* 8. 1–2 (1986); for the visual arts see *Difference: On Representation and Sexuality*, catalogue of the exhibition curated by Kate Linker and Jane Weinstock (New York, 1984–5); for film theory see *Deconstructing 'Difference'*, special issue of *Screen* 28. 1 (Winter 1987). For a critique of this debate with particular reference to lesbianism see Mandy Merck's introduction to the last volume, 'Difference and its Discontents' (pp. 2–9). The most extensive and sophisticated account of the relationship between feminism and (male) theory remains Alice A. Jardine, *Gynesis: Configurations of Woman and Modernity* (Ithaca, 1985). For a polemic against theory in women's studies see Germaine Greer, 'The Proper Study of Womankind', *TLS* (3–9 June 1988), 616, 629.

[5] The production was directed by Lluís Pascual for the Centro Dramático Nacional. The programme was published by the Ministerio de Cultura: Instituto Nacional de las Artes Escénicas y de la Música (Madrid, 1987). For representations of the male body in advertising see Alasdair Foster, 'Exhibitions: Heroes, Fools, and Martyrs', *Ten. 8: International Photography Magazine*, 28 (1988), 54–63.

the protagonist, in which the question of masculinity is subject to a radical interrogation. Moreover, there is the hint that, in spite of his apparent mastery of money and time, the modern man may be imprisoned by the discourses of leisure and consumerism: is there life outside the life-style? Could any identity be recognized without the appropriate clothing? For men, as more frequently for women, such images serve as an address or interpellation. They instruct the subject to work (on) the body until it is perfect.

The advert thus hints at a knowledge that it cannot make explicit: that there is no essential masculine identity. But it also points quite openly to a recent change in the image repertoire of popular culture, namely the emergence of the male body as protagonist in the mass media, as in academic discourse. Thus *Marxism Today* recently devoted a special issue to 'Men' (April 1988); and *El país* had a pull-out dossier on 'Masculinidad' (5 May 1988). In the United States masculinity has indeed become (in *El país*'s phrase) a 'topic of the day'. In the wake of feminism there has emerged the discipline of 'men's studies', the attempt to read man not as the universal representative of humanity, but as peculiar to himself. The scope of published work is already varied, ranging from Harry Brod's mainly sociological collection *The Making of Masculinities* (Winchester, Mass., 1987) to Alice Jardine and Paul Smith's more theoretical *Men in Feminism* (New York, 1987).[6] Whatever their approach, such studies stress the difficulty of even considering the subject of men. Rosalind Coward's description of the 'invisibility' of the male body still holds true to a large extent. She writes in *Female Desire* (London, 1984) of the 'strange contradiction' at the heart of heterosexual culture: 'There has been a massive investigation of "women the enigma", and an obsessive quest to understand women's sexuality. . . . Nobody seems to have noticed that men's bodies have quietly absented themselves. . . . It is in reality

---

[6] See also Declan Kiberd, *Men and Feminism in Modern Literature* (London, 1985); Anthony Easthope, *What a Man's Gotta Do: The Masculine Myth in Popular Culture* (London, 1986); and for an anticipation of this debate see Stephen Heath, *The Sexual Fix* (London, 1982). A seminar on 'Male Order: Unwrapping Masculinity' took place at the ICA on 6 July 1988, addressing the question 'Are men's sexual politics changing with the changing image of masculinity?'. See the collection of essays of the same title, ed. by Rowena Chapman and Jonathan Rutherford (London, 1988).

men's bodies, men's sexuality which is the true "dark continent" of this society' (p. 227). The erasure of the male body thus has a contradictory effect. It both ensures the persistence of male dominance and prevents men from knowing themselves: 'Men know exactly that in rendering women the aesthetic sex they also render women the subordinate sex. . . . Men neglect their bodies and the bodies become strange to the men themselves' (p. 229).

This book is offered as the first contribution to men's studies in Hispanism. But I am well aware of the difficulties of focussing on a male identity which is so naturalised as to be invisible. Hence, even after the first chapter (a homage to feminism and women writers) it will prove scarcely possible to prevent the question of woman from returning, however hard it is repressed. Any attempt to move man to the centre of the stage must also examine that stage itself. And the ground on which man takes up his position is, inevitably, woman.

If the concept of gender is difficult to approach, that of sexuality is notoriously resistant to definition. On the one hand it cannot be reduced to genital acts; on the other it should not be abstracted into a universal, creative spirit. Freud himself struggled against the reductive and the absolutist definitions of sexuality, and in the second half of this introduction I will give a reading of his *Three Essays on the Theory of Sexuality* and contrast them with the views of the later theorists on whom I draw in the rest of the book.[7]

Freud's *Three Essays* were first published in 1905, but were subject to a continuing process of revision. They deal, in turn, with sexual aberrations, infantile sexuality, and the transformations of puberty. Freud begins by claiming that his 'enlarged' concept of sexuality is similar to the Platonic Eros (p. 45). But, as we shall see, this does not mean that it is idealist. On the contrary, Freud consistently resists the temptation to ascribe any essential identity or unchanging characteristics to deviants, to women, or, indeed, to men. Thus he states that 'inversion' (homosexuality) is neither innate nor degenerate, and that physiological hermaphroditism is not the cause of psychological disturbance (pp. 51, 52).

[7] I cite from the Penguin text in *On Sexuality* (Harmondsworth, 1977).

Freud rejects the claim that homosexuality can be defined as 'a feminine brain in a masculine body' on the grounds that a brain has no gender (p. 54), and a footnote of 1915 comes to the more radical conclusion that homosexuals cannot be considered 'a group of a special character'. The heterosexual condition is equally problematic: 'the exclusive sexual interest felt by men for women is also a problem that needs elucidating and not a self-evident fact based upon an attraction that is ultimately of a chemical nature' (p. 56 n., 57 n.). For Freud the relation between the sexual drive and the person to whom it is directed is arbitrary: 'the sexual instinct and the sexual object are merely soldered together . . . the sexual instinct is in the first instance independent of its object' (p. 59). He is well aware that the understanding of sexuality is historically determined, and notes that for the ancients it was the instinct not the object which was emphasized (p. 61 n.). Once the object recedes into the background there can be no simple distinction between the normal and the perverted: 'No healthy person . . . can fail to make some addition that might be called perverse to the normal sexual aim; and the universality of this finding in itself is enough to show how inappropriate it is to use the word perversion as a term of reproach' (p. 74). If there is something innate lying behind the perversions it is *'innate in everyone'* (Freud's emphasis).

This generalization of the aberrant is also found in the second essay, on the child. Infantile sexuality, deprived of any object but itself, is, in the famous phrase, 'polymorphously perverse' (p. 109). But the argument takes an unexpected turn when the child's multiple potential for pleasure is also attributed to 'the average uncultivated woman', before being acclaimed 'a general and fundamental human characteristic'. Here the child, the woman, and (implicitly) the pervert are presented not as deviations from an adult male norm, but rather as originary models for that norm.[8] This is not to deny that there is an undercurrent of prescriptive biologism in this essay. At one point Freud invokes Nature as authority for the belief that it is no accident that the zones selected for the

---

[8] See Sander L. Gilman, *Difference and Pathology* (Ithaca, 1985), for an analysis of the link Freud makes between the polymorphous perversion of child and prostitute in the context of contemporary pornography and literature.

stimulation of pleasure tend to favour the reproductive act (p. 101). But in a note of 1920 he glosses this statement in a way which seems to admit the inadequacy of such anatomical determinism: 'In biological discussion it is scarcely possible to avoid a teleological way of thinking.' Here Freud points himself to the necessary limits of his own discourse.

The third essay, on puberty, seems at first glance even more prescriptive. We are told that in adults 'sexual instinct is now subordinated to the reproductive function'; and that 'one of the tasks implicit in object choice is that it should find its way to the opposite sex' (p. 152). Yet the latter quote is qualified by the admission that this process 'is not accomplished without a certain amount of fumbling'. The fumbling is perhaps that of Freud himself rather than his adolescent patients, as he struggles to free himself from a narrowly teleological view of sex, only to be seduced, repeatedly, by its continuing lure. Such contradictions recur throughout his text. Thus at one point we are told that 'the strongest force working against a permanent inversion of the sexual object is the attraction which the opposing sexual characters exercise upon one another'; but at the next this idealist bias is contradicted by the recognition that social and criminal prohibition has a marked influence on the prevalence of homosexuality.

The *Three Essays* thus offer themselves up for two irreconcilable readings: the one progressive, the other reactionary. The progressive reading would take even Freud's 'negative images' of women and the perverse as a description of a particular historical order which need not be accepted as universal; the reactionary reading would take them as prescriptions for an unchanging nature which must be rejected as erroneous. To take a specific example, Freud makes the scandalous claim that 'the sexuality of little girls is of a wholly masculine character . . . libido is invariably and necessarily of a masculine nature, whether it occurs in men or in women and irrespectively of whether its object is a man or a woman' (p. 141). Many women will find this insulting, even absurd. But it has proved useful to French feminists who claim that the ubiquity of the male order must be confronted before women can attempt to escape it. In other words they read

Freud's dictum as description, not prescription; and as description of a state of affairs normally veiled by good intentions. This brings us to the very complex question of the relationship between Freud's texts and those of the later theorists to whom I appeal in this book. As I have just suggested, feminists such as Luce Irigaray have attempted to remobilize psychoanalytical concepts for their own purpose: the male system is to be examined, not taken for granted. A male theorist such as Barthes charts in his career the movement from a scientific structuralism to a more subjectivist post-structuralism which owes much to psychoanalysis. One area in which Barthes would agree with Freud is in the latter's stress on the plurality of sexual constitution and on the reversibility of the 'pathways' of desire (p. 125). Lacan's work is presented as a 'return to Freud'. One of Lacan's fundamental concepts is repetition, a term used by Freud when he defines the sexual aim as the desire for repeated stimulation of a zone previously experienced as pleasurable (p. 101). Foucault is generally hostile to psychoanalysis, and tends to treat it as just another of those disciplines which serve in the surveillance and punishment of the body. But in the first volume of his history of sexuality he treats the same three 'deviants' chosen by Freud: women, children, and homosexuals. And Freud's use of the term 'instinct for knowledge' (p. 112) in relation to sexuality prefigures Foucault's definition of it as 'la volonté de savoir'. Finally, structural Marxists such as Althusser attempt fusions of historical materialism and psychoanalysis, generally by assimilating the unconscious to ideology; and postmodernists such as Lyotard celebrate, like Freud (p. 84), the surface of a 'skin' which forms a seamless erotogenic zone. What all of these writers share with Freud (and there are many factors which differentiate them from him and from each other) is a scepticism towards both common sense and mystification. They take it for granted that sex can neither be brought down to the level of genital acts, nor borne up to the level of universal ideal.

If I take one image as exemplary of the way in which I read the body in this book, it is the bearded lady from Covarrubias's *Emblemas morales*.[9] I refer to this emblem in Chapter 1. On the

---

[9] Madrid, 1610 (ii. 164).

reverse of the picture the commentator retells the fable of Hermaphrodite, the mythical product of the fused bodies of heterosexual lovers. It would be tempting to take the image as one of the ideal transcendence of gender division. But the text which follows prevents any such easy resolution. It is very diverse. Covarrubias notes that some babies are indeed born with genitals of both sexes and goes on to cite Cicero on the disgust aroused by the sight of effeminate men. He ends by noting that the picture is of a real woman: 'the bearded lady of Peñaranda'. The modern reader will no doubt feel sympathy for this unfortunate, notorious woman, who is posed so starkly against a background we may presume to represent her native town. Her long gown and ruff confine her to a particular place and time. But she is secured all the more tightly by the (invisible) lines of discourse which run through her. Covarrubias fails to distinguish between hermaphroditism and effeminacy; and he links a specific disturbance in secondary sexual characteristics (the facial hair) to a fear of female sexuality in general. Secure in our 'scientific' knowledge, we modern spectators will find the confusion absurd or naïve. But the moral of the bearded lady is that the bundle of practices and discourses we call 'sex' has been subject to a wholly discontinuous development: that each age considers its articulation of sexuality to be natural and each is deluded.

Androgyny is thus no escape from the rigours of sexual identity. Indeed, in this case (as often in botany), hermaphroditism is associated with protandry, the precedence and supremacy of the male term or organ. Even the 'monster' can only be conceived in terms of its deviation from the masculine. It is no accident that Freud also refers to the hermaphrodite at the start of the *Three Essays*. He cites 'the poetic fable which tells how the original human beings were cut up into two halves—man and woman—and how these are always striving to unite again in love' (p. 46). Freud's aim is to deny the myth and the compulsory heterosexuality it serves to legitimate. But in doing so he has himself repressed part of the fable. In Plato's *Symposium* the original beings were of three kinds: male/female; male/male; female/female.[10] In his very attempt

---

[10] This reference occurs in Aristophanes' speech (189 C–193 E).

to escape the discursive prison which surrounds him, Freud unwittingly reconfirms its limits. No less than the bearded lady, he is a prisoner of sex.

To conclude, then, my model of the body is not to be identified with the individual or self. The body goes beyond experience (because it admits determinants unknown to the empirical subject); but it falls short of transcendence (because it admits no essence beyond or within itself). As a continuing enigma, it will give rise to endless theorising.

WRITING WOMEN IN THE GOLDEN AGE

I. WOMEN'S STUDIES AND FEMINIST THEORY

IN the presidential address he delivered to the Modern Language Association of America in 1986 J. Hillis Miller[1] notes how the 'triumph of theory' has been linked to an additional (and sometimes contradictory) move towards the study of the material base: history, culture, society, politics, and gender (p. 283). This internal cleavage (which cannot be reduced to simple opposition) is reproduced within the most successful of the new critical movements, that of women's studies. One great contribution made by this field is that it has superseded the old dichotomies of public and private, literary and social, by proposing a politics of the body which cannot be confined within the traditional restraints. There has also been a secondary benefit. Women's studies have opened up a discursive space in which men can also attempt to examine their own practice as critics.

But if few universities now lack courses or programmes in women's studies, then feminist theory still provokes strong resistance. Toril Moi is perhaps the scholar who has made the greatest contribution to the diffusion of feminist theory. In her influential manual *Sexual/Textual Politics* (London, 1985) she marks out the shifting boundaries between Anglo-American criticism and French theory, the former based on a broadly empiricist approach to 'images of women', the latter on a psychoanalytic concern for feminine subjectivity. Her objections to the empiricist school are set out in the introduction to her book, in which she claims that such critics have been unable to give an adequate account of a founding mother of feminism, Virginia Woolf:

---

[1] 'The Triumph of Theory, the Resistance to Reading, and the Question of Material Base', *PMLA* 102 (1987), 281–91.

By their more or less unwitting subscription to the humanist aesthetic categories of the traditional male academic hierarchy, feminist critics have seriously undermined the impact of their challenge to that very institution. The only difference between a feminist and a non-feminist critic in this tradition then becomes the formal political perspective of the critic.' (p. 18)

For Moi, then, political engagement is insufficient when it goes unsupported by the intellectual commitment to revise (male) critical methodologies.

Two British feminists have also been amongst those who have treated the question of theory and practice (thought and action). In *Female Desire* (London, 1984) Rosalind Coward lays bare the process by which women's bodies are constructed in and through the discourses of the media, of fiction, and of consumerism. She writes: 'To be a woman is to be constantly addressed, to have our desire constantly courted—in the kitchen, on the streets, in the world of fashion, in films, and fiction' (p. 13). Of course, these discourses are not neutral. Rather, they serve to perpetuate patriarchy by enforcing certain modes of pleasure: 'The aim of *Female Desire* is to examine how presumptions about female pleasure and female desire are shot through so many cultural practices . . . Female desire is constantly lured by discourses which sustain male privilege' (p. 16). This objectivization of woman means that her desire is transformed into labour: 'Women become *the sex*, the sex differentiated from the norm which is masculine. Women are the sex which is constantly questioned, explained, defined. And as the defined sex, women are put to work by the images' (p. 82). However, for Coward it is no easy matter to transcend the imposed definitions: to do so, she confesses, may be to abandon cherished pleasures. Her theoretical learning, worn lightly in this volume, does not allow her to adopt the comfortable position of the Anglo-American empiricists, who submit 'images of women' to 'objective' examination, and frequently find them wanting. On the cover of *Female Desire* there is a pair of high heels, trussed like a turkey and served up on a platter. The image is a witty commentary on the complicity between consumerism and femininity, on a sexual fix which it may prove difficult to dissolve.

Jacqueline Rose also approaches the problem of theory and

practice, but in rather more technical terms. In the introduction to *Sexuality in the Field of Vision* (London, 1986) she gives a dense account of the relation between the latest trends in feminism and psychoanalysis. Rose suggests that there are at least two vital areas which cannot be accounted for by a committed, political criticism: fantasy and the compulsion to repeat (p. 14). She appeals to deconstruction as an ally in the struggle against doctrinaire fixity and the prison of binary opposition: 'Against the [male] order of representation, Derrida posits *différance*, the sliding of language which only arbitrarily and repressively fixes into identity and reference alike. *Différance* is explicitly opposed to sexual difference in which Derrida identifies a classic binarism that closes off the potentially freer play of its terms' (p. 19). Derrida thus proposes 'an endless dispersal of subjectivity' (p. 20). The question for the (woman) critic, however, is whether the work of Derrida (and of Lacan) serves truly to demystify the dominant order or simply reproduces its subtlest configurations. Is it 'an exposure of fantasy at the basis of language—or its mere repetition?' (p. 22). As we shall see, this problem of mimicry or repetition is even more acute for women writers than it is for men. Ultimately, however, Rose has no hesitation in rejecting the false dichotomy of thought versus action. Theory is itself an urgent political necessity: 'To understand subjectivity, sexual difference, and fantasy in a way which neither entrenches the terms nor denies them still seems to me to be a crucial task for today. Not a luxury, but rather the key processes through which—as women and as men—we experience, and then question, our fully political fates' (p. 23). As we shall see, Rose goes on to reject the common view which holds that theorists such as Julia Kristeva have in their later work retreated into apolitical individualism.

One aim of feminist theory, then, is to make us aware of the possible complicity between women's studies and traditional, male disciplines. This problem is more complex than it may appear at first sight. On point frequently made by philosopher Luce Irigaray is that the male order is always 'the same', that it permits no genuine difference from itself. Theory would thus teach both women and men to be sceptical of images such as that which appears on the cover of the Spanish Ministry of

Culture's programme for equal rights (Madrid, 1987). Against the background of anonymous women's faces we find a female sign, a mathematical equals sign, and a male sign: women equals man. Of course, the public commitment of the Spanish authorities to women's rights (a commitment conspicuously absent in Britain and the United States) is not to be minimized. But the erasure of difference between female and male is by no means a goal to which thinkers such as Kristeva or Irigaray would lend their support. The necessary struggle for socio-economic equality cannot be abstracted into a mathematical formula, or sublated into a nominally androgynous or unsexed body politic.

There are two options available to contributors to women's studies. The first is the study of representation: the images of women produced by (male) writers. The second is the study of women themselves as writers: the question of whether a 'female writing' can exist within a dominant male culture. At first the Golden Age does not appear to be a promising field of study for either approach. For the images of women offered by male authors are rarely sympathetic and often overtly hostile. It is not difficult to imagine a check-list of misogyny in which the burlesque poetry of Quevedo and the wife-murder tragedies of Calderón are only the most conspicuous examples of verbal and physical violence inflicted on women. Even those 'manly women' who figure so largely in both the *comedia* and the *novela* are elicted by and directed to a male audience. They tell us little about the historical conditions of women's lives in the period, and less about the enabling conditions of gender and sexual difference as a whole. The reversal of male and female roles serves merely to reinforce the status quo, through its actual intermittence and perceived incongruity.

On the other hand, there are very few women writers in Spain in the period, even fewer than elsewhere in Europe. The Spanish obsession with domestic privacy often prevented the publication of memoires and personal letters. If we feel the lack of a Saint-Simon in Spain to recount the minutiae of courtly life, then even more acute is the absence of a Castilian Mme de Sévigné, who might have shed light on the darkest of continents, the relationship between mother and daughter. In this study I treat two women writers; St Teresa and María de

Zayas. The first is sixteenth-century and religious, the second seventeenth-century and secular. Apart from their gender these two figures may seem to have little in common. Indeed, the genres of the texts by them which I treat (autobiography and short story, respectively) are quite different from one another. However, as I hope to show, if these writers do share certain characteristics, they are to be found not in the images of women that their texts offer us, but rather in the texture of their very language. Hence I am concerned not so much with representation, as with what we might call stylistics or textuality.

Beth Miller has edited a volume of studies on women in Hispanic literature.[2] These essays attempt to recover forgotten female authors and to examine the depiction of women in male texts. What this valuable work fails to address, however, is the question of sexual difference itself as a cultural or historical formation. This is the kind of theoretical problem with which French (and some Anglo-Saxon) feminists are indeed concerned. In the introduction to her recent anthology of pieces on English writing, Mary Jacobus asks whether it is possible for woman both to retain her 'alien and critical' heritage (a sense of self as separate from the institutions of patriarchy) and to transcend a historical experience of oppression (the attempt to bridge that gap or separation).[3] Or again, Jonathan Culler in his essay 'Reading as a woman' suggests that the woman's position as reader is exemplary of a division inherent (but repressed) in any 'reading subject', namely that between the experience of self represented within the text and of self in the world beyond the text.[4] The artifice and marginality of the feminine thus have a general significance for all writers and readers. This 'gesture towards androgyny' (in Jacobus's phrase) is, however, fraught with difficulty. Where once woman was marginalized or excluded, her perspective repressed or devalued, now she expands to encompass the space of discourse and society in general. In this synecdochic movement, the part ('woman') displaces the

[2] *Women in Hispanic Literature: Icons and Fallen Idols* (Berkeley, 1983).
[3] *Women Writing and Writing about Women* (London, 1980), 20.
[4] In *On Deconstruction: Theory and Criticism after Struturalism* (London, 1983), 43–64 (p. 64).

whole ('Man') and is absorbed into a nominally neuter totality ('humankind'). Jacobus suggests in her conclusion that the 'difference of view' offered by women is 'a question rather than an answer, and a question to be asked not simply of women, but of writing too' (p. 21). Thus the dialectic between woman as same and as other (between assimilation and exclusion) cannot be limited to women alone. It requires the interrogation of literature and language themselves.

One much debated question is whether the characteristics of women's writing (if, indeed, such a writing exists) are determined by biology, history, or a combination of the two. Those who stress the former may be called 'essentialists' in that they take women's qualities to be inevitable and unchanging. Those who stress the latter may be called 'relativists' in that they see no innate connection between women's experiences and their expression at different moments in history. These are extreme views, caricatures of actual positions. But one way of keeping both nature and nurture in play at the same time is through a conception of the woman's body as historical construct, not biological essence. Such an understanding would neither sever woman from an awareness of the specificity of her body, nor shackle her to an unwieldy biological determinism. This concept may seem obscure, but is exemplified by two images of women taken from a Golden Age paraliterary text, Sebastián de Covarrubias's *Emblemas morales* of 1610.[5] One emblem shows a mermaid with arms extended. It bears the motto 'Atrum desinit in piscem' or 'She ends in a black fish', and its Spanish verse reads in translation: 'The vice of the flesh is a lady: the top half of her body is very beautiful, but the bottom half is that of a hard, scaly fish, horrible, abominable, and terrifying' (i. 94). The second depicts a bearded lady, standing solemnly in front of a rural landscape. The motto reads 'Neutrumque et utrumque' or 'Neither and both', and the verse reads in translation: 'I am *hic*, *haec*, and *hoc*. I decline myself. I am man and woman, and I am a third which is neither one nor the other, and it is not clear which of these things I am' (ii. 164). Superficially different, the two images have much in common. Both depict

---

[5] Fac. edn. (Madrid, 1978).

operations performed on the female body by the male artist or chronicler: the addition of a fish's tail in the first, and of a beard in the second. And both define woman as a sexual being. In the first emblem, she is endowed with a dangerous excess of sexuality, and lures weak men to their doom. In the second she suffers from a painful lack of sexuality, and serves as a warning to effeminate men. Though the moral is different, the effect is the same: the woman is monstrous and produces horror in those who witness her. Less obvious is the implied equation between the woman's body and the world of literature and language. The motto 'Atrum desinit in piscem' is taken from Horace's *Ars poetica*, where it is used to warn the poet against the lack of unity in his plot and of decorum in his diction. Its original message is literary or discursive, not ethical or biological. In the second emblem biological categories are traced back to their grammatical equivalents: 'hic, haec, hoc' equals 'masculine, feminine, neuter'. This kind of linguistic correspondence is not uncommon in the seventeenth century. It also occurs in a similar context when Emmanuele Tesauro treats the hermaphrodite as a verbal conundrum in his *Cannocchiale aristotelico* of 1670.[6] Though the Italian's monster is the object not of horror, but of wonder ('meraviglia'), it bears equal witness to the system of correspondences within which knowledge is still articulated in the later Renaissance. This system permits freedom of movement between the bodily and the discursive (anatomy and grammar), and finds one of its most potent allegories in the ever varied and contradictory figure of woman.

The sense of woman as both superfluity and deficiency of sexual desire is also reflected in contemporary medicine. On the one hand, women are burdened with passionate humours and wandering wombs, both of which are unchecked by (male) reason, and on the other, they are disabled by the lack of a phallus, which renders them wounded or deficient males. Even Juan de Espinosa, who argues for the perfection of women in his *Diálogo en laude de las mujeres* (1580), argues in part from a biologist position. Following Aristotle and Galen he claims that women are produced in the left testicle:

[6] Fac. edn. (Bad Homburg, 1968), 77–8.

'Women are engendered from the left side of the man, which is the side of the heart and therefore the nobler.'[7] Espinosa's claim that the left side is more noble than the right is a clear example of those attempts to reverse a prevailing hierarchy that are always doomed to failure. The 'difference of view' can never displace its more potent rival, and the female term remains negative and inferior.

The problem of reverse hierarchy and the refusal to create a new order equal and opposite to that of the dominant male are typical of the questions raised by the two French writers to whom I appeal in my readings of St Teresa and María de Zayas. If Julia Kristeva and Luce Irigaray are often difficult to follow it is partly because they share a mistrust of that univocal and repressive 'clarity' of both style and perspective that seeks to enforce its will on the passive reader. More particularly, Kristeva and Irigaray move freely between the critical and the creative modes of writing in an attempt to break down the boundaries between personal experience and public practice. Each is trained in psychoanalysis, a discipline often accused of sexism. Yet their works unsettle any received notions that Freudian analysis need be dogmatic prescription. And they supplement this ahistorical model with a broadly Marxian awareness of women's role in the relations of production and reproduction. Thus the approach of each, though very different from each other, combines the abstract and the material. And often it does so in the figure that I introduced earlier, the discursive or historical body.

The single concept or area which I borrow from Kristeva is the 'semiotic', a term she uses in a precise, technical sense.[8] The semiotic is a stage of pre-verbal consciousness characterized in the child by discharges of energy or impulses which orientate the body with reference to the mother (p. 26). It is both positive (in that the impulses give pleasure) and negative (in that they are linked to death and destruction). The semiotic subject is discontinuous and fragmented: it cannot yet perceive its body as an integrated whole, and thus has no sense of identity. But if the semiotic is arbitrary, it is not

---

[7] Ed. Angela González Simón (Madrid, 1946), 147.

[8] See 'Sémiotique et symbolique', in *La Révolution du langage poétique: L'Avant-garde à la fin du XIXe siècle: Lautréamont et Mallarmé* (Paris: 1974), 17–100.

random. Rather, it is articulated according to deep linguistic structures. What Kristeva calls the 'thetic' (or propositional) is a break or threshold in the semiotic in which the separation of the subject from its image ensures the possibility of meaning through the perception of difference (pp. 41–2). At this 'mirror-stage' the child identifies with its own image and thus fixes, temporarily at least, the endlessly mobile flux of impulse (p. 45). This rupture corresponds to the emergence of the child from auto-erotic or maternal closure into the world of difference and language. The continued incursion of the semiotic, however, destabilizes the thetic, even in its most basic logical structure of subject and predicate (p. 54). But the semiotic is not the opposite of the thetic: the former is rather a necessary precondition for the latter. Indeed the semiotic is characterized by stases as well as impulses, when a mobile desire fixes temporarily on a fetishistic object (p. 63). Without such fetishes the subject or text would disintegrate. Thus for Kristeva, the artistic text is produced not, as one might expect, by the free-play of the semiotic, but by a persistent attachment to the thetic which is constantly menaced by negation (p. 68). The artist provokes a partial return to the semiotic state by reproducing or mimicking aspects of the signifying practice. This mimicry produces a temporary breakdown in social and linguistic order which permits the release of 'jouissance' (p. 77).

Kristeva's argument is dense and intricate. But the main point is that the semiotic, for all its fragmentation and discontinuity, can neither be reduced to chaos nor isolated from social and linguistic determination. What is more, although it is associated with the mother's body and with the child's uneasy dependence on that body, it is not biologically female. Indeed, the writers who exemplify the semiotic for Kristeva are the male authors of the French avant-garde, such as Lautréamont and Mallarmé. Elsewhere in her work, Kristeva is hostile to what she calls the naïve romantic belief in an essential female identity. This, she suggests, is just the mirror image of phallocratism.[9] Yet she also defines sexual difference as the 'exile' of woman from meaning (*Polylogue*,

---

[9] *Polylogue* (Paris, 1977), 519.

p. 8), a repressed position somewhat similar to that of the semiotic. Moreover, the principal motif in the semiotic is also associated with woman: it is the *chōra*, a mobile and provisional articulation, which Plato identifies with the mother or nurse as both source and receptacle of desire (*Révolution*, p. 23).

Luce Irigaray's work is much more overtly concerned with the figure of woman and the nature of her language: 'parler femme'. Yet, like Kristeva's, it procedes at such a level of technicality that it is often difficult to decide what sense of the word 'woman' is implied at any given point. Is it the biological female, the historical construct of the feminine, or woman as archetype of the marginal and oppressed? Nevertheless, at times Irigaray seems to invoke an undisguised biologism in her theories of the discursive body. Thus in one essay she contrasts an experience of the male genitals with that of the female.[10] As the former are single and visible they seek to recreate in woman an equal and opposite correlative, based on the clitoris (p. 23). But female sexuality, like Kristeva's semiotic, is auto-erotic. Its figure is the two lips or labia, which constantly touch one another and thus offer a plurality of sensation which is irreducible to the single (unity) or the dual (opposition). But if woman's sex is plural or dispersed, it is by no means incoherent. She may lack the interiority men attribute her, but her *jouissance* lies in a freedom of exchange or reciprocity. Yet, traditionally, woman's role is that of object of exchange within a male economy. And to invert this economy (if such a project were possible) would merely reinstate a new kind of phallocratism (pp. 26–32). Irigaray suggests in another essay that the roles of the male homosexual and the wife are important here. Homosexuality is forbidden by male law; yet it is the logical result of a productive economy amongst men which excludes women, even from pleasure.[11] The wife's role is merely to ensure this 'circulation of the same' (male with male) by adopting the travesty of the feminine. The essay ends with a Utopian vision of a pure, gratuitous exchange of commodities, outside the

---

[10] See the title essay in *Ce sexe qui n'en est pas un* (Paris, 1977), 23–32.
[11] 'Des marchandises entre elles', in *Ce sexe*, 189–93.

tyrannical male economy of capitalization and appropriation
(pp. 191–3).

An apparent essentialism thus alternates with a more
openly political and historical awareness. Yet, as Jane Gallop
has suggested, Irigaray's 'body' is more strategic than
biologist. For it is not biology that determines thought, but
phallomorphic logic that 'reconstructs anatomy in its own
image.'[12] We cannot take these figures literally: women do not
experience their genitalia in such a way. But by sticking so
closely to the contours of the body, Irigaray forces her readers
to reconsider the status of referentiality itself. The question
she poses is whether it is possible to speak of female experience
within a language and culture saturated with male values.
Thus, although our perception of sexual difference may be
historically produced, we cannot simply deny the persistence
of the appeal to 'nature': there is no easy middle way between
essentialism and relativism. But perhaps the most resonant of
Irigaray's images of woman is the *korē*, a Greek term which
(like the Spanish 'niña') can mean both 'a young girl' and 'the
pupil of the eye'.[13] The pupil is both the central point of vision
and the most purely reflective part of the eye. It thus suggests
that women are caught in the mirror of representation, central
to a male perspective but ultimately excluded from it. The
woman as *korē* combines reflection, absence, and death.

As I suggested earlier, the work of Kristeva and that of
Irigaray are quite different from one another. In particular it
would be absurd to restrict Kristeva to some ghetto of
'women's studies' when her books are concerned quite
explicitly with general theories of language and subjectivity.
Yet both writers are alike in their resistance to the positivism
and empiricism employed, perhaps unknowingly, by traditional
literary critics. They thus offer the opportunity for radically
new readings of literary works by women. And the texture of
their own writing, which moves freely from the technical to
the effective and revels in paradox, ellipsis, and discontinuity,
is not so different from that of some Golden Age Spanish
authors. In her most recently published work Irigaray
suggests that if there is a female literary tradition then it is to

[12] '*Quand nos lèvres s'écrivent*: Irigaray's body politics', *RR* 74 (1983), 77–83 (p. 78).
[13] *Speculum, de l'autre femme* (Paris, 1974), 183–8.

be found in religious writing, and particularly in that of the mystics. The slow 'sedimentation' of this tradition may now be complete.[14] Perhaps the time has come for a reassessment of St Teresa's autobiography.

2. TERESA AND THE MYSTIC BODY

Until recently criticism of St Teresa has been marked by overt sexism. Thus Américo Castro gave a lofty diagnosis of Teresa's condition, claiming that she was a 'feminine soul' who displaced her desire into her thought, and thus obliged her emotional sensibility to trail behind her intellect.[15] As we shall see, for María de Zayas the soul can have no gender. Castro, on the other hand, has no difficulty in defining the essence of womanhood: as in the Renaissance, it is volatility, inconstancy, and emotionalism. This essentialism is linked to a debased Freudianism: desire is held to be hydraulic or homeostatic. If it is frustrated in one area (desire) it must be displaced into another (thought). The female intellect or womanly whim is merely the product of repressed sexuality and must be dragged behind its unfortunate owner like a ball and chain. The way in which male critics can both denigrate and idealize female writing is very evident here. For Teresa is made to represent a female 'experience' that is at once inaccessible to men and unworthy of them.

This kind of essentialism is often combined with praise of Teresa's easy 'spontaneity' of style. This belief is strangely persistent. As early as 1915 Menéndez Pidal had suggested that Teresa's frequent checking of her speech (her claims to be ignorant of the appropriate word or phrase) may be read as a wilful act of humility, reflecting her wish to avoid the charge of conspicuous linguistic display (cited (p. 97) in Victor García de la Concha's *El arte literario de Santa Teresa* (1978), where Pidal's tendency to find hidden structure in Teresa's supposedly 'natural' writing reaches a climax). García treats in some detail Teresa's aesthetics, poetics, rhetoric, and grammar. By submitting the texts to an analysis based on Renaissance

---

[14] *Éthique de la différence sexuelle* (Paris, 1984), 111.
[15] Cited by Víctor García de la Concha in his *El arte literario de Santa Teresa* (Barcelona, 1978), 126.

criteria he shows that they display a tendency towards linguistic precision, and that the style Teresa calls 'desconcertado' or 'disordered' is by no means chaotic (pp. 100, 107). For García much of Teresa's apparent waywardness may be attributed to her rhetorical awareness of the audience for whom she is writing (pp. 190–4). In particular, she is sensitive to the woman reader's relative lack of education (pp. 142–4). Even the supposed anomalies of her style may be seen not as ingenuous mistakes, but as sophisticated rhetorical figures: ellipsis, anacoluthon, hyperbaton (pp. 298–300). Yet, though García acknowledges that such figures produce an effect of spontaneity in the reader, he fails to accept that the 'voice' or 'personality' he perceives in the text may also be a rhetorical construct. He concludes traditionally enough by praising the boundless wealth of form and feeling with which Teresa dissolves linguistic and literary structures (p. 376).

Critics thus offer a choice between natural effusion and artful reticence, or between biology and history. According to the first view, Teresa is spontaneous because she is a woman; and according to the second, she is ingenious because she is the product of a sophisticated, Renaissance culture. Yet perhaps we should not be surprised that both views are often proposed simultaneously, as they are by Menéndez Pidal and García de la Concha. For the 'historical' view of Teresa as artfully enforcing her will on the reader is as phallocratic as the 'biological' view of her as a little woman, incapable of logical expression. By attributing to the woman writer the productive strategies of the male text, critics fail to examine those presuppositions on which both sexual difference and literary value are founded. Teresa may be admitted, albeit with some difficulty, into the ranks of authoritative male authors, as long as the supposed deficiencies or excesses of her style remain ignored or repressed. The canon itself is undisturbed.

Teresa's own comments on her mode of writing offer no escape from this trap. Indeed, while few modern critics take at face value her repeated claims that she lacks education and fluency of style, she herself often attributes such 'faults' to the weakness of the female sex. There also seems little material for a feminist reading in her overt depiction of herself as a woman in the *Vida*. Her initial motive for writing is out of obedience to her male confessor, the addressee of the *Vida*, an act seen by García as an absolute submission of identity (p. 92). The first chapters are dominated by the figure of Teresa's father, his benign influence and exemplary death.[16] The other influence on the young Teresa is literature: chivalric romance and (later) devotional works. The opening of the *Vida* thus appears to shackle Teresa to what Kristeva calls the 'symbolic' or 'thetic': the world of social and linguistic difference presided over by the Father. The halting progress of Teresa's career, constantly interrupted by visions of Christ as a young man and attempts to ensure her confessor's ratification of those visions, reads (overtly once more) as a continuing submission to male authority, as the persistent self-denial of a strong-willed woman. On the other hand, we do indeed find in the *Vida* a minute attention to the domestic and personal conditions of women, and the creation of the affective 'personality' which has so engaged modern critics. But this 'feminine soul' is defined and delimited by both the material restrictions of a male culture and the psychological constraints of a received female consciousness. Our spurious sense of intimacy with Teresa, our perception of her as an integrated personality, derives not from any direct intuition of her essential nature, but from the indirect action of a society which permitted women only an internal or psychological space in which to express themselves. Feminist theologians today seek (like Teresa before them) a new religious awareness at the margin or 'outside' of institutions.[17] But to appeal, as some have done, to 'experience' in this context is to risk reinscription into the very system which they seek to transcend.

Yet, in the case of Teresa, we are not obliged to choose between biology and history, or between progressive and reactionary images of women. Nor need we attempt to juggle with opposing terms, and reduce the text to the simple alternation of the one and the other. For my own thesis is, quite simply, that the mystical sphere in Teresa corresponds

---

[16] I refer to the eighth edn. of the text in the Austral series (Madrid, 1978).

[17] See Ursula King, 'Mysticism and Feminism or Why Look at Women Mystics?', in *Teresa de Jesús and her World*, ed. Margaret A. Rees (Leeds, 1981), 7–17.

(in all its contradictions and discontinuities) to Kristeva's semiotic; and that the visions themselves (and the language in which they are represented) form a *chōra*, a receptacle or space within which the semiotic drives are articulated.

We note from the earliest chapters how physical or bodily the religious experience is for Teresa. When she begins she is wracked by an illness, which makes her mute and paralysed (iii, iv). Her tongue is bitten to pieces, her whole being disjointed, and her head full of nonsense. She is left unable to move anything but a single finger, and must learn once more to integrate her body and crawl like a baby (vi, pp. 37–8). The physical and mental fragmentation caused by suffering is similar to that produced by divine *jouissance*. In the sublime state, the imagination takes over from the intellect (ix, p. 56) and she feels a pleasure without pain: 'there is no suffering, only a pleasure which cannot be understood' (xviii, p. 97). This pleasure derives in part from an experience of non-difference: she cannot distinguish between the mind and the soul, between the mind and the spirit. Like the child in the grip of the semiotic, then, the mystic body is fragmented and torn between positive and negative impulses. It is also innocent of those divisions or differences (such as male and female, self and other) which permit both the integration of identity and the articulation of logical meaning. Yet, like the semiotic once more, the mystic body is not chaotic, but structured by deep psychic and linguistic principles. Kristeva suggests that the *chōra* consists of a play of discharge and stasis (*Révolution*, p. 28). In Teresa's narrative this alternation registers in the constant movement between exaltation and depression. Yet these moments of stasis are necessary, for they also appear in the fetishization of the visionary image when desire fixes on the face, hand, or wounds of Christ. Yet Teresa's text cannot be purely semiotic, a free play of drives and pre-verbal impulse. For any linguistic act is necessarily thetic or propositional, requiring the separation of the subject from his or her own image. And the experience of division between self and other is perhaps as characteristic of the mystical sphere as is the sense of non-difference and amorous fusion. For example, during her levitations Teresa is at once rapt by communion with the Holy Spirit and shamed by an awareness of the physical incongruity of her position. The mystic state is both internal and external, psychological and social.

How, then, can we read the texture of Teresa's writing in a womanly or semiotic way? At the most general level, the autobiography reveals a progressive defacement or alienation from self, as the formality of narrative comes up against the random accident of experience and the rigid rules of dogma. Teresa appeals to allegories or extended metaphors in order to communicate ineffable states. The longest of these is that of the four waters which stretches over some thirteen chapters (xi–xxiii). Yet by the second water we have already reached communion with God, and the rest of the allegory seems increasingly redundant and ineffective. As with the proliferating rooms within rooms of the *Moradas*, the more figurative language is employed, the more it is deprived of logical or propositional authority. Thus if Teresa compares the mystic state to any material object or sensual phenomenon, she immediately strips that object or phenomenon of the qualities by which it is recognized. Thus the light of heaven is similar to the light of the sun, except that it is infinitely brighter and knows no darkness (xviii, p. 156). Here we find once more the gesture towards non-difference typical of mystic expression: light is no longer opposite to dark. Yet it is couched none the less in propositional form, a mimicking of logical argument. The semiotic and the thetic are inseparable.

At a smaller linguistic level the unrealizable urge towards the dissolution of contraries can be seen in the use of chiasmus at the moments of greatest tension. Thus, famously, when Teresa finds the child Jesus on the staircase, her proposition is matched exactly by his: 'Yo soy Teresa de Jesús'; 'Yo soy Jesús de Teresa.' Or again, Christ explains towards the end of the *Vida*: 'Ya eres mía, y yo soy tuyo' (xxix, p. 239). Here chiasmus is not merely a neat verbal trick. The prominence of its position with the narrative suggests a more profound resonance: it reproduces, through its symmetry, the perfect pre-verbal mirroring of the child in the mother, before the child accedes to linguistic and sexual difference. By means of chiasmus Teresa's Christ disrupts and relativizes the most basic distinction in the thetic, that between subject and predicate. Each is reflected magically in the other. But this ideal auto-affection is necessarily provisional and intermittent. Teresa reproduces aspects of the signifying process in distorted form and thus offers the reader brief access to the semiotic *chōra* on the 'other' side of linguistic and social order. Her (and our) *jouissance* is produced by a fragmentation of language and representation, which takes place, none the less, within the boundaries of each.

We began with two problems for critics of the *Vida*. First, to what extent is the text personal (determined by an individual's experience) or social (determined by the institutions to which she belonged)? Second, to what extent is Teresa's writing spontaneous (deriving from an essential nature) or artificial (deriving from an acquired culture)? Both questions may be circumvented if we accept the hypothesis that there is a pre-verbal stage of human consciousness, associated with the female body, to which the reader may regain access through certain kinds of writing. The contradictory texture of the *Vida* would then result from the 'drift' of the speaking subject from the mobile articulation of drives and pleasures typical of a fragmented, pre-verbal body to the more rigid disposition of images and statements characteristic of a unified, yet alienated, personality. Or to put it more briefly, from a shuttling between the semiotic and the thetic. Thus a scene such as the transverberation would be read not (or not merely) as the woman's passive submission to male Law, but as an active pleasure in the disintegration of the body and the dissolution of difference (xxix, pp. 165–6). In the last vision of the *Vida* Teresa sees herself as an infinite mirror in the centre of which is Christ. As she watches, the mirror flows amorously into the form of the Lord, sculpting itself into his shape (xl, p. 243). The image is typically paradoxical. But in the fluidity of its movement it suggests that love of non-difference common to both mystical rapture and infantile *jouissance*. Christ is reflected in the mirror, but he is also the mirror itself: subject and object are indistinguishable. What Teresa fails to articulate (overtly at least) is whether the fusion of image and medium she attributes to Christ is also accessible to women. Recent French criticism has seen Teresa as the revolutionary conqueror of female identity and the creator of a space equal

to woman's infinite desire.[18] The alternative view, however, is
that Teresa remains trapped (like the *korē*) in the mirror of a
man-made language, her only escape the womanly space, at
once exalted and fettered, of maternal, bodily enclosure.

Kristeva's work after the early *Révolution* has circled around
the (linked) questions of femininity, maternity, and spirituality.
As we shall see, it sometimes deals explicitly with mysticism in
this context. For Jacqueline Rose the shift in Kristeva's
position does not signal a retreat from politics into random
subjectivism. Rather, it is to be seen in context as 'a
continuing focus on questions of psycho-sexual identity whose
basic insight has not changed: that identity is necessary but
only ever partial and therefore carries with it a dual risk—the
wreck of all identity, a self-blinding allegiance to psychic
norms' (*Sexuality*, p. 150). The link between 'early' and 'late'
Kristeva, then, is to be found in a conflict which also lies at the
heart of mystic experience: how can the subject acknowledge
the liberating effect of the dissolution of identity without being
menaced by psychic annihiliation? Kristeva proposes for
herself a project which is not dissimilar to Teresa's, the 'effort
to take transcendence seriously . . . believing that God is
analysable. Infinitely' (cited by Rose, p. 163).

Kristeva has always refused to define femininity. In *About
Chinese Women* (London, 1977; first published 1974), she
claims that the role of women is simply that of permitting
representation to take place: 'the separation of women from
power ensures that power remains representable, and that it is
up to men . . . to represent it' (p. 200). In an interview in
Polylogue she repeats the view that femininity can be defined
only in negative terms: woman is 'never that', she must be the
marginal term which can neither be represented nor spoken
(p. 519). But an essay in the same volume (on a Virgin and
Child by Bellini) offers a more positive model for this feminine
difference. The radical division of the maternal body speaks in
an anti-logical form: 'That is happening, now I am not there';
or again 'I cannot think it, but it is taking place' (p. 409).

---

[18] Pierre Boudot, *La Jouissance de Dieu ou le roman courtois de Thérèse d'Avila* (Paris,
1979); Béatrice Didier, 'Thérèse d'Avila et le désir de Dieu', in *L'Écriture-femme* (Paris,
1981), 51–70.

Maternity, as the engendering of a body or space that is at once same and other, is thus linked to representation once more: it is an analogue of the painter's 'luminous spatialization', the point at which a new identity (in the picture, in the womb) comes into being (p. 435). In *Histoires d'Amour* (Paris, 1983) it is love rather than maternity which serves as the constructor of space. The amorous (hi)stories provoked by psychoanalysis are not so much a code as a 'pact' which underwrites the shifting and provisional 'contracts' of emotional crisis (p. 355). Psychoanalysis is thus an enabling discourse, not a prescriptive one. What the three terms of femininity, maternity, and psychoanalysis have in common, then, is (a kind of) transcendence. But it is a transcendence which cannot be taken for granted, which must endlessly be analysed.

Curiously, when members of the Carmelite order praise Teresa today it is not for the 'spontaneity' beloved of literary critics but for her investigative acumen. Thus Ruth Burrows's *Inner Castle Explored* (London, 1981) ends with a reference to 'Teresa's ability to analyse mystical experience' (p. 122). And in his introduction to *The Interior Castle* (London, 1979) Kieran Kavanaugh points to her 'analytical abilities in probing the mystery of God's workings in the Soul'. He cites Pope Paul VI who 'spoke of her as a teacher of "marvelous profundity"' (p. 1). Such readings rely on an unexamined depth metaphor (the 'penetration' of a supposed outer surface) which literary theory would question. But they suggest, when taken in conjunction with Kristeva's later work, an attention to the problem of the infinite which avoids the appeal to ineffability or emotionalism. We can now return to the most famous passage of the *Vida* (the transverberation) and attempt a new reading of it.

En esta visión quiso el Señor le viese [al ángel] ansí: no era grande sino pequeño, hermoso mucho, el rostro tan encendido, que parecía de los ángeles muy subidos, que parece todos se abrasan. . . . Veíale en las manos un dardo de oro largo, y al fin del hierro me parecía tener un poco de fuego. Este me parecía meter con el corazón algunas veces, y que me llegaba a las entrañas: al sacarle me parecía las llevaba consigo, y me dejaba toda abrasada en amor grande de Dios. (pp. 165–6)

In this vision God willed it that I should see the angel in this form:

he was not tall, but short, very handsome, with a face so fiery that he seemed to be one of those whose place is high up, who are all aflame . . . . I could see that he held in his hands a long, golden dart, at the end of which there seemed to be point of fire. He seemed to put it in my heart several times, and it reached my innards, and when he took it out it seemed to take them with it, leaving me burning with a great love for God.

This passage marks out the limits of representation. Teresa, as woman, is excluded from power: it is the divine will which stages the vision for her. Her exclusion is, however, necessary for the depiction of transcendence to take place. She is defined by her passivity, her negativity. The burning shaft is plunged into her heart and pulls out her viscera when it is removed. Her pleasure and her pain circle around that penetration. Like the experience of maternity this is a moment of pure difference, of the setting up of an alien presence within the woman's body. Expressed in an anti-logical discourse which blurs the boundaries between inside and outside, the mystical experience marks out the margins of spatialization, of a process which is at once material and immaterial. Teresa's history of love is addressed to an absent listener (God or the reader), necessary for the construction of that space within which her drama unfolds. Hers is a rhetorical or investigative text which seeks to persuade the reader through an appeal to personal ethos. Like Kristeva, Teresa thus combines a negative definition of woman with a positive attempt to examine an experience which is resistant to representation.

In her most recent book, *Soleil noir* (Paris, 1987), Kristeva draws a comparison between the depressive and the mystic. Depressives, she claims, are narcissists in mourning for a primal Thing outside language which will satisfy their eternal sense of loss. Unlike happy people, they are unwilling to accept 'objects' for their desire, mere substitutes for the Thing (p. 22). Depressives are mystics in so far as they lend no credence to any human other but hold tight to their own ineffable form (p. 24). Unwilling to trust to the treacherous displacements of language they cling to feeling or affect itself as the only consolation. In Kristeva's formula: 'L'affect, c'est sa chose' (p. 24). The value of Kristeva's account of melancholy for a reading of Teresa is clear. It suggests that Teresa's concern for the affects need not be trivialised. That concern can be read more properly as an investigation of the process of loss and projection (absence and substitution) through which human identity is formed. The mystic body thus reproduces, in its exaltation and despair, that instability at the core of our sense of self which is generally repressed. But, less positively, Kristeva's work also suggests that this quest for identity is thoroughly narcissistic: woman remains frozen in front of the mirror, unable to escape from the traffic of reflection. It is an image central to the philosophy of Luce Irigaray.

3. ZAYAS AND WOMEN'S LANGUAGE

The question of woman's position in history is posed more openly by María de Zayas than by Teresa. In the foreword to her first volume of stories *Novelas amorosas y ejemplares* (1635), Zayas scolds the male reader for his surprise that a woman dare write and publish fiction.[19] Such men believe women have no talent. But if souls are neither male nor female, then why should men think themselves wiser than women? It is not biology but history that stops women writing. If they were given books to study, instead of samplers to embroider, they would be as fit as men for academic posts. But Zayas herself also argues from a biological position, and appeals to the Aristotelian or Galenic medicine we saw in Juan de Espinosa: since women's humours are cold and wet they must be more intelligent than men, for the intellect itself is moist by nature (pp. 21–2). Thus although Zayas's defence of women should not be underestimated, given the historical circumstances under which it was written, it cannot transcend the phallocratic logic of her own time: if cold and wet displace hot and dry as the dominant humours then the traditional hierarchy is reversed for a moment, but its prestige remains fundamentally undisturbed.

In another well-known passage taken from her second and final volume of stories, *Desengaños amorosos* (1647), Zayas claims for herself a natural simplicity of style, free of *culto* affectation and rhetorical exaggeration. Her style is functional

---

[19] 'Al que leyere', in the edn. by Agustín G. de Amezúa (Madrid, 1948), 21.

or instrumental in character. It is determined by her awareness of a diverse male audience, united only by its thoughtless hostility towards women. She must make herself understood to even the least educated of these. Elsewhere she calls her own style simple and unaffected.[20] Yet the constant concern for the effect of her writing on an audience (which we have also seen in Teresa) is itself a rhetorical posture. Indeed, the desire to change men's minds and impose one's will on the public is the traditional aim of rhetoric, the art of eloquent persuasion. Zayas thus attempts to dislodge men from the positions of power, both social and stylistic. But she can only do so by adopting those same weapons used by men against women: biological essentialism and linguistic mastery.

Modern critics have tended to agree with Zayas's estimation of her own qualities. Where nineteenth-century scholars attacked her 'libertine' enumerations of amorous adventure and her persistent descent into the grotesque and obscene,[21] twentieth-century critics praise her for the same naturalness and spontaneity they attribute to Teresa. Thus Amezúa claims that Zayas has not the slightest concern for style: she writes as she would speak, for the imaginary audience of her frame-tales (*Novelas*, p. xxx). Yet if her style is 'natural', Amezúa himself acknowledges that the dichotomy between Art and Nature is a source of controversy in the period, and lists four elocutionary virtues of the time which are evident in her stories: invention, artifice, grace, and morality (pp. xiii, xvi–xvii). Likewise he sees no contradiction in praising both her love of the supernatural and her unswerving commitment to 'realism' (pp. xviii, xxv). These difficulties are resolved by appeal to 'female intuition' (p. xix), that ineffable, internal sphere which serves (as in Teresa, once more) to reconcile all logical contradictions.

Even recent women critics have praised Zayas's 'clarity' of style, 'personal' perspective, and 'successful' manipulation of the reader (see Foa, pp. 105, 109, 183). And when they turn from stylistics to representation, they have taken it for granted

---

[20] Both passages are cited by Sandra M. Foa in her *Feminismo y forma narrativa: Estudio del tema y las técnicas de María de Zayas y Sotomayor* (Valencia, 1979), 105.

[21] See the judgement of Ludwig Pfandl, cited by Amezúa in the intro. to his edn. of the *Novelas* (p. xxxiv).

that Zayas's overt feminist 'message' registers directly in the
action by the rewards granted the various characters or the
punishments inflicted on them. Apparently marginal or
superfluous elements (the narrative 'frame' inherited from
Boccaccio; the frequent interventions of the narrative voice)
are made subordinate to this supposedly essential sphere of
action. For one critic, Zayas sets up opposite modes of
behaviour which her wives or fiancées may adopt (obedience
or rebellion; passivity or dominance) and then suggests an
easy synthesis of the two terms. The moral of the stories is that
women must be androgynous or hybrid, combining both male
and female qualities.[22]

What this approach fails to explain is the frequency with
which Zayas treats acts of extraordinary and unmotivated
violence against women, more bloody in their way than those
represented by Quevedo or Calderón. Thus one wife is
immured by her husband, and is released only when her flesh
has been eaten away by worms; another is confined in a casket
under the table on which the men feast; and a third is forced to
drink from the skull of her presumed lover. It is indeed true
that these passive women, victims of male violence, are
counterbalanced by active women who avenge themselves on
their male tormentors. Thus Hipólita in 'Al fin se paga todo'
plunges her dagger 'five or six times' into the heart of her
sleeping husband. Once more, the woman displaces the man,
but only by reproducing masculine actions and values. Zayas
implies an acceptance of the patriarchal code of honour, and
does not question the belief that blood can only be cleansed
with blood. Women are thus permitted to adopt a travesty of
man, but cannot transgress the law of the dagger and the
phallus.

Yet, if we abandon traditional modes of criticism, it may be
possibile to offer a progressive or feminist reading of a
superficially conservative text. Such a reading would focus not
on Zayas's overt, but limited, calls for female rebellion, but on

[22] Mireya Pérez-Erdelyi, *La pícara y la dama: La imagen de las mujeres en las novelas
picaresco-cortesanas de María de Zayas y Sotomayor y Alonso del Castillo Solórzano* (Miami.
1979), 113–15.
    Subsequent references to Zayas are to *Novelas completas*, ed. María Martínez del
Portal (Barcelona, 1973). This edn. includes both volumes of stories, but omits the
forewords and preliminaries to each.

covert contradictions in the fabric of her writing. My own thesis is that the relationships between men and women depicted by Zayas and the language in which those relationships are couched may be read in terms of Irigaray's 'parler femme' or women's discourse. It seems best to consider a single story in detail and one, *a fortiori*, which seems least promising for this kind of analysis. 'Mal presagio casarse lejos' is one of those stories in which an innocent woman is murdered by her husband. Doñ Blanca's three sisters have already been killed or mutilated by foreign husbands when she herself is forced to marry the Flemish suitor who has courted her assiduously for a year in Madrid. Once the couple leave Spain, however, her husband becomes indifferent and her satanic father-in-law is openly hostile. In her solitude she becomes friendly with her husband's sister who is garrotted by her own husband and father for an imaginary offence. When Blanca surprises her husband making love with a favourite page-boy, she knows she has little time left to live. She is bled to death by her husband and father-in-law, an event which precipitates (or so we are told) the Duke of Alba's subsequent campaign in the Low Countries.

The story seems unambiguous, truly exemplary: as the title suggests, 'It bodes ill to marry far away from home.' Yet the presentation of this thesis is by no means clear or self-evident. There are arbitrary contradictions in the main characters: why does the husband woo Blanca so ardently for a year, only to change so abruptly on their marriage? We may speculate that he is concerned only with her dowry. What seems more important is that Zayas offers no plausible motivation. Again, Blanca herself is witty and outspoken before her marriage. For example, she argues that if it is common practice to inspect merchandise before buying it, surely the same should apply to husbands? Unlike clothes or jewels, they cannot be returned to the manufacturer (p. 522). Yet after the marriage, she simply collapses, and is unable to offer the slightest resistance to the dangers which threaten her. And if the characters are arbitrary, so is the plot. It is wildly 'overdetermined': neither the character nor the reader requires *all* of Blanca's sisters and female companions to be murdered or mutilated in order to get the point that foreign men are not to be trusted. The curious coincidences and illogical consequences of the narrative are so overstated and under-explained as to be almost farcical: the corpses of the two dead sisters and the mutilated body of the third (her legs amputated at the hip) return to Madrid on the very day that Blanca is setting out for Flanders; Blanca's death is not in vain, for her fellow countrymen battle against the treacherous Flemings in her name. We could explain such pecularities by invoking contemporary theories of genre and verisimilitude: these stories are closer to romance than to novel, and their plots are based on possibility rather than probability. Similarly implausible moments could be found in Cervantes or Castillo Solórzano (not to mention Boccaccio and Bandello). It remains the case however that the communication of Zayas's feminist 'message' is severely restricted by the very literary artifice of which she claims herself to be innocent. Her stories could hardly be taken as the 'natural' recreation of historical incident or lived experience even at the time they were written.

But perhaps this very inability (or refusal) to recreate an integrated female subject and a coherent female narrative may lead us to a new reading of this story. Blanca's lack of 'personality' confirms Irigaray's suggestion that women do not possess that resonant, mysterious interiority attributed to them by men. What the women in the story do share, however, is a freedom of social exchange outside the world of men. Thus Blanca is constantly surrounded by female characters whose fortunes reflect and mimic her own: the dead and mutilated sisters; the maid who travels with her to Flanders; the husband's sister who is killed before Blanca herself. Within this shifting female group there is a fluidity of circulation, a lack of division: the lady, the maid, and the friend speak freely and intimately to one another. Indeed, Blanca and her friend are mirror images of each other, in spite of their differing nationalities. As the title of one of Irigaray's texts has it: 'The one does not move without the other.'[23] This reciprocal female exchange, so different from the fitful and halting relations between men and women in the story, is continuous and undifferentated, like the touching of two lips.

---

[23] *Et l'une ne bouge pas sans l'autre* (Paris, 1979), a short text on the relationship between mother and daughter.

Yet these women can only reflect each other's absence, represent for each other a common impotence and exclusion. Blanca is defined (if at all) by her absence of sexuality: her one positive act is to burn the bed in which her husband and his page have made love, a symbolic rejection of desire in all its forms. But this negative female exchange his its counterpart in the equally hermetic social system of the male. For Blanca's investment with the attributes of the wife (passivity, muteness, subservience) is required by the alien productive economy of men. The husband, the father, and the page form a group as self-sufficient as that of the wife, the friend, and the servant. So self-sufficient in fact that even sex takes place within the male grouping. The husband and his lover are not ashamed by their discovery: rather, they revel in it. And this is because (according to both Zayas and Irigaray) 'hom(m)osexualité' (sexual commerce between men) is the logical result of a system which persists in excluding women. In this 'circulation of the same' women can figure only as objects of exchange and can never transcend a state of permanent exile. The dominant male culture thus promotes an overt exogamy (marriage across the national boundaries requiring the exchange of women) and a covert endogamy (exclusive relations between men which ensure the oppression of women).

Blanca's name, then, is exemplary not only because it suggests purity and innocence, but because it denotes both absence (white as lack of colour) and currency (the 'blanca' as unit of money). At once central and peripheral to the logic of the text, she may be identified with Irigaray's *korē*, the virgin trapped in the eye of the mirror, purely reflective, and purely absent. But Irigaray also asks us to read the 'blanks' of patriarchal discourse and suggests the possibility of a space beyond its dominion (*Speculum*, pp. 176–7). Can we escape from the bloodless corpse at the end of the story and propose a new version of the body that is neither absence (negativity) nor pure presence ('personality')? If such a reading is possible then it lies (as it does in the case of Teresa) in the intermittence of Zayas's narrative and syntax. Thus the stories as a whole are burdened by a narrative framework recounting the loves of Lisi and her companions, that becomes increasingly emphatic in the second volume. These narrators tend to intervene at inappropriate moments. For example in 'Mal presagio' we are given a digression on the Spanish love of formal address ('don' and 'doña'), which is not only irrelevant to the main theme, but also tends to detract from it (p. 530). For if Spaniards are indeed as haughty as the narrator suggests, then Blanca's chilly reception in Flanders is not quite so difficult to understand. Much of the story is taken up with descriptions of the year spent in courtship (a mere preliminary to the action proper) and in the transcription of songs and poems often irrelevant to the main narrative. At a smaller level, even the most dramatic of scenes are curiously over-burdened with precious or unmotivated detail. Thus when Blanca lies dying, Zayas speculates as to the possible causes of her husband's brief and tardy compassion: is he moved to see this 'lily stripped of its leaves', or enamoured by such a noble death' (p. 542) When she is finally dead, the fact that Blanca can no longer envy the fate of her sisters, the military deeds of the Duke of Alba carried out in her name, and the desperate mourning of Blanca's lady servants are all packed together in a single massively proliferating sentence, full of subordinate clauses (pp. 542–3). It is not surprising that the only English translation omits much of this detail and cuts the lengthy period up into several shorter sentences.[24] Thus the climactic moment in the story (the one which seems to require the most perfect 'clarity' of style) produces the most opaque and perplexing syntax. It is as if the final exclusion of the woman from the narrative provokes a linguistic compensation on the part of the writer.

Muerta la hermosa doña Blanca tan desgraciadamente, por que no envidiase la desdicha de sus hermanas, si es don para ser envidiado, dexando bien que llorar en aquellos Estados, pues los estragos, que tocaron en crueldades, que el duque de Alba hizo en ellos, fue en venganza de esta muerte . . . como doña María y las demás pudieron salir adonde estaba, no lo rehusaron, antes llorando se acercaron todas de ella, españolas y flamencas, . . . que de todas igualmente era amada . . . (p. 542–3)

When the beautiful doña Blanca had died so unfortunately, in order that she should not envy the fate of her sisters (if it is a gift to be envied) she left much to be wept over in those Territories, since the

---

[24] *A Shameful Revenge and Other Stories*, trans. John Sturrock (London 1963), 150–1.

dire deeds, verging on acts of cruelty, which the Duke of Alba performed there were in revenge for this death . . . since doña María and the other ladies were able to come out to where doña Blanca was, they did not neglect to do so, and rather weeping all drew near to her, both Spaniards and Flemings, . . . for she was loved the same by all of them . . .

The reaction of critics to such passages is complex. For the same men who praise Zayas for her simplicity and naturalness chide her for the inclusion of irrelevant detail and the failure to conform to grammatical precept (see Amezúa, i. p. xxx; ii, p. xiv). Disrupted syntax is the same 'fault' found by critics in Teresa. Already Luis de León complains that Teresa begins a new topic before she has finished the old one, mixes up arguments, and breaks the thread ('rompe el hilo') of logical discourse (*Vida*, p. 15). In both Teresa and Zayas this lack of grammatical linking (known technically as anacoluthon) is said to contribute to the spontaneity of the style. Yet there is an alternative reading of this phenomenon, a 'womanly' one. Irigaray calls for a text that will overturn syntax ('bouleverser la syntaxe') and suspend teleology through the breaking of linguistic threads ('la rupture des fils', *Speculum*, p. 177). Such a practice must resist the enforced return to a single textual origin by means of a limitless expansion and diffraction. To read Zayas (and Teresa) as a 'woman's writing' would thus be to refuse the temptation to construct a 'personal identity' as source of the text, and to attempt (provisionally at least) to experience *all* writing as an alternating play of continuity and rupture, stasis and impulse. This does not mean that we should isolate these texts from all historical or subjective determinants. To acknowledge their plurality need not be to celebrate their incoherence. Rather, it would be to accept that woman's experience cannot be spoken in a man-made language without gaps and discontinuities; and that the utopia of a purely female space must be a break or threshold in a dominant male order.

It could be argued that 'Mal presagio' is atypical of Zayas's work as a whole. In his *María de Zayas* (Boulder, 1923) Edwin B. Place claims it is 'a revolting story of cruelty', an example of 'feministic propaganda', and 'the most blood-curdling of the whole collection' (p. 47). The first volume of *novelas* is less relentless in its depiction of women as victims, and an analysis of a very different story from that volume ('El prevenido, engañado') will shed new light on the roles of women and men in Zayas's work. As its title suggests, this story concerns a male protagonist who although cautious ('prevenido') is deceived ('engañado') none the less. The noble Fadrique is led through a catalogue of amorous misfortunes. First, he sees Serafina, the woman he hopes to marry, give birth in secret to a daughter whom she abandons. Next, he discovers that Beatriz, the rich widow he is courting, has taken a black servant as her lover, and has indeed exhausted him with her exorbitant passion. Finally, he is tricked into sharing a bed with the husband of a relative of his latest fiancée. After a night defending his honour from the sleepy advances of his bedmate, he discovers that it is no man he has been resisting, but rather the beauteous Violante whom he loves. Disillusioned with worldly women, he returns to his home town where he had placed Serafina's abandoned daughter (Gracia) in a convent. Now grown up, she corresponds exactly to his desire: she is 'the very subject he was seeking' (p. 168). After they are married the cautious Fadrique tests his bride's ignorance by telling her that the role of the wife in marriage is to stand guard over her sleeping husband. This she does over a number of nights. However, a youthful lover takes advantage of Gracia's *naïveté* and introduces her to a different kind of married life, one for which she need not wear helmet and breastplate. When Gracia ingenuously confesses what she has learned from her 'other husband' Fadrique at last realizes his mistake: women cannot be virtuous if they are kept in ignorance.

Unlike 'Mal presagio', 'El prevenido, engañado' has many comic elements. Indeed the tone is sometimes farcical. Gracia embodies once more the negative definition of woman we saw in Blanca, but in a lighter tone. She is passive, ignorant, and prone to repetition, only too willing to mimic the words told her by the two 'husbands' and to represent the (contradictory) roles they require of her. She has no desire in herself. Her desire is of or for the other. As an armed guard, she keeps watch over patriarchy in the form of her husband; as a pliant sexual partner, she adapts herself to the pleasure of a younger suitor. From the moment of birth, when she is abandoned by Serafina, she is destined for confinement; and she ends her life stupidly happy ('boba') in the same convent as her mother (p. 173).

On the other hand, Fadrique is scarcely more active than his wife. He is frequently reduced to voyeurism: he spies on Serafina's confinement and Beatriz's illicit liaison. It is ironic that he is so anxious to avoid homosexual rape, for access to female sexuality is wholly denied him. Woman's desire remains an exotic spectacle. Fadrique is literally unable to recognize a woman even when he shares a bed with her. The patriarch thus suffers repeated humiliation, and is finally parodied in the figure of the 'Amazon' Gracia, who keeps watch, in full armour, over her sleeping husband. Thus although it is the women who complain of melancholy (to mask pregnancy or illicit intercourse), it is the men who are left frozen in front of the mirror, petrified by a lack of self-knowledge. We are told that Vicente, one of Serafina's unsuccessful suitors, dies of melancholy (p. 168); and Fadrique must die with an awareness that he is the cause of his own deception. He has foolishly relied on women as the supplement to his lack, the key to his own identity. His only relation to himself is one of exteriority.

The later work of Irigaray has addressed this same problem of heterosexual relations and male identity. Irigaray reiterates, in a very different register, the twists and turns of Zayas's novella. Thus in *Amante marine* (Paris, 1980), she claims after Nietzsche that woman cannot adopt the position of truth, that she is foreign to any essence (p. 92). Like Ariadne she is the double of man, lending her thread to his explorations (p. 125). Woman is always stillborn, subject to an endless arrest or sentence of death: 'Arrêt, et de mort, sans fin' (p. 127). The mimicry and negativity of characters such as Gracia are visible here. But so too is the isolation of Fadrique. In the more lyrical *Passions élémentaires* (Paris, 1982) Irigaray continues to investigate the paradox that the negativity assigned to woman is related to a certain deficiency in man. *Passions* is a text addressed by a female voice to a male love object. The woman is given a white or blank mouth, through which she sings a song for him who does not listen. With his tongue in her mouth, how can she do other than speak to him (pp. 7, 9)? He seeks her, but inside himself, making her serve as 'virgin matter' on which he constructs his world (p. 10). Man is thus dependent on the woman he ignores: his body is her prison, but they will die together if he allows her outside his self/same (p. 17). He will remain enclosed for ever by his skin, and can only touch himself from the outside.

If *Passions* has a moral it is similar to that of 'El prevenido engañado'. It is that truly heterosexual relations will remain impossible until women are allowed self-knowledge. This is not the banal message that foolish women will prove resistent to male logic. Rather, it is the more complex suggestion (implicit in Zayas, explicit in Irigaray) that a woman's language would transform the current order of knowledge, would open up the space for new gender identities defined in the light of a genuine difference.

4. A CHANCE OF LIFE

Walter J. Ong has suggested that women writers played a significant role in the evolution of the novel, because they were uncompromised by the rhetorical education of their male counterparts.[25] In Golden Age Spain the position seems rather more complicated. Although we can only speculate about the exact degree of formal education that Teresa and Zayas received, what is plain is that both were aware of a male rhetorical tradition, which they sometimes mimicked and sometimes subverted. The occasional disintegration of syntax we find in both writers may derive from an inability or unwillingness to find coherent expression for female subjectivity in male literary conventions. This is not, of course, to suggest that anacoluthon or ellipsis are absent in Cervantes or Góngora. A feminist reading cannot claim syntactic disruption as an essential characteristic of women's writing, or as an eternal threat to male hegemony. After all, such disruption is also typical of Kristeva's nineteenth-century avant-garde, not to mention twentieth-century modernism. But we should be

[25] *Orality and Literacy: The Technologizing of the Word* (London, 1982), 111–12, 159–60.

aware of the mobile articulation of some women's writing (the *chōra*) and of the deadly fixity with which she is sometimes represented (the *korē*). If such an awareness is supplemented by a knowledge of contemporary rhetoric, the discursive 'body' which emerges is at once biological and historical.

Ironically, perhaps, what Teresa and Zayas have most in common is the qualities falsely attributed to them by male readers: idiosyncrasy, spontaneity, naturalness. If we reject such terms as being irretrievably compromised by a male system which both idealizes and denigrates women, then we are thrown back to the male system as an object of study in itself. In this system, Teresa might be seen as the siren: the mobile body, drifting on the semiotic sea of drives and desires, threatening male composure, while remaining the object of its fascinated gaze; Zayas might be seen as the bearded lady: the monster deprived of feminine charm by an attempt to mimic male potency that was always doomed to failure. Mary Jacobus, we remember, calls for a work of revision, that will preserve woman's alienation while transcending her marginality. Such a project is not merely Utopian or theoretical. It creates the space for new readings of women writers such as Teresa and Zayas. But it also requires us to look once more at the male writer and reader, stripped of his spurious potency and now relative, particular, and marginal himself.

What is the role of mysticism within this revised view of the relation between the sexes? Irigaray addresses this question directly in a chapter in *Speculum* which bears the title 'La Mystérique' (pp. 238–52). The neologism refers to 'mystery', 'mystic', 'hysteric', and even 'soul' ('l'âme'). For Irigaray the main value of mysticism is that it offers a public space for the articulation of female desire. Here, the most poverty-stricken are the richest in visions (p. 239). The mystic takes (her) pleasure in a phantom play of reciprocity in which each partner enjoys the other. But even here woman cannot escape repetition: at the centre of mystic experience we find, once more, the mirror (pp. 245, 246). The mystic cannot escape the One, the self-same of the male order. Her text remains a flaming speculum, the reflection of male examination.

The model seems appallingly passive. But Irigaray's minute attention to the subtleties of power does not preclude the possibility of resistance. Rather, the one is the necessary precondition for the other. Irigaray recently read a lecture in London on the theme of political resistance: 'A Chance of Life: Limits to the Concepts of the Neuter and the Universal in Science and Knowledge.' In this paper she stresses once more her rejection of an 'objective' rationality which excludes women, and of a society between-men ('entrehommes') which presents itself as natural. And she proposes a social 'sexuation', the transformation of society through the acknowledgement of women's particular relation to time and to war. She concludes by advising women to hold on to subjective experience, but not at the risk of emotionalism. It is a strategy reminiscent of Teresa: a rejection of rationality which does not require the abdication of public discourse; a concern for the affects which does not permit sentimentality.

We are left none the less with the problem of repetition and subversion. Can feminists remobilize traditional 'images of women' (as emotional, as maternal) without reconfirming prejudices? As Rose says of Kristeva's later work: '[It] splits on a paradox, or rather a dilemma: the hideous moment when a theory arms itself with a concept of femininity as different . . . only to find itself face to face with . . . the most grotesque and fully cultural stereotypes of femininity' (*Sexuality*, p. 157). For Irigaray *all* women are subjected by such images, even those who believe themselves to be liberated.

One of Zayas's fictional narrators is 'Zelima', a moorish slave who has the letter 'S' branded on her cheek. After telling her story, which is one of captivity, Zelima reveals that she is in fact 'Isabel', a Christian lady who has faked the signs of slavery in paint: the surface branding merely points to a deeper servitude 'in the soul' (p. 373). 'Zelima' may wipe off her make-up, but she cannot erase the trace of a difference which is at once sexual and linguistic. She is scarred by the mark of the Signifier. Teresa's body was pierced and burned in the transverberation, and quite literally dispersed after her death by seekers of relics from Europe and Mexico. Zayas's narrator is mutilated and her characters abused. But if woman is wounded, what will become of man? This is the main question to be addressed in the chapters which follow.

2

GÓNGORA AND BARTHES

1. 'BEYOND' TRANSGRESSION

BARTHES is the least systematic of writers: we will find no consistent theory of sexuality to abstract from his texts. The label 'feminist' or 'deconstructionist' can perhaps be taken as referring to a particular body of criticism, however multiple and contradictory that body may be. But to proclaim oneself a 'Barthesian' would be senseless, since Barthes's own career is one of continuous displacement and self-contradiction. Thus it is conventional, if not quite accurate, to draw a distinction between the early 'scientific' Barthes and the later 'subjectivist' Barthes. The watershed is taken as occurring in 1970 with the publication of the books on Balzac and Japan (*S/Z* and *L'Empire des signes*, respectively).[1] *S/Z* in particular, a work which sets out a complex system for the analysis of narrative to which Barthes himself never returned, has been taken as emblematic of this insistent displacement and dispersal of self. The emphasis in Barthes's later work would seem to shift from language to the body. While some critics (such as Culler)[2] have seen this move as a retreat into subjectivism and mystification, it could also be read (in broadly Marxist fashion) as an attention to the materiality of the subject and to his or her position in history. These are questions which were neglected or repressed by the implicitly transcendental model of the subject implied by an earlier structuralism. More particularly, although some feminists have objected to Barthes's apparent indifference to the status of woman,[3] I would argue that his presentation of the self in all its contingency, even randomness, enables us to read his work quite explicitly as that of a man writing, a man who has abandoned any claim to be

---

[1] The first published in Paris, the second in Geneva.
[2] See Jonathan Culler, *Barthes* (London, 1983).
[3] See Morag Shiach, 'Roland Barthes: Some Feminist Fragments', unpublished paper read at the conference on Barthes held at Warwick University in 1985.

'representative'. Barthes's body, then, is not natural, but cultural.

In this chapter I read two texts by Góngora (the *Soledades* and the *Polifemo*) in the light of the two questions raised above. The first question is that of displacement: is it possible to go 'beyond' transgression, to escape that structural rigidity to which sexual and textual movement is always prone? The second question is that of the body: is it possible to read narrative as a body (an arbitrary collection of texts) and to read the body as discourse (a mosaic of linguistic fragments)? As we shall see in the conclusion, even the most shockingly subjective of Barthes's texts does not necessarily reconfirm the reactionary values of unity and transcendence conventionally attributed to the bourgeois 'individual'.

At first the conjunction of Barthes and Góngora will seem perverse, even preposterous. After all, Barthes himself expresses little interest in European literatures and languages other than the French, still less in Spanish poetry of the Golden Age. Yet on closer examination the conjunction seems more plausible. Commonplaces about both writers tend to coincide: thus Barthes is a professed hedonist, the theorist of 'pleasure' in its various forms, and Góngora is the poet of the senses, the eulogist of pagan luxury and bodily delight. Yet both couch pleasure in the language of difficulty, and both are attacked by contemporaries for their use of 'jargon'. Góngora's extreme linguistic disruption, his separation, say, of noun and adjective, of article and noun, are as radical as the disintegrative poetics championed by Barthes in the experimental works of a Robbe-Grillet or of a Sollers. In particular the formal characteristics of Barthes's and Góngora's 'jargons' have much in common: a love of neologism and Latinism; a reliance on the figures of contrast and disruption: antithesis, asyndeton, anacoluthon. Like the modern text praised in *Le Plaisir du texte* (Paris, 1973), Góngora's formal difficulty exacts a reading which is leisured, in Barthes's word, 'aristocratic'. And like the modern text again, Góngora's later works are 'writerly', requiring the active participation of the reader in the reproduction of syntax, viewpoint, and (eventually and provisionally) meaning. The perspective they offer the reader is multiple and discontinuous, an aspect enhanced by the learned nature of Góngora's verse, by its saturation in erudite reference and allusion. The space of these poems is (in Barthes's image again) the echo-chamber, of a generalized and constantly deployed 'citation without speechmarks', which remains both anonymous and highly tangible. If all writing may be seen as the intersection of a multiplicity of discourses, then few poets have foregrounded this intertextuality as emphatically and knowingly as Góngora.[4]

Barthes, like Góngora, raids the texts of the past in the production of his own works, which typically take the form of a collection (or 'circle') of fragments. The first poems I treat by Góngora might be seen as equally fragmentary and discontinuous. The *Soledades* or *Solitudes* (written around 1612–13), perhaps Góngora's greatest achievement, are unfinished and (arguably) ill-defined works. They consist of two poems (of what may have been a projected four) of about one thousand lines each, framed in a loose and flexible metre, the *silva*.[5] The narrative is elliptical: in the first poem the (nameless) hero is shipwrecked on an unnamed island, and is welcomed by the local rustics, one of whom makes a lengthy oration on the perils of navigation. He witnesses a marriage and the games by which it is celebrated. In the second, he is entertained by a fisherman who tells of his daughters' exploits in the catching of marine monsters; there follows an alternate song between two amorous sailors, and the work ends, abruptly, with the description of a hawking party.

Pleasure, difficulty, intertextuality, discontinuity: these are the general areas which Barthes and Góngora seem to have in common. There is one point, however, at which Barthes himself in his own writing refers explicitly to Góngora. It is a fragment in *Roland Barthes par Roland Barthes* which has the title 'Actif/passif':

Viril/non viril: ce couple célèbre, qui règne sur toute la Doxa, résume tous les jeux d'alternance: le jeu paradigmatique du sens et

---

[4] See Antonio Vilanova's monumental *Las fuentes y los temas del 'Polifemo' de Góngora* (Madrid, 1957).

[5] For a discussion of the *silva* see Maurice Molho, *Semántica y poética* (*Góngora, Quevedo*) (Barcelona, 1977), 79–81. The texts and translations to which I refer in this chapter are: *The Solitudes*, trans. E. M. Wilson (Cambridge, 1965); and *Polyphemus and Galatea: A Study in the Interpretation of a Baroque Poem*, ed. Alexander A. Parker, trans. Gilbert F. Cunningham (Edinburgh, 1977).

le jeu sexuel de la parade (tout sens bien formé est une parade: accouplement et mise à mort). (p. 136)

Virile/non-virile: this famous couple, which reins over all the Doxa, comprehends all kinds of the play of alternation: the paradigmatic play of meaning and the sexual play of the parade (all well-formed meaning is a parade: coupling together and putting to death).

The transgression of the deadly coupling of opposites is fraught with danger: thus in 'Arab countries' (unnamed) the practice of homosexuality, potentially transgressive and libertarian, merely reinscribes the subject in the tyrannical paradigm of performance and acceptance: active/passive. There remains, nevertheless, the possibility of escape, both sexual and textual:

Cependant, dès lors que l'alternative est refusée (dès lors que le paradigme est brouillé), l'utopie commence: le sens et le sexe deviennent l'objet d'un jeu libre, au sein duquel les formes (poly-sémiques) et les pratiques (sensuelles), libérées de la prison binaire, vont se mettre en état d'expansion infinie. Ainsi peuvent naître un texte gongorien et une sexualité heureuse. (p. 137)

However, once the alternative is refused (once the paradigm is scrambled), Utopia begins: meaning and sex become the object of a free-play, in the midst of which (polysemic) forms and (sensual) practices, freed from the binary prison, will reach a state of infinite expansion. In this way there can be born a Gongorine text and a happy sexuality.

The transgression which will transcend transgression itself and free the subject from the binary prison is thus given a name: happiness, or alternatively, Góngora. Barthes's use of the name here is no doubt (to use his own term) 'reactive'. It serves a rhetorical function in his argument, by denoting the exclusion of the term he rejects. The 'Gongorine' text is implicitly opposed to the supposed characteristics of French classical writing attacked in *Le Degré zéro de l'écriture* (Paris, 1972), 32–40, and in the essays on La Bruyère and La Rochefoucauld: continuity, metonymic progression, closure. French 'clarity', ridiculed by Barthes in *Critique et vérité* (Paris, 1966), is superseded by Spanish 'baroque' convolution, its obscurities supposedly more open to the free-play of sense or meaning.

The fragment 'Actif/passif' itself however suggests a heuristic or exploratory movement which I shall employ in the

reading of the *Soledades* which follows. First, the construction
of the paradigm: the conventional gendering of language and
discourse in which culture causes sex and text to lie down
together in an apparently natural and eternal union; secondly,
transgression: the ways in which Góngora's reproduction of
gender roles and observation of genre rules might be seen as
'scrambling' the paradigm constructed above; thirdly, recuperation: the 'reading out' of these apparent innovations in the
light of contemporary poetic practice outside Spain; fourthly
and finally, evacuation: the provisional and hazardous attainment of a state of non-meaning or indeterminacy immune to
the coercive policing of generic determinism. This journey
through signification ('le chemin du sens') is exemplified in a
passage from the first *Soledad* on a wrestling match, to which I
shall give particular attention.

But an initial question remains to be resolved: why the
association of sex and text? There is some anxiety in modern
criticism that genre is trivializing and external. Indeed,
Barthes himself makes this objection at one point (*Degré zéro*,
p. 42). The attempt by a theorist such as Todorov[6] to claim
speech-acts as the origin of genre-forms reflects the desire to
upgrade genre by associating it with the supposedly natural
and authentic spoken word. Yet I would suggest that genre
needs no justification, for its very name reveals an essential
and often repressed condition of writing: that language is
always already gendered, that sex is never absent from
discourse or value. The play I make on gender and genre
(frequent now in feminist criticism)[7] is of course impossible in
Romance languages where one word designates both concepts:
the Spanish 'género', Italian 'genero', or French 'genre'. The
common origin of these words, the Latin 'genus', is cognate
with 'gignere', to produce (of plants and animals): Nature
supplies the language of culture. Quintilian's genders of nouns
and kinds of discourse are denoted by the same word: 'genera
nominorum' and 'genera dicendi', respectively. The slippage
between sex and text is almost imperceptible, because of its

---

[6] See Tzvetan Todorov, 'L'Origine des genres', in *Les Genres du discours* (Paris,
1978), 44–60.
[7] See e.g. Susan Kirkpatrick, 'On the Threshold of the Realist Novel: Gender and
Genre in *La gaviota*', *PMLA* 98 (1983), 323–40.

very omnipresence. If language is a system of differences, then the sexual distinction is uniquely efficacious, because uniquely 'natural'. Thus Quintilian, again, speaks in *Institutio oratoria* of a 'natural order' which *precedes* rhetorical invention: 'men and women, day and night, sunrise and sunset' (9. 4. 23). In classical rhetoric (as in Barthes) text or discourse is a body: the figures of speech articulate the oration as the movements of the limbs do the body (2. 13. 9). But the virtues of this body are male: 'a solid and robust eloquence' (10. 1. 2). A typical passage is Quintilian treating a delicate subject (ornament), hedges it about with appeals to male virtue and attacks on female vice:

But let this ornament be manly ('virilis') and strong and holy, and not seek effeminate smoothness and the lying colour of cosmetics, but shine with blood and strength. (8. 3. 6)

The male text is authentic and true, the female counterfeit and mendacious. The former is like a male athlete whose muscles have been formed by exercise: handsome, yet well-equipped for competition (8. 3. 10). This image of eloquent discourse as the rivalry of trained men, recurs in a passage in which the utility of figures of speech is compared to the employment of weapons by armed combatants: the orator will defeat his opponent with the devious thrusts and counterstrokes of the linguistic sword (9. 1. 20).

By the sixteenth century, literary genre is divided according to gendered conceptions of matter and form. Thus Scaliger's *Poetices libri septem* (Lyons, 1561) state succinctly that the subjects of the epic, the highest genre, are 'dux, miles, classis, equus, victoria' ('the commander, the soldier, the fleet, the cavalry, victory') (p. 45). The inferior lyric, on the other hand, treats the matter of love: 'curas amatorias' (p. 47). The status quo is supported, as ever, by appeal to Nature, changeless and eternal guarantor of meaning and value. The virtues required of the text are abstracted from an idealized Nature and projected back on to Art as concrete realities. Thus Tasso in the *Discorsi dell'arte poetica* (first published in 1587) seeks to defend the epic's unity of plot from the wayward violations of Ariosto's *romanzo* by appeal to Nature.[8]

[8] See Bernard Weinberg, *A History of Literary Criticism in the Italian Renaissance* (Chicago, 1961), 647.

But the object of this 'natural' imitation in its highest mode is
unequivocally masculine: 'The illustrious of the epic poet is
founded on the deeds of a supremely virtuous warrior, on acts
of courtesy, of generosity, of piety, of religion' (cited by
Weinberg, p. 648).

And this masculine prestige is also that of the epic poet who
seeks to coerce his audience into belief by the recitation of
manly exploits (Weinberg, p. 686). Compare this example of
'mediocrità lirica' taken from the *Discorsi del poema heroico* (first
published in 1594): 'La verginella è simile a la rosa | ch'in bel
giardin su la nativa spina | mentre sola e sicura si riposa | né
gregge né pastor se le avvicina'. ('The coy maiden is like the
rose | which in a beautiful garden on her native thorn | while
she remains alone and in safety | no flock or shepherd will
approach her').[9] Here, lyric is a lady is a flower: gender,
genre, and Nature link hands once more. And the floral motif
recurs on the following page in the association of lyric poetry
and linguistic ornament.

Thus the gender-paradigm constructed under the auspices
of Nature is (of course) in no way innocent, not merely a case
of 'separate development'. When male, utility, virtue, and
epic are contrasted with female, decoration, sensuality, and
lyric then the contrast is in each case not one of true
opposition but rather of deprivation. In scholastic terms, the
female elements are not a *species relativa* (different, but equal
and even mutually constituting) but a *species privata* (different
because of a lack in the second term of the defining
characteristic of the first).[10] Thus lyric irredeemably lacks the
gravity of the epic, while epic (if necessary) can encompass the
delightfulness of the lyric: Tasso's examples (p. 224), tellingly,
are Virgil's depictions of Dido and Venus as huntresses in the
Aeneid. Classification is always already valorization. And this
sense of woman as deprivation is a commonplace of other
disciplines of the period. Physiologically, woman is held to be
an imperfect version of the male: while man is hot, woman is
cold. She consequently lacks the moral qualities associated
with high body temperature: courage, liberality, honesty. In

  [9] Torquato Tasso, *Discorsi dell'arte poetica e del poema heroico*, ed. Luigi Poma (Bari,
1964), 197.
  [10] See Ian Maclean, *The Renaissance Notion of Woman* (Cambridge, 1980), 44–5.

the case of ethics, too, woman lacks man's powers of judgement. Where woman is allowed to possess a quality unknown in men it is always a failing, such as the love of ornament and decoration with which she is charged by both theologians and, as we have seen, rhetoricians (see Maclean, pp. 32, 50, 15).

The final element in the paradigm, and one peculiar to Góngora and his time, is that of nationality. The poets of sixteenth-century Spain borrowed and assimilated both verse form and poetic lexicon from Italy; yet in spite of, or perhaps because of, this indebtedness, there remained a persistent anxiety as to the enervating influence of the florid Tuscan on the severe Castilian. For the poet and rhetorician Fernando de Herrera (in a work published in 1580) the terms of this relationship are implicitly gendered: Tuscan is soft and lascivious, Castilian grave and moral.[11] Where Italian has the feminine vices (sensuality, promiscuity), Spanish has the manly virtues, canonic already in Quintilian's prescription for robust and solid eloquence: virility, nobility, religiosity.

The Spanish poet of the late sixteenth century is thus uniquely bound in the discursive prison of binary, reactive oppositions. But this constriction is not experienced as such; indeed, it is assumed to be eternal and attributed to Nature. And these oppositions are the enabling conditions of writing: epic gravity is read for its difference from lyric sensualism; Spanish severity for its manly divergence from the genetically effeminate Italian (and vice versa). Such hierarchic taxonomies are not extrinsic to the practice of writing, but rather constitutive of it. Hence their extraordinary prestige.

2. THE *SOLEDADES*: GENDER AND GENRE

Virile/non-virile: as Barthes suggests, this is indeed the arch-distinction, enforcing value throughout the Doxa. How, then, does Góngora appear to transgress the (extended) paradigm constructed above? First, in the reproduction of gender-roles. Spanish poetry of the period is massively male: man is the viewer and speaker; woman, the object of his gaze and of his

---

[11] The work is the *Anotaciones* to Garcilaso, reprinted in Antonio Gallego Morell (ed.), *Garcilaso de la Vega y sus comentaristas* (Madrid, 1972), 313.

amorous discourse. There is no Spanish equivalent of Louise Labé or Gaspara Stampa, a woman poet to speak in praise of man as object of desire. Góngora's presentation of women and of men seems non-standard when taken in this context: they tend not to conform to the codes of expectation by which they are conventionally defined. Thus the anomymous protagonist is curiously non-virile, led apparently at random from one incident to another by the rustics he meets on his way.[12] The supposed cause of his wanderings (misfortune in love) is revealed only belatedly and plays no part in the narrative. His sole defining characteristic is an unmanly one: beauty. When tossed naked by the waves on to the island in the opening lines he is defined with reference to the most common of homosexual myths, that of Ganymede: 'el que ministrar podía la copa | a Júpiter mejor que el garzón de Ida' ('fitter cup-bearer than Ganymede | for Jupiter') (lines 6–7).[13] Such passivity is hardly compatible with the hero of epic. As one of Góngora's contemporary critics complained, he is merely a 'mirón' or 'watcher'. One object of his gaze is indeed woman: concealed in the trunk of a tree he watches the country girls dancing and singing (262–5). But in one other scene at least (the wrestling scene, to which I will return later) the display of male bodies is offered explicitly for the gaze of women.

More frequently, female and male attractions are counter-poised: 'tanto garzón robusto, tanta | ofrecen los álamos zagala' ('So much sturdy youth | So many maids the poplars could display') (i. 643–4), 'vírgenes bellas, jóvenes lucidos' ('splendid youths and lovely maidens') (i. 732), 'del galán novio, de la esposa bella' ('Of handsome lover and of lovely bride') (i. 1043). In such typically elegant and balanced parallelisms the antitheses of gender difference are subsumed and neutered by aesthetic equilibrium. It is the movement which Gérard Genette proposes as the 'structural poetics' characteristic of French baroque: difference becomes contrary;

[12] For a detailed study of Góngora's impersonal protagonist see Antonio Vilanova, 'El peregrino de amor en las *Soledades* de Góngora', in *Estudios dedicados a Menéndez Pidal*, iii (Madrid, 1952), 421–60.

[13] For a study of the different representations of male beauty in Spanish and Italian lyric of this period see Paul Julian Smith, '*Descriptio pueri*: Praise of the Young Hero in some Poets of Renaissance Spain and Italy', *SS* 24 (1983), 57–66.

contrary, symmetry; and symmetry, equivalence.[14] The play
of alternatives offered by the paradigm (either male or female)
becomes a reconciliation of opposites lent equal status by the
poet's ornamental superfluity (both male and female).

The rhetorical 'body' of the *Soledades* is characterized by the
facile aestheticism and gratuitous decoration enacted in such
antitheses and chiasmuses. Its promiscuous ornament is
emphatically female, based primarily on verbal patterning
rather than conceptual coercion. In rhetorical terms, the
stress is on figures of speech, rather than figures of thought. In
particular, Góngora favours those linguistic strategies condemned by the rigorous Herrera: the piling-up of nouns or
adjectives for cornucopian display, as in the catalogue of birds
of prey in the final hawking scene; the affective emotionalism
of the diminutive, so compromising to masculine gravity: the
calves and kids of domestic animals; the 'bunny rabbit'
('conejuelo') which here need not fear man. And these
features are, as we have seen, associated with Italian language
and poetry. For all its classical reference, the immediate
precursors of the *Soledades* are Italian: Guarini's tragicomedy
and Sannazaro's piscatorial eclogues.[15]

Góngora, then, seems consistently to valorize the traditionally
negative, privative side of the gender paradigm: woman,
ornament, lyric, Italy, these are the emphases of a work which
aspires nevertheless to the highest regions of cultural prestige
and to the utmost limits of linguistic complexity. To what
genre, then, do the *Soledades* belong? Not surprisingly, the
question is a complex one, and the source of much controversy
at the time of their appearance. Góngora is immediately
attacked for treating matters more suited to lyric in an epic
style.[16] The plot is said to be inconsequential and incoherent,
wholly lacking the 'natural' unity required by such theorists
as Tasso, in whom amorous adventure is safely subordinate to
heroic purpose and civic utility. If place is uncertain, then so
is time: one critic complains (perhaps unfairly) that at one

[14] 'Une poétique structurale?', *TQ* 7 (1961), 13–19.
[15] Molho cites Poliziano's *silvae* and Tasso's *Aminta* as precursors of the *Soledades* (pp. 44–6). Wilson claims in his intro. that Góngora's world is 'more robust, less effeminate' than that of Sannazaro and Montemayor (p. xv).
[16] See Ana Martínez Aracón, *La batalla en torno a Góngora* (Madrid, 1978), 32.

point the rustics huddle over a log fire as in winter, and at another sweat drips from their faces as in high summer. The poet is unequal to the demands of the heroic style (Martínez Arancón, p. 189).

This rhetoric of abuse is of course blindly and unknowingly gender-based. Góngora's improper mixture of languages produces a 'hermaphroditic' text whose lack of unity is inevitably compared to Horace's exemplum of the unnatural imitation in the *Ars poetica*: the torso of the handsome woman which ends in the tail of a black fish. For Quevedo, Góngora's great enemy, Góngora's verses are 'per-verses', an 'adulteration' of 'chaste' poetry (Martínez Arancón, p. 84). The prudent poet (that is, man) will scorn reckless ornament and sing (in Propertius's much-quoted phrase) 'things which any girl can understand' (Martínez Arancón, p. 103). Lyric is here assimilated to seduction, the male speaker overcoming female listener by the force and subtlety of his eloquence, as before in Quintilian the orator defeats his opponent with the tricky sword-play of his tongue. Góngora's obscurity, his 'jargon' effectively remove him from this standard economy of seduction and domination, his monstrous conjunctions are irreducible to the binary poles of emission and reception (active and passive) implicit in any model of discourse based, like the rhetorical, on the primacy of audience and of communication.

Góngora himself is not insensitive to these charges. In a famous defence he claims the utility of his poetry is in the sharpening of the reader's wits with its erudition. The reader is to take off the 'corteza' ('bark' of a tree or 'skin' of a fruit) to reveal the mysterious truth within (Martínez Arancón, p. 43). This commonplace of hermeneutic with its organicist metaphor reinserts the text into the general poetic marketplace: it may be peeled like an orange (albeit with difficulty) and consumed with pleasure and profit by the discriminating reader or gastronome. But if the *Soledades* are a natural product, their form, substance, and origin (in a word, their genus) is uncertain even to their admirers. Thus one supporter proposes, with the poet himself, that matter and style are not bucolic but heroic (Martínez Arancón, p. 141). The authority cited, as so often, is Tasso's *Del poema heroico*.

But Góngora's principal commentator (Salcedo Coronel) proposes an elaborate myth of origin based on the poem as natural effusion of the solitary forest which is its subject. The *Soledad* is a *silva*, that is 'forest': as the wind moves through the trees, causing them to vibrate in rustic harmony, so the poem flows from the poet, rude and unpolished.[17] This model of spontaneous generation is evidently incompatible with both the heroic dignity associated with the high style and the manifest poetic craftsmanship of the text itself. The embarrassment of Góngora's supporters is in proportion to the generic indeterminacy of his creation, a monster which appears to transgress the constrictive paradigm of sixteenth-century poetics.

However, this temporary and provisional triumph of pleasure and generic confusion as supreme poetic criteria is no sudden innovation, but is rather foreshadowed by developments in the second half of the sixteenth century. The history of poetics in the period is to a large extent the history of the controversy over new genres: Ariosto's *romanzo* and Guarini's tragicomedy. Tasso himself, defender of heroic unities, is the precedent for the wholesale incursion of lyric into epic, though he feels obliged to justify the amorous adventures of his Christian knights by lending them an allegorical meaning. Góngora's defensive strategies are rather similar. But at times in *Del poema heroico* Tasso's distinction between epic and lyric becomes tenuous indeed. He speculates that 'se l'epico e 'l lirico trattasse le medesime cose co' medesimi concetti, adoprerebbe per poco il medesimo stile' ('If epic and lyric were to treat the same subjects with the same ideas they would adopt more or less the same style') (Tasso, p. 227). As Bernard Weinberg describes the process, the abstracted, Platonic forms attributed by the moralists to a changeless and eternal Nature are superseded by pragmatic literary forms based on individual literary production and the desires of specific audiences (p. 1104). There is something of this sense of fluidity in Góngora's cavalier approach to the generic Doxa which he inherits, in his production of a work irreducible to pre-existent genre forms.

Construction, transgression, recuperation: the final stage of

---

[17] *'Soledades'* . . . *comentadas* (Madrid, 1636). fo.1ᵛ.

the paradigmatic movement outlined in the introduction remains: that of evacuation, or the achievement of a potential non-sense or third term which transcends the deadly play of alternation. I would suggest that the *Soledades* aspire to this (unrealizable) ambition to the extent that the space and time they offer the reader is (in Barthes's distinction) a-topian rather than U-topian. As we have seen, commentators are uneasy at the indeterminacy of Góngora's island, which remains unnamed. Yet for all its classical and Italianate resonance, the rustic topology is not merely literary, not purely reducible to Utopian fancy. Thus the newly-weds are greeted with an epithalamium reminiscent of Catullus, and Cupid and Neptune participate in the narrative; but the speech on the perils of seafaring refers to Columbus, Magellan, and the historical circumstance of Spanish discoveries in the New World.[18] The dignity of classical myth is repeatedly disrupted by gratuitous humour in which homely matter and elevated diction are made to clash head-on: take, for example the periphrastic eulogy of the ram: 'El que de cabras fue dos veces ciento | esposo casi un lustro' ('He who for near a lustrum was the spouse | Of twice a hundred she-goats') (i. 146–47). Góngora tells us that the goat's death redeemed countless vines ('vides'), a blasphemous pun on the death of Christ, which redeemed lives ('vidas'). The burlesque debunking of mythology, whether classical or Christian, is of course common in the period. What seems unusual is the intermittence of this bathetic stance, the inconsequentiality of its effect. In burlesque, the literary is deflated by the real; in panegyric, the real is elevated by association with the literary. In Góngora's twilight zone of generic indeterminacy both terms float in an evaluative void and the status of each is called into question. Likewise, praise of the country and vituperation of the town is a contemporary topos, rehearsed at length at one point in the

---

[18] For the most sophisticated attempt to establish a relationship between Góngora's practice as a writer and the historical moment in which he lived see the work of the theoretical Marxist John Beverley, including: intro. to Luis de Góngora, *Soledades* (Madrid, 1979); *Aspects of Góngora's 'Soledades'* (Amsterdam, 1980); and 'Barroco de estado: Góngora y el gongorismo', in *Del 'Lazarillo' al Sandinismo* (Minneapolis, 1987), 77–99. Beverley's work is a necessary antidote to the frequent aestheticism of traditional approaches to Góngora, but he does not consider the question of gender which is my subject here.

poem (i. 88–129). But Góngora's villagers do not live in harmony with Nature as one might expect, but ravage and despoil it for their very cultured purposes.[19] One example, as I will demonstrate in a moment, is the chopping down of trees to construct a classically inspired arena for the nuptial games. Once more, it is not that cultured shepherds are infrequent in contemporary pastoral, but rather that Góngora's rustics are alternately coarse and sophisticated, that they represent no 'gold standard' of immutable and natural goodness by which the inauthentic deviants of the city may be measured. Nature itself is 'denaturalized' and can no longer be taken as origin and focus of permanent value.

We come now to a particular passage, the wrestling match at the end of the first *Soledad*, in which I hope to show that by following the path of meaning ('le chemin du sens') to its very end the conventional values of nature, myth, and gender may be 'exempted' or neutralized and the expansive free-play of sense and sex achieved, albeit momentarily. The topos itself is a test case, in that the description of games is a set-piece of the epic which comes to Góngora saturated with the heroic value and resonance of the *Iliad* and the *Aeneid*.

> Llegó la desposada apenas, cuando
>   feroz ardiente muestra
> hicieron dos robustos luchadores
> de sus músculos, menos defendidos
> del blanco lino que del vello obscuro.
> Abrazáronse, pues, los dos, y luego
> —humo anhelando el que no suda fuego—
> de recíprocos nudos impedidos
> cual duros olmos de implicantes vides,
> yedra el uno es tenaz del otro muro.   (963–72)

> And hardly had the bride arrived there, when
>   Two sturdy wrestlers showed
> Fierce burning sinews, hidden more from sight
> By bodies' hair than by their linen white.

---

[19] For the relationship between town and country see M. J. Woods, *The Poet and the Natural World in the Age of Góngora* (Oxford, 1978), 158–66; and J. F. G. Gornall, 'Góngora's *Soledades*: "Alabanza de aldea" without "Menosprecio de corte"', *BHS* 59 (1982), 21–5.

> The one embraced the other next, and then
> —One panted smoke, the other fiery glowed—
> The double knot thwarting their joint intent,
> (Like the tough elms with clinging vines around)
> One, ivy, hung upon the other, wall.

This description may be seen in itself as an intertext, a space or gap between the successive movements of epic narrative. Thus in the most authoritative precedent (Virgil's *Aeneid*) the games occur in Book 5, a necessary interlude between the lyric and heroic highpoints of Books 4 and 6: the love of Dido and Aeneas and the descent into the Underworld, respectively. In Virgil, however, the games have a place in the martial and civic vision of the poem as a whole: the same men now competing at sport will soon be engaged in the genuine battles required for the founding of Rome itself, the transcendental mission of the epic as a whole. The ethos is patriarchal: the games are in remembrance of Aeneas' dead father, symbol of the values and culture the soldier-athletes are transporting from Troy.

In the inconsequential narrative of the *Soledades* the games have no such function: the participants are unknown, their motive derisory—the celebration of a marriage between two (equally anonymous) villagers. Yet the passage occurs in an emphatic, indeed climactic, position at the end of the first poem, and (as the contemporary commentators demonstrate) it is sonorous with classical echoes. Sons of the earth, the wrestlers are subsequently compared to Antaeus, opponent of Hercules, who regained his strength on touching the ground. But this is only the most emphatic of heroic resonances: the image of the fallen man as uprooted pine that follows the passage also occurs in Virgil's boxing match. The appeal to the blind forces of Nature (earth and tree) suggests the un-mediated closeness of the peasants to their land. But, typically, the space in which they meet is that of classical culture: the colosseum or Olympic palestra formed by the chopping-down of the trees. And the trees themselves are by no means innocent, are described as having 'feigned the forest'. Even nature in its primal, virgin state is a deceit, an imitation, no less mendacious than the fictions of classical myth. The wrestlers are naked, but they are clothed by Culture—the literary reminiscence of a practice (the nakedness of athletes) common in antiquity but unknown in Catholic Spain. Inversely, this classical abstraction and intemporality is compromised by specific, material detail: the dark body hair ('vello obscuro') which covers their limbs. The wrestlers are at once and alternately natural and cultural, classical and contemporary.

This spectacle of the male body is explicitly proposed for the female witness: 'Llegó la desposada apenas' ('And hardly had the bride arrived there'). The contemporary commentator, Salcedo Coronel, goes on to suggest that the shady auditorium is intended for the 'serranas' ('village girls') and other female spectators to sit in (fo. 185^v). At this point, then, Góngora seems to be proposing an alternative perspective to that of the hegemonic male gaze. Salcedo Coronel cites Julius Caesar Scaliger as an authority on classical games. But Scaliger himself notes that Augustus prohibited women from watching athletic contests, lest they be stirred to lascivious thoughts by the naked bodies of the male contestants, smeared with oil and scattered with dust (*Poetices*, p. 37). Góngora's insistence on the presence of women at his wrestling match thus seems to carry a particular significance, for it implies that the possibility at least of a female desire can be acknowledged and celebrated within the poem. Moreover, the public display of physicality entailed by wrestling itself is alien to the prudish Spanish male: the commentator refers to bouts he has witnessed in Italy 'donde mas ordinariamente se exercitan en este certamen' ('where they more commonly participate in this contest') and is anxious to assure the Spanish reader that even there, in dangerously lascivious Italy, contestants wear tunic and shorts (fo. 186^v).

The significance of the *Soledades* is thus, in the final analysis, literary, self-reflexive. The games are the space of a motivelesss versatility and ingenuity, of a poetic performance in which the textual body flexes its figurative limbs. For Barthes, we remember, meaning is a deadly parade: 'tout sens bien formé est une parade: accouplement et mise à mort' ('all well-formed meaning is a parade: coupling together and putting to death.') In Góngora, the threat of death is dispersed (the wrestlers' performance is derisory) and evaluative meaning with it. My equation of poetics and gymnastics may seem far-fetched, but it also occurs in Renaissance theorists. Thus Scaliger treats the origin and practice of the classical games under the heading of 'Historicus' in his *Poetices libri septem*, affirming that games are mute fictions ('fabulae'), while fictions are speaking games (p. 37). Like the 'well-lit body' to which Barthes draws attention in what he styles the small textual 'theatre' of the marquis de Sade,[20] Góngora's wrestlers benefit from the sensual privilege of enshrinement in desire. The evacuating process is similar to that described by Barthes in his famous essay on wrestling in *Mythologies*.[21] The audience has no concern for an authentic outcome to the combat, but rather trusts to the primary virtue of spectacle, the abolition of all causes and effects (p. 14). Góngora's text, motiveless and inconsequential, embodies the virtue of pure spectacle.

3. THE *POLIFEMO*: NARRATIVE AND CATACHRESIS

The *Fábula de Polifemo y Galatea* (1613) is written not in the flexible *silva* verse form, but in the more rigid *ottava rima*. In other ways, however, it is rather similar to the *Soledades*. Its narrative structure seems somewhat arbitrary: near the beginning we find a lengthy description of the giant Polyphemus' cave, and near the end an extended account of his love-song for the nymph Galatea. The climactic moment, however, in which the giant's rival Acis is murdered as he attempts to flee, is in contrast rather cursory. We also find, as in the *Soledades*, a relative lack of concern for a consistent or authentic representation of the real. Although the *Polifemo* is set in a pre-classical Sicily, there are wilful anachronisms, such as the reference to Swiss pikemen in the love-song (428). Another feature shared by both texts is the idiosyncratic treatment of gender-roles. As we shall see, the handsome Acis presents his naked or lightly-clothed body for the contemplation of his female partner.

Critics tend, once again, to erase or suppress questions such as these. Thus Parker [22] vindicates the symmetry of the poem's

---

[20] *Sade, Fourier, Loyola* (Paris, 1971), 137.
[21] 'Le Monde où l'on catche', in *Mythologies* (Paris, 1957), 13–24.
[22] In the intro. to his edn. (see note 5).

structure: the thirteen stanzas of the Cyclops' song are said to 'balance' the fifteen which precede the love-making of Acis and Galatea (p. 73). For Parker the form and structure of the *Polifemo* are 'rounded and finished' (p. 80). Critics have also attempted to ascertain or elucidate the 'reality' to which Góngora refers: does he conceive nature as an exemplum of Platonic harmony or of anarchic violence?[23] This debate has restricted itself, however, to the verification of a referent beyond the text (or in Barthes's phrase) 'behind the page'. It dare not consider the possibility that the contradictions are of such a kind as to elude resolution in any referent, even that of conflict. The bias towards unity of form and reproduction of the real shared by modern critics derives from an appeal to 'nature' which remains unexamined: both text and world are held to be informed by an underlying principle of organic order, even when (as here) that order is seen to break down. It is no accident that the critics keep returning to the apparent naked-ness of Góngora's lovers and their passionate instincts. I will argue that in the *Polifemo* there can be no nakedness unclothed by culture, no instinct uncompromised by textuality.

Seventeenth-century readers are often less eager than modern critics to impose meaning or symmetry on the work. In his defence of Góngora, Gonzalo de Hoces claims that the poet flees from simplicity ('sencillez') as the child abandons its first garments, and frees its arms from swaddling clothes.[24] Natural development is here inseparable from the proper acquisition of culture and language. And if a supporter of Salcedo Coronel claims that the latter's commentaries have stripped away the 'veil' which covers the light of Góngora's text, then the commentator himself acknowledges more modestly that the literary precedents to which he could have compared the *Polifemo* are 'infinite' and would make 'many books' in themselves.[25] Here there is no primary text (no nakedness), no access to a single, instinctive origin. Rather, we find an endless proliferation of textuality in which Góngora

---

[23] See Parker's intro. for an account of this debate, referring to critics such as Dámaso Alonso, R. O. Jones, and C. C. Smith.

[24] *Todas las obras de don Luis de Góngora* (Madrid, 1634), 'Vida del autor', unnumbered.

[25] *El 'Polifemo'* . . . *comentado* (Madrid, 1629), sonnet in praise of Salcedo Coronel by Miguel de Silveyra; and the ed.'s preface 'Al lector' (both unnumbered).

takes up a position that is particular, but by no means isolated. My own view is not incompatible with that of seventeenth-century commentators: it is that the *Polifemo* is constituted by a plurality of narrative codes; and that those codes engage figures or commonplaces of love, not icons of authentic or instinctive sentiment.

As I stated in the introduction to this chapter, Barthes's most systematic account of narrative structure is *S/Z*, a dogged, even perverse, reading of the Balzac novella *Sarrasine*. Barthes begins by rejecting both the quest for a single model adequate for all narratives and the desire to impose meaning on a text in the name of 'interpretation' (pp. 9, 11). The critic should rather attempt to appreciate the plurality of the codes of which the text is composed, a plurality which admits no totalization and no 'foyer': centre, refuge, source of luminous truth (pp. 12, 14). The text is not to be reconstructed but to be pierced or broken off (pp. 20, 21). What the author writes is the 'already-made', 'already-read', the 'furrow' left by the passage of the codes which precede the text he or she writes (pp. 26, 28). At this point, Barthes invokes the Spanish verb 'citar' ('to quote' or to 'make a date') in a specialized sense: the bullfighter gestures for the bull to charge him, but steps aside at the last moment (p. 29). In just such a way the writer invokes a signified or referent which is called into being by his gesture but can never be wholly present to the reader. But this model of text as citation is no theoretical nicety. Rather, it is intimately related to the body, and in particular, to the woman's body. For Barthes, feminine beauty has no referent in the real, always feeding back to the cultural code from which it derives: Woman copies the Book and all bodies are a quotation of that which is already written (p. 40). Thus beauty can never be explained, but can only be affirmed, enumerated in each (fetishized) part of the body. If a woman is said to be as beautiful as Venus, to what is Venus to be compared (p. 41)? In this endless circulation the primary term of the comparison (the referent) remains empty of meaning. The figure of beauty, then, can be named as 'catachresis': like the 'arms' of a chair or the 'sails' of a windmill, it is always already distanced, metaphorical, and has no unmediated access to the real.

From these opening sections of *S/Z* we can see that Barthes's model of narrative is inseparable from his model of the body. The latter is not so much an object represented in the text as a sequence of figures which are constitutive of it. A number of Barthes's arguments seem particularly appropriate for the *Polifemo*. Like Barthes's connotative text the *Polifemo* has no 'foyer', or stable centre: the focus shifts from the Cyclops' cave and complaint to the amorous dalliance of the lovers in the fields. As the commentators have demonstrated, every line of the *Polifemo* is a tissue of voices, a complex furrow ploughed out for Góngora by the passage of earlier poets. In this intertextual landscape, Góngora 'quotes' or 'invokes' ('cita') a series of referents which are called into visibility, only to vanish without trace. One example is the 'carpet' of flowers which, we are told, Tyrian dyes would imitate in vain (313–15). Here the poet gestures towards a real which is nominally anterior to the artificial or secondary term to which it is compared. But he cannot do so without appealing to the figure of catachresis: the 'carpet' of flowers is always already metaphorical, can have no literal name. In cases such as this, or the 'wall' of ivy shattered by the giant (272), nature is displaced by an originary culture, just as the referent is displaced by a primary use of language.

Elsewhere Góngora tells us that before Galatea lays eyes on Acis a 'brush' has sketched him in her imagination (251–2). It is symptomatic of the way in which painting is taken as a model for a mode of writing which keeps the referent at one remove, in an indefinite suspension. The *pintura* of Galatea is made up of a series of examples of transferred attributes and epithets: her beautiful eyes make her 'the peacock of Venus' and 'the swan of Juno' (104); and the roses and lilies of her complexion produce 'snowy red or red snow' (108). This fluidity of metonymic exchange and substitution reveal how the textual portrait is produced by the superimposition of multiple elements. But it also suggests that the (woman's) body is itself articulated according to pre-existing codes: the figures which stand in for a conventional beauty (divinities and flowers) come to serve as primary terms which mask the absence of an original referent. Góngora's topoi serve, in Barthes's term, as *indices* (p. 69): they 'point' without saying

(invoke, but do not embody). If Galatea's beauty seems 'real'
(in spite of the impossibility of the reader visualizing what the
poet describes) it is because the real is always that which can
be represented, not that which can be executed or put into
practice (p. 87). Thus it does not matter that the reader cannot
conceive of red snow. The figure engages, immediately, a
formalized and autonomous code of representation which has
no need to depend on the real. But such codes resist
totalization. In Góngora (as in Balzac) the female body is
presented as a sequence of partial objects (eyes, complexion,
lips) which cannot be reassembled to form an organic whole
(p. 118). In other words, the catalogue of anatomical attributes
cannot be predicated from a single subject (p. 120). Another
rather similar example is when Galatea is described as giving
to a stream 'as many jasmines as the grass hidden by the snow
of her limbs' (179–80). Commentators cannot agree whether
the flowers refer to her limbs stretched out on the grass or
reflected in the water (Parker, pp. 142–3). The question has
proved undecidable. What seems more important is to
recognize that the image is emblematic of a shimmering
linguistic surface which refuses to be anchored safely to the
solid materiality of a pre-existing referent.

   Góngora's catachreses (metaphors deprived of primary
terms) thus point to an absolute attribute (beauty, femininity)
which they necessarily fail to embody. But there are other
points in the poem at which realism stands revealed as that
which is not 'opérable', which can be represented but not put
into practice. One of these is the scene in which the Cyclops
looks at his reflection in the sea (421–2). The image derives
here, as so often, from Virgil's second *Eclogue*; and it is one
which the earliest Latin commentators attack for its implausibility. Góngora makes the scene more 'opérable' than Virgil
by saying it is the time of perfect calm when the halcyon lays
its eggs (417). But it remains the case that the resonance and
indeed humour of the passage relies on the reader's awareness
of the textual furrows left in the poetic ocean by the passing of
earlier poets. What is more, this highly cultivated nature is
prone (like Góngora's roses and lilies) to metonymic disturbance: the single eye reflected in the water changes place with
the disk of the sun (423–4). As Barthes suggests, the ceaseless

play of the codes can be arrested only outside nature by the sublime or the monstrous (p. 62). The single eye of the Cyclops spreads, pandemically, through the text. It is a fitting image of the (male) order of representation, of the endless traffic of reflection.

Traditional criticism tends to look 'behind' or 'beyond' such passages, stripping away the veils of language to reach the naked truth within. It is Barthes's contention, however, that inside the textual body there is precisely nothing. This can be illustrated by a close reading of Góngora's portrait of male beauty, Acis. As I mentioned previously, Acis presents his body for the woman's gaze. Having come across the sleeping Galatea by accident, he prepares an offering of rustic gifts for her and then feigns sleep as she awakes. Galatea hovers like an eagle over a kite fledgling (261–4): the roles of victim and aggressor are reversed for a moment. And she sees reproduced 'in colour' the sketch already drawn in her imagination (269–72): representation precedes experience of the world. Góngora gives a *pintura* of Acis' beauty in which his hair is compared to the setting sun and his downy beard to flowers at twilight:

> Del casi tramontado sol aspira
> a los confusos rayos, su cabello;
> flores su bozo es, cuyas colores,
> como duerme la luz, niegan las flores.   (276–80)

> In mingled hues his locks aspire to trace
> The cloudy brilliance of the sunset's sheen;
> Down blooms upon his cheeks, though sleep denies
> That bloom the hidden daylight of his eyes.

Salcedo Coronel stresses the scantiness of his beard: just as the colours of flowers cannot be distinguished when sunlight grows faint, so Acis' down cannot be recognized as he sleeps (*Polifemo*, fo. 67ʳ). The similitude is imperfect, and the argument obscure. It is more significant to note that here Góngora trusts to the same lyric topos and rhetorical figure on which he relies for the invocation of feminine beauty: the flowers of catachresis. Elsewhere, when Góngora mentions the 'pearls' of sweat on Acis' brow, the commentator cites a precedent in Tasso, where the sweet disorder of dust and

perspiration adds piquancy ('grazia') to male beauty (fo. 51ᵛ).
As in the case of the portrait of the woman, the image of the
man (however aestheticized) is never self-sufficient or identical
to its referent: it is always reliant on the collaboration of a pre-
existing code. When Acis pretends to awake he shakes his
limbs and proudly shows off his 'persona' (298). Critics have
disagreed as to whether this phrase implies he is naked.
However it should be stressed that there can be no absolute
nakedness in poetry. As Barthes says of Balzac's use of
euphemism, the meaning of the text lies in the plurality of its
(contradictory) registers (p. 126). It is precisely the superimposition of various levels of association which produces the
texture, and indeed, the eroticism of such passages. Like the
wrestlers of the *Soledades*, the lovers of the *Polifemo* have no
decidable or consistent state of (un)dress. In just the same
way there can be no final unveiling of the text: for Barthes
'dévoilement' leads to the knowledge that what is revealed at
the end of a text is, quite simply, the end (p. 193). Narrative
has no object but itself (p. 219).

   This is not to minimize the power of Góngora's poetry, nor
to suppress the particularity of its vision. But I would suggest
that if the *Polifemo* reveals anything beyond itself it is what
Barthes finds in *Sarrasine*: the trouble of or in representation
(p. 222). By his adoption of a constantly shifting sign system
Góngora calls into question the ability of one term to stand in
for (to represent) another. In the *Polifemo* we find an unregu-
lated circulation of signs, and, indeed, of sexes. In the text
of Góngora (as, incidentally, in that of Balzac) the narrative of
love is also a narrative of death and castration. At the end, of
course, Acis is crushed by a boulder hurled by the giant, and
is transformed into a river which flows to the sea. But there is
also a curious item in Acis' list of rustic tributes to Galatea
which deserves closer examination in this context. The
reference is to 'the celestial fluid, recently solidified, | which
the almond kept between green and dry' (201–2). One
modern editor (R. O. Jones)[26] writes that Góngora is probably
referring to nuts which were shelled but not dried (p. 148).
But what of the 'celestial fluid'? Another scholar[27] has claimed

---

[26] *Poems of Góngora* (Cambridge, 1966).
[27] *Antología poética*, ed. Antonio Carreira (Madrid, 1986), 183, n. 97.

that Góngora is citing the Phrygian myth of the origin of the almond: Zeus' sperm engendered Agdistis, a hermaphrodite whose genitals were cut off by the gods. Where the genitals fell there arose almond trees. Acis offers his gifts in exchange for sexual favours. But they bear hidden within them the marks of castration and death which are wholly at odds with the overt intentions of both character and author in the passage. Both language and desire bring with them the possibility of an uncontrollable excess of connotation. The feminization of Acis (as aesthetic icon, as object of the active gaze) suggests not so much a simple reversal of the paradigm, as the collapse of the economy of meaning. It is but a symptom of a prevailing metonymic contagion in which predicates such as beauty or femininity are constantly displaced in the search for an original subject always already lost. As Barthes shows, this form of catachresis is habitual even in 'realistic' writing. The extremity of Góngora's text, however, suggests a topography of the body wholly alien to the codes on which it draws none the less: one in which the difference between inside and outside is abolished, in which the underncath is empty, in which the contract of desire is broken (*S/Z*, p. 220). A body, in short, which, deprived of both interiority and essence, is all surface, all text.

4. FIGURES OF SEXUALITY

If the *Soledades* and the *Polifemo* can be read as love stories, then it should perhaps be in the way suggested by Barthes in his *Fragments d'un discours amoureux* (Paris, 1977). Barthes compiles a dictionary of 'figures', defined as gestures of the body seized in action, not contemplated in repose (p. 7). The frozen movement of the figure is often a commonplace, even cliché; and it shares with the cliché a certain emptiness of meaning (p. 9). These figures are outside any syntagm or logical sequence of terms, and cannot be integrated at a higher level or absorbed into a transcendental 'work' (pp. 10, 11).

In just such a way Góngora's poems are composed of a sequence of figures (of bodies arrested in motion), which are wholly reliant on conventional, topical context (the elm and the vine, the rose and the lily). They resound only in the space of a citational culture. And they are scandalously resistant to narrative impetus and conceptual resolution: each fragment remains isolated and particular. The *Soledades* and the *Polifemo* have successfully resisted critical attempts to reduce them to formal integration and evaluative cohesion.

But to say that Góngora invokes the empty commonplaces of love is not, of course, to deny the particularity of his poetry: it is marked throughout by very specific determinants of place, time, and person. Góngora's pagan landscapes may be made up quite literally of poetic 'places' (topoi), but in the extremity and density of their repetition of conventional motifs they stake a claim to a unique difference. As Barthes claims in *Incidents* (Paris, 1987), the most recent of the posthumous collections, the only way to 'read' a landscape is through the body, that is, through the necessary mediations of our subjectivity (p. 20). Most of *Incidents* is taken up with the repetition of the figures of sexuality, fragments of intimacy which seem all the more real because they are rewriting a corporeal text we seem always to have known. But it would be naïve to take such glimpses of the private as a confession of Truth. If these texts have any significance it is in their refusal to integrate the discontinuous, and to attribute value to erotic experience. This is also the case with the *Soledades* and the *Polifemo*, texts which defy integration and resist transcendent meaning.

3

GALDÓS, VALERA, LACAN

1. PSYCHOLOGISM AND PSYCHOANALYSIS

To attempt a reading of the nineteenth-century novel in the light of psychoanalytic theory is to be confronted by a series of obstacles. Would-be psychoanalytic critics often deal in archetypes (the negation of history) and prescription (the normalization of the subject). They seek to dissect the author or character, as if the first were immediately accessible and the second endowed with autonomous existence. And they are frequently tempted by the lure of the allegorical reading, that which substitutes latent for manifest (penis for pen) in the quest for 'original' or 'authentic' meaning invisible, yet accessible, beneath the surface accident of the text. All of the above tendencies I call 'psychologist' rather than 'psycho-analytical'. That is, they constitute a vulgarized simplification of the enterprise initiated by Freud. In her book *Psychoanalytic Criticism: Theory in Practice* (London and New York, 1984) Elizabeth Wright suggests an attractive model for the critic who seeks to reconcile history and subjectivity, language and mind, in a properly rigorous manner. She writes: 'Psycho-analysis explores what happens when primordial desire gets directed into social goals, when bodily needs become subjected to the mould of culture. Through language, desire becomes subject to rules, and yet this language cannot define the body's experience accurately' (p. 1). The lack of correlation between desire and culture is stated very clearly here: the linguistic and the somatic intersect (but do not coincide) in the figure of the body. If we follow through Wright's account of psychoanalysis and apply it to literary studies, then the fixity of the archetype will give way to the unstable process of socialization; and prescription will yield to description. The object of study will become not the author or character but the structure of the text itself; and the quest for stable or original meaning abandoned for the movement of desire in language. Indeed, Jane Gallop has gone further by suggesting that if there is a 'method' to be abstracted from psychoanalysis it is not the compulsion to transform accident into meaning, but a rigorous attention to the *reste* or remainder, to that which is marginal, irreducible, which stubbornly resists interpretation.[1] One image of this unassimilable remainder is 'the letter'. Another is 'the woman'.

The major exponent of this anti-psychologist psychoanalysis is Jacques Lacan, who consistently rejects any conception of psychoanalysis as a metalanguage, as the ultimate test of authoritative meaning. Why is Lacan central to the present volume? First, because he is concerned with the primacy of language or the signifier in the constitution of the subject. Two *Écrits* to be discussed later in this chapter are of particular interest to the student of narrative: the seminar on Poe's *The Purloined Letter* and 'L'Instance de la lettre' (translated as 'The Agency of the Letter', but perhaps better rendered as 'Insistence'). Both texts (written in 1956 and 1957 respectively) make the uncompromising point that it is language (or the letter) which calls the subject into being. But for Lacan language cannot be separated from sexuality. And the two texts on sexuality to which I shall appeal in this introduction are 'La Signification du phallus' of 1958 (translated as both 'signification' and, more simply, 'meaning'); and *Encore*, a late and notoriously difficult seminar of 1973.[2] The extreme difficulty of even the earlier texts prevents the Lacanian formula 'There is no metalanguage' from being taken as a polite, theoretical commonplace. Meaning is continually deferred as we move along the chain of Lacan's paradoxes and catachreses. For Lacan psychoanalysis is a clinical practice: he asks what it can learn from literature, but not what literature can learn from it. And it seems impossible to envisage any critical model which would remain faithful to

[1] *Feminism and Psychoanalysis: The Daughter's Seduction* (London, 1982), 92–3.

[2] 'Le Séminaire sur *La Lettre volée*' and 'L'Instance de la lettre dans l'inconscient ou la raison depuis Freud', in *Écrits*, i (Paris, 1966), 19–53, 249–89; 'La Signification du phallus', in *Écrits*, ii (Paris, 1971), 103–15; *Le Séminaire: Livre xx: Encore* (Paris, 1975). Trans. of these texts in Alan Sheridan, *Écrits: A Selection* (London, 1977); and Juliet Mitchell and Jacqueline Rose (ed.), *Feminine Sexuality: Jacques Lacan and the école freudienne* (London, 1982). My refs. throughout are to the French originals.

the fearsome complexity of Lacan's own texts. But one feminist reader of Lacan (Jane Gallop, once more) has suggested that infidelity is precisely the position that should best be adopted by women critics (*The Daughter's Seduction*, p. 48). Female (and perhaps male) readers should not take upon themselves the labour of reproduction, of mirroring the great man in all his authority. Rather, they should explore the gaps and detours in his writing which prevent it from achieving a seamless totality and an ultimate meaning. But this faithlessness does not imply a wholly random or subjectivist approach. Rather, it suggests a heavier responsibility: an increased attention to the specificity of both theoretical and literary texts, to the materiality of the letter. It is perhaps significant that what is at stake in the two novels I treat later in this chapter is precisely the fidelity of the woman protagonist to the patriarchal system which defines her position, a fidelity which is always precarious and unstable.

Malcolm Bowie makes a rather similar point to Gallop's when he argues that Lacanian psychoanalysis does not offer the critic an authoritative system but rather makes him or her sensitive to the 'commodity fetishism' implicit in the idea of the literary 'text' itself.[3] Just as capitalism represses the process of production and presents the commodity as a pure organic form, innocent of human labour, so literary criticism suppresses the intersubjective relations inherent in any act of writing and presents the text as a hermetically sealed abstraction. As we shall see, commodity fetishism (the alienation of people from objects and from one another) is a dominant theme in at least one of the novels to be read here, Galdós's *La de Bringas*. But Bowie's observation also suggests the possibility of an overlap or community of interest between psychoanalysis and Marxism. For example, Marxist alienation might be compared to Lacanian castration: the process by which people become estranged from themselves through enforced submission to an economic order beyond their own control seems similar to that by which subjects gain access to language and society only at the cost of psychic integrity. There are indeed close similarities between Marxist readings

[3] 'Lacan and Literature', *RS* 5 (1984–5), 1–26 (p. 20); repr. in *Freud, Proust, and Lacan: Theory as Fiction* (Cambridge, 1987).

of the nineteenth-century novel (perhaps the most stimulating on Spanish material) and my own psychoanalytic reading. However, it is not possible simply to displace one set of terms by another: the two fields are not concentric. Marxism must, finally, assume the existence of a science (itself) and a material base (the concrete) which lie beyond problematization. Lacanian psychoanalysis, however, rejects any claim to authoritative knowledge, and has little use for the 'real' (the irreducible and inaccessible substance outside representation). It is hardly surprising that much Marxist literary criticism has tended to neglect both language and sexuality, the two constant motifs of Lacanian psychoanalysis. For to acknowledge that either of these motifs could be a determining factor in the production of the subject would be to abandon those vestiges of autonomy and authenticity which even the most sophisticated structural Marxists still claim for the proletariat. Hence the relish with which Lacan cites (in a mischievous footnote) Stalin's decree that language is base, not superstructure.[4] Even the champion of Socialist Realism (the unmediated reflection of the real conditions of existence) is forced to acknowledge that language is not pure transparency, that it is not wholly immaterial.

Having sketched out the parameters of the psychoanalytical field, we can now look more closely at Lacan's theoretical accounts of male and female sexuality, accounts which will serve later in the chapter to suggest new readings of novels by Galdós and Valera. Lacan begins 'La Signification du phallus' with a reference to what is perhaps the most controversial of his borrowings from Freud, the castration complex. The boy-child's discovery that the mother is not gifted with the phallus he had assumed her to possess leads to the traumatic belief that he too will suffer similar deprivation. The position of the girl-child in relation to the castration complex is obscure in both Freud and Lacan (p. 104). What is important to stress here, however, is first, that Lacan is dealing with unconscious fantasy, not lived experience; and second, that the assumption by the subject of adult sexual identity is made only at the cost (for both sexes) of a traumatic

---

[4] *Écrits*, i. 252, n. 6.

sense of loss and absence. The moment of castration signals an opening-out from the narcissistic 'imaginary' dyad of mother and child into the alien world of the 'symbolic', where needs are clothed imperfectly in language and the 'third term' of the father intrudes in all its violence. But, once more, these terms need not be linked to any phenomenal reality. The materiality on which Lacan insists is not biological but linguistic. Indeed, the phallus itself is not flesh, but the 'passion of the signifier', the empty site on which meaning is continually erected and dismantled in the endless displacement of language. This radical disjunction between imaginary and symbolic (narcissism and socialization) suggests that language can never be coterminous with the movement of desire. For Lacan 'désir' (a controversial rendering of Freud's *Wunsch*) is the gap which opens up between demand and need. These last two terms are irreconcilable or, in Lacan's term, ec-centric: the demand for love is absolute, the need for material satisfaction particular. It thus follows that for Lacan desire is, by definition, insatiable: it takes up its position between the shifting poles of the psychic and the somatic, the absolute and the particular, the cultural and the biological. Childhood trauma recurs in adult encounters: each partner is for the other not the object of love, nor the subject of need, but the cause of desire. The role of the phallus in this process is to serve as the empty and provisional marker of the point at which language intersects with desire. It can only serve this function when veiled (pp. 109–11). To summon it into visibility would be to reduce law to flesh, to expose the arbitrary nature of what Lacan calls the 'mascarade' or 'comedy' of sexual relations. The positions adopted by men and women in relation to the phallic function are asymmetrical: the woman gives what she does not have (a fantasy of wholeness), the man seeks what he has already (the phallus of which his mother was deprived). But the universality of the phallic order has a final, perverse consequence: in its preoccupation with the 'mask' of feminity the virile parade is itself emasculated, feminized (pp. 113–15).

Much of the detail of Lacan's polemic in this short text remains obscure. What seems evident, however, is that 'the meaning of the phallus' is no fixed or stable signified. Rather, the phallus is the site of meaning, the signifier *par excellence* which serves to enforce value in the linguistic and sexual economy. While some feminists have reacted angrily to this apparent phallocratism, others have taken Lacan's extreme position as the starting point for a critique of the dominant order. In other words, they have taken his text as the description of a prevailing order, not the prescription for an unchanging state of affairs. As Gallop suggests: 'Feminism does not necessarily find its ally in the man who theorizes the relation between the sexes according to how, in all fairness, it ought to be' (p. xiii). By flaunting his phallic prestige Lacan pricks the bubble of male presumption at the same time as he asserts its ubiquity. And it should be stressed that for Lacan the phallic function cannot be reduced to the biological male. Indeed, I shall argue myself that Galdós's heroine places herself on the 'male' side of the phallic paradigm, while Valera's virile comedy subverts its own too-visible masculinity.

The seminar *Encore* offers a yet more extreme version of the lack of correlation between male and female. Indeed, Lacan states polemically that there is no 'rapport sexuel' (no relation between the sexes). There is only 'something of one', a residue of male narcissism. Love is always directed towards the subject presumed to know ('sujet supposé savoir'), and the resulting imbalance or frustrated reciprocity is neurotically rehearsed by men in their invention of obstacles to the achievement of gratification which prevent them from discovering the truth: that the lack of sexual relation makes gratification impossible already. One such case, for Lacan, is the phenomenon of courtly love in which men acted out the comedy of infinite deferment and thus endowed themselves with an illusion of autonomy (pp. 63–5). Why is it that no relation between the sexes is possible? Because, according to Lacan, man relates to the *objet petit a* (a narcissistic, infinitely labile other set in motion by the subject himself), while woman relates to the 'Autre' (an absolute Other of which she has no knowledge). Male desire is thus fantasy, woman's nonsense. Woman is 'pas-tout', not all, or incomplete, defined by her exclusion from language. In Lacan's scandalous sentence, 'Women do not know what they are saying', and their *jouissance* is taken without knowledge. Such is the case with the mystics. For Lacan the ecstasy of Bernini's Saint Teresa cannot be reduced to fucking ('foutre'). Rather, it denotes the complicity between female sexuality and authoritative knowledge. The male divinity is supported by (and is perhaps even dependent on) the pleasure which woman experiences, but cannot express (pp. 67–71).

It should be stressed once more that this is no global definition of an essential feminity. Lacan cites male mystics to the same purpose: subjects place themselves wherever they wish. And more particularly, woman is not to be defined as absolute absence, 'elle n'est pas pas du tout' (p. 69). Woman is precisely that which resists generalization. Thus Lacan refuses to write 'La femme' and strikes the article with a bar ('Ła'). Just as the phallus offers universality without authority (a phantom erection, a vacant site), so the 'pas-tout' offers negativity without essence (a persistent gap which cannot be closed). The slippery Lacanian terms cannot be reduced to a biologist paradigm of penis and penis envy (pure presence and pure absence).

Both of the novels I treat in this chapter have a feminine definite article in their title: *La de Bringas*; *Juanita la Larga*. In the light of Lacan's account of this same signifier, I would suggest that it should be read in the following ways. First, as a reminder of the materiality of the letter, of the determining force of language in human psyche and society. Second, as a pointer to the irreducibility of sexual difference, a difference which is, however, neither fixed nor innate. Third, as a sign of the woman's curious position, shuttling between a spurious universality and a genuine, but unknowable, specificity. This may seem to lend disproportionate weight to a single syllable. But for Lacan 'la' is the one signifier which cannot mean nothing. And for the psychoanalytic critic it may serve as the exemplary instance of the term which is too obvious to examine, too apparent to be significant, and which can serve, none the less, as the key to the interpretative process.

2. *LA DE BRINGAS*: THE FACTOR OF TRUTH

The definite article and genitive particle of the title *La de Bringas* point all too plainly to the socio-linguistic drama to be played out within the novel: it is the status of women as man's possession which is at stake here, a status which will prove to be more problematic than the (ironic) title at first suggests. Published in 1884, but set some sixteen years earlier on the eve of the Revolution, *La de Bringas* is the story of Rosalía, wife of the modest bureaucrat Francisco; of her passion for clothes which she cannot afford; and of her bungled adultery with the slippery diplomat Pez. There is a gallery of supporting characters, mainly impoverished aristocrats or would-be aristocrats like Rosalía herself, and an elaborate setting: the Palace in Madrid, where the Bringas family are housed and where Queen Isabel holds court.

Critics have tended to focus on two general areas: the psychology of Rosalía and the intricacies of Galdós's narration (that is, on the question of woman and on that of language). Typical of traditional psychologist critics is Marie-Claire Petit, who praises the emotional coherence of Galdós's women characters, which she traces back to the experience and memories of their creator.[5] More recently, Stephen Miller has claimed as a 'feminist' reading his proposal that *La de Bringas* be read as a *Bildungsroman* in which Rosalía discovers her 'true self' by winning her independence from a male-dominated society.[6] Bridget Aldacara's reading (earlier than Miller's) condemns the sexism of earlier male critics who are eager to attack Rosalía's 'immorality' and to defend her small-minded husband.[7] But Aldacara goes further than Miller by hinting, at least, that the critic's quest for authentic being is not to be taken for granted: Rosalía's passion for clothing cannot simply be dismissed as a substitute for 'deeper' sexual yearning. Indeed, the very possibility of psychic interiority is called into question by a society which has almost erased the distinction between public display and private sentiment. Alicia Graciela Andreu's excellent work on Galdós's relation to popular literature suggests that he often reproduces stereotypical images of women derived from 'literatura de consumo', images which are elicited by the class interests of the new

---

[5] *Les Personnages féminins dans les romans de Benito Pérez Galdós* (Lyons, 1972).

[6] '*La de Bringas* as *Bildungsroman*: A Feminist Reading', *RQ* 34 (1987), 189–99.

[7] 'The Revolution of 1868 and the Rebellion of Rosalía Bringas', *AG* 18 (1983), 49–60.

bourgeoisie.[8] The epigraph to her study, taken from a contemporary magazine, exhorts women to let their virginal purity serve as the mirror image of men's black wickedness. This image unwittingly reveals the role of women in the period: it is the traditional one of reproduction, of echoing back to man his own message, albeit in an inverted form. If this is the case, then the critic's quest for Rosalía's 'true nature' must of necessity be in vain. There can be no authentic woman under patriarchy.

I shall return later in this section to the problem of gender. It is enough here to say that the position of the phallus as signifier *par excellence* makes the identification of an intrinsic female subjectivity problematic indeed. This leads us to the second area of critical debate, Galdós's achievement in the realm of narration. Recent Anglophone criticism has tended towards relativism. For Diane Urey, Galdós's ironic treatment of characters such as Francisco Bringas reflects back on the reader: specularities within the narrative (Rosalía imitates her aristocratic friends, who in turn imitate the Queen) are mimicked or reproduced in the text's necessary failure to offer an adequate 'imitation' of a reality which must always escape language.[9] Both inside and outside the fiction, all is counterfeit, a mere play of reflections. Elsewhere Urey suggests that Galdós himself is subject to a reflexive paradox: he cannot write the history of his own writing of history (he cannot see his blind spot).[10] Peter Bly's position is rather similar when he comments on the unreliability of *La de Bringas*'s narrator and on the lack of any other authoritative figure within the fiction who can serve as a reliable guide for the reader. For Bly the events in *La de Bringas* have no 'outside', no verifiable

---

[8] *Galdós y la literatura popular* (Madrid, 1982). For woman as reader and character see D. J. O'Connor, 'La mujer lectora y protagonista de la novela española del 1870', *Hispanófila*, 84. 3 (1985), 83–92. See also Geraldine M. Scanlon, *La polémica feminista en la España contemporánea (1868–1974)* (Madrid, 1986).

[9] *Galdós and the Irony of Language* (Cambridge, 1982), 32, 38, 46, 52. For a critique of realism which cites Barthes's 'effet de réel' see Hazel Gold, 'Francisco's Folly: Picturing Reality in Galdós's *La de Bringas*', *HR* 54 (1986), 47–66. For a critique of the 'transparency' of language which cites Freud and Foucault see Luis Fernández Cifuentes, 'Signs for Sale in the City of Galdós', *MLN* 103 (1988), 289–311.

[10] 'Isabel II and Historical Truth in the Fourth Series of Galdós's *Episodios Nacionales*', *MLN* 98 (1983), 189–207.

context.[11] Thomas F. Lewis had earlier offered a slightly similar reading of *Fortunata y Jacinta*, but in structural Marxist terms. For Lewis there is indeed a referent in Galdós's fiction, but one produced in the (Lacanian) imaginary: the novel offers the progressive, bourgeois readership those elements of their ideology which are absent from the historical period in which Galdós is writing. Such readers are 'replenished' by this supplement to the real.[12] For Lewis the relation between fiction and history is thus eccentric or deviant, not simply one of mirroring or reproduction.

One problem raised but not answered by the liberal relativists is the status of the author in relation to the ironic, specular narrative he has called into being. It is not always clear whether he has cleverly contrived this play of relativities or whether he is himself a victim of forces beyond his control. The Lacanian view would seem to be that the position of subjects (whether writers or readers) is determined by the insistence of the signifying chain along which they move, by the endless displacement of language in which they are caught up. Just as the primacy of the phallus deprives woman of authentic identity, so the primacy of the signifier deprives all subjects of genuine autonomy. This hostility towards the autonomous ego is shared by Marxist critics. And before attempting a Lacanian reading of *La de Bringas* it is worth considering in detail a recent Marxist interpretation of the text. In the introduction to their edition,[13] Alda Blanco and Carlos Blanco Aguinaga cite Marx's (uncharacteristic) statement that 'language speaks itself' (p. 38). Language, like culture, is a material phenomenon and there can therefore be no simple distinction between appearance and reality (between words and deeds) (p.46). In spite of Galdós's minute attention to manners and costumes in the novel, the transformation of society which it depicts is not merely 'superficial'. Rather Galdós bears witness to the emergence of new subjectivities in

---

[11] *Galdós's Novel of the Historical Imagination* (Liverpool, 1983), 61, 71, 72.

[12] '*Fortunata y Jacinta*: Galdós and the Production of the Literary Referent', *MLN* 96 (1981), 316–39 (p. 339). For another complex account of the relation between history and literature see the same author's 'Galdós's *Gloria* as Ideological *Dispositio*', *MLN* 94 (1979), 258–82. For the latest essays on this topic see Peter A. Bly (ed.), *Galdós y la historia* (Ottawa, 1988).

[13] Published in Madrid, 1985.

response to emergent class antagonisms. This new order is based on exchange value: the ceaseless circulation of commodities (pp. 30–1). Amongst these commodities is woman: her only access to the world of men is through the medium of money (p. 19); and because of her economic dependency, she is forced to exchange her only possession (her body), whether inside or outside marriage, for the chance to play a role in the theatre of capitalism (pp. 33, 37).

All of these points may be reread in terms drawn from Lacan's famous seminar on *The Purloined Letter*. First, language (or the letter) is material by nature, in spite of its ability (shared with the economic order) to render itself invisible. The insistence of the linguistic chain (again, like that of the economic order) leads to the alienation or 'ex-sistence' of the subject. Language operates by displacement (exchange) and woman in particular is at once situated and alienated by its passage. She is both inside and outside its Law, excluded from participation and forced to play a subordinate role. The Poe story glossed by Lacan is one in which a letter circulates (unopened) from one male hand to another. All the reader knows of it is that if its content were revealed it would cause irreparable damage to the honour of the illustrious lady to whom it is addressed. For Lacan the story is exemplary of the primacy of signifier over signified (of movement over meaning); and of woman's role as the factor of truth (at once marginal and indispensable). His paradoxical conclusion has become a favourite axiom of literary theory: a letter, even when mislaid, always reaches its destination.[14] By this he suggests that any message received by the subject is one he has already sent himself, which returns in an inverted form.

It seems banal to state that letters play an important role in the narrative structure of *La de Bringas* (as indeed they do in *Juanita la Larga*) Rosalía's long-dreaded bill from the fashion house arrives in the form of a letter (xxxvii; 235), as does Bringas's medical bill (xxxviii; 241). An unexpected letter from Agustín Caballero in France (xxxix; 246) heightens

[14] *Écrits*, i. 19, 20, 25, 53. For woman as factor or messenger of truth see Jacques Derrida, 'Le Facteur de la vérité', in *La Carte postale de Socrate à Freud et au delà* (Paris, 1980), 441–524. This text is Derrida's reading of Lacan's seminar on Poe.

Rosalía's longing to escape Madrid. Finally, a letter from Pez informs Rosalía that she has sold her honour for nothing (xliv; 272). Lacan's rule of inversion seems to apply in most of these cases: the addressees receive messages contrary to their desires, but precipitated, none the less, by their own initiatives. Thus Rosalía procures her own ruin as she attempts to alleviate it, and Bringas provokes the expenditure he seeks to avoid. This kind of reading, however, is not merely banal, it is also allegorical: the characters are reduced to fixed counters who are forced to 'represent' a stable meaning, to stand and deliver to the critic. What seems more interesting about these examples is the way in which they suggest a network of references throughout the text, linking language to clothing, to money, and to sexuality. These references cluster around the body in its various states: decorated, maimed, and desired, respectively.

We may begin with clothing. Fashion is presented in the novel as women's language: Rosalía and her friend Milagros can indulge in their passionate conversations only when Bringas is absent (ix; 93). The 'exotic language of clothing' is overlaid with French terminology, which the narrator attempts to suture to his Spanish fabric ('tejido') with verbal 'pins' (x; 94). When Rosalía undresses we are told that her body seems to seek release from the prison of her restrictive clothing (xiv; 114), and when she is making up her costumes her skirts become enmeshed in bales of cloth (xv; 120). But the signifying system of fashion is not merely negative or alienating. The names of French fabrics and Parisian couturiers compulsively repeated in the text suggest both woman's exile from male, Spanish society and the inability of that society to absorb her. Fashion exemplifies the curious status of Lacan's letter: it is intersubjective, demanding the participation of a number of individuals; it places those individuals in a succession of different, indeed incompatible, positions, by means of its continuous displacement; finally, it tends towards invisibility even as it produces these very material effects (it cannot draw attention to its own movement). Lacan speaks of the subject 'en possession de la lettre', that is, both possessing and possessed by language. Such is the position of Rosalía in *La de Bringas*: at once relentless in her acquisition of clothing and

seduced by the shimmer of fabric. For Rosalía, deprived of a
native language (a mother tongue), fashion is a foreign idiom
invented by men, which must endlessly be made familiar,
moment by moment. She is repeatedly described as an 'exile'
even at home (xxxii; 235). For her there is no nakedness
beneath the clothes (no nature beneath the culture): deprived
of its decorations the body is reduced to one of the tailor's
dummies cited so frequently in the novel, merely a prop for
the signifying system which shimmers around it.

At the end of the novel Rosalía pays a begging visit to the
fallen woman Refugio. The latter takes from a drawer a mass
of scraps of cloth, tangled threads, and banknotes (xlvi; 279).
This heterogeneous mixture is characteristic of the way
clothing and money are interwoven in the fabric of Galdós's
text. For money, too, is a signifier. Rosalía counts syllables 'as
if they were coins' (xviii; 137). The circulation of money (from
husband to wife to money-lender to fashion house) determines
the course of the narrative. Yet, for all its material effects,
money is curiously insubstantial, and indeed frequently
invisible. Like the counterfeit notes made by Rosalía to
deceive her blind husband (xxxiv; 218), the possession of
money is at best a charade, a pretence. This is not simply for
the banal reason that those who claim to be wealthy in the
novel are frequently destitute, but because money relies for its
potency on intersubjective consensus, on the conventional
attribution of value. Like a letter, money can have no
significance to a wholly isolated individual: it exists only in
circulation, only (in Lacan's phrase) when it is 'missing from
its place'. And it is on this 'manque à sa place' or original lack
of debt that the narrative is founded. Circulation serves to
maim the body. In marriage, prostitution, or medicine, the
body is alienated from its possessor, reduced to exchange
value. We have already seen his process in Rosalía. But in the
case of Bringas too the physical and the financial are
exchanged or substituted one for the other. When stricken by
blindness Bringas has to choose between his purse or his sight
('La bolsa o la vista.') (xxix; 197); and he fears a specialist will
cost him 'un ojo de la cara' (an idiom corresponding to the
English 'an arm and a leg') (xx; 149). This is not simply a
ridiculous pun inflicted on a foolish character by an ironic

author. It is also an (unintended) pointer to the inextricability of sight, money, and language in the realm of the phallus.

What links the letter to desire? For Lacan, the very exclusion of woman from circulation makes her the factor of truth: the purloined letter is to be undressed 'like the immense body of a woman' (p. 47). This coincides with the traditional view of truth as that which has been hidden and is brought to light: *alēthēs* (p. 31). *La de Bringas* at once provokes and frustrates the (male) desire for knowledge (of the woman), a desire known technically as epistemophilia. By entering the woman's mind and offering us her innermost thoughts the narrator promises to bring to light her true nature. Yet that nature is revealed as wholly artificial or superficial: Rosalía has no desire 'deeper' than that for adornment. Psychic revelation or bringing-into-light is thus continually deferred throughout the novel. *La de Bringas* also calls into question the ability of woman to serve as purveyor of truth through its insistence on intersubjectivity. Different characters adopt the same roles at various points in the story: for example Rosalía dupes Bringas, but is herself duped by Pez. In the slippery network of the narrative people come to fill unexpected positions. This scepticism towards stable identity and psychic autonomy is also suggested by the use of ironic or emblematic names. The lubricious, phallic Pez is only the most conspicuous example of a name which proclaims the primacy of the signifier (the determining force of language) as it denies the psychic integrity of the individual. It is in this context that the complex play of narrative perspective should be taken. The mixture of reported speech, free indirect style, and dramatic dialogue; the discontinuity of the narrator's status, alternatively ignorant and omniscient; the interminability of the narrative incidents, which begin before the novel has started and continue after it has ended—all these have prompted critics to seek some unique, totalizing vision which could explain and unify the work as a whole. I would suggest that these techniques both block the reader's access to any objective reality 'behind the page' and promote an awareness of a discursive truth: that all knowledge is intersubjective, that it cannot be confined to a single transcendental 'viewpoint'. The notion of intersubjectivity unsettles any belief in either the controlling ego of the author or the essential nature of the character.[15] The narrator's repetition of the phrase 'à la lettre' is thus highly ironic (see, for example xix; 140): by promising to reproduce his characters' speech with absolute fidelity, the narrator merely calls attention to the impossibility of fulfilling such an aim. There is no position of absolute knowledge from which he could speak, and accuracy is not to be confused with truth. His faithfulness is thus a model for the critic. It offers both minute attention to detail (to the letter) and radical instability.

We have already touched on the link between language and sexuality in *La de Bringas*. How can Lacan's reading of the phallus supplement this model? Just as psychologist critics would look for (literal) letters in Galdós's novel, so they would be tempted to look for moments of (symbolic) castration. The most obvious would be Bringas's blindness: the loss of potency which deprives him of his money and his position as head of the household. The process complementary to this would be Rosalía's emergent virilization. As she engages in amorous intrigue with Pez the narrator dwells fetishistically on her swelling nostrils (xxv; 174–5, xxxix; 247). By the end of the novel Rosalía is emancipated and Bringas infantilized. If it is indeed legitimate to lend significance to such moments, the Lacanian reading would stress not the supposed prestige of the phallus, but the arbitrary nature of its function. If the male-female dichtomy is replaced by the phallic/castrated distinction then it must be recognized that the latter does not coincide with the former: individuals place themselves on either side of the bar and indeed may migrate from one side to the other. Galdós insists (like Lacan) that the relation 'between' the sexes is a *mascarade*: the words 'comedia', 'artificio', and 'teatro' frequently recur in this context (xvi; 124, xxxv; 228, xlviii; 293).

Lacan says that the phallus must remain veiled in order to perform its function as empty marker of difference. Thus it cannot be embodied by a single character, still less by the all too visible figure of Bringas, the 'little mouse'. Rosalía's fear of

---

[15] This is perhaps the most important point at which a Lacanian criticism would diverge from a traditional criticism which stressed the link between psychological coherence and aesthetic unity. See e.g. Ricardo Gullón, *Psicologías del autor y lógicas del personaje* (Madrid, 1979), 19; and José F. Montesinos, *Galdós*, ii (Madrid, 1980), 151.

her husband seems disproportionate to what we are told of his character. But this is because her terror corresponds not to the particular man but to the power of the phallic order which, initially at least, speaks through or in him. Pez offers another example of this veiling. The narrator's description of him in chapter xii alternates between asserting and denying his material presence. Pez is at once entirely sure of his identity and wholly lacking in inner life. He is the image of Saint Joseph, the step-father of Christ, but he dresses like a tailor's dummy. His conversation consists of redundant repetition, but it is this very repetition which lends him authority. Pez, then, seems to exemplify the emptiness of the phallus, the way in which patriarchy erects meaning over a vacant or provisional site. He also displays the most curious characteristic of the phallus: its tendency to feminization. The narrator stresses his 'woman's hands' and subtle use of perfume (xxiv; 171, xxv; 172). This feminization is once more intersubjective, shared between more than one character (Bringas and Pez).

   The dominance of the phallic function (however precarious it is revealed to be) determines the asymmetrical relations between women and men in the novel. There can be no communication between wives and husbands here. Woman's desire is exorbitant: Rosalía's passion for clothes has begun before the novel itself, stimulated by gifts from Agustín Caballero (ix; 92). It provokes a womanly discourse which the narrator calls 'interminable' (x; 94). This is because (as Lacan suggests) desire is the space which opens up between need and demand (between particular gratification and absolute love). No scrap of flesh can satisfy this desire, and it need not be directed to men. As Pez says, women are like bulls, they aim for the rag ('trapo') not the man (xxxvi; 229). Elsewhere the narrator talks of Rosalía's 'pasión trapística' (that is, both 'devotional' and 'vestimentary') (xxxviii; 244). These two images illustrate, perhaps too neatly, two of Lacan's intuitions. The first suggests that desire is eccentric or deviant and always surpasses the object it claims for its origin. The second suggests that there is a complicity between women's desire and the authority of male discourse, that the unspeakable female *jouissance* serves as a prop for the Name of the Father.

   We shall return to the relation between woman and the

Other in the reading of *Juanita la Larga*. As a supplement to this section, however, there follows a gloss on a typical passage of *La de Bringas*, typical not only of the texture of the novel, but also of its stress on the circulation of the letter and the meaning of the phallus:

> —¿Tu mamá . . ?
> —Está en la *Saleta* con la marquesa—replicó la niña . . . La marquesa estaba llorando porque estamos a siete.
> —Estamos a siete—había dicho Milagros a la Pipaón . . . y si para el día diez no he podido reunir . . . ¡A mí me va a dar un ataque cerebral! . . .
> Se habían encerrado en la soledad de la habitación, sin luz, porque el amo de la casa era partidario frenético del oscurantismo en todas sus manifestaciones . . . Mirando [Milagros] a las estrellas, creía sentir inexplicable consuelo . . . las estrellas lanzaban a lo interior de su alma un cierto destello metálico. (xxx; 199)

> 'Where's your mother?'
> 'She's in the *Saleta* with the marquess', answered the little girl . . . 'The marquess was crying because today is the seventh.'
> 'Today is the seventh', Milagros had said to Rosalía . . . 'and if I haven't got the money together by the tenth . . . It will give me a stroke!'
> They had closed themselves off on their own in the room, without any light, because the head of the household was obsessive about darkness in all of its forms . . . When Milagros looked at the stars she thought she felt an inexplicable sense of consolation . . . the stars sent into the inner reaches of her soul a kind of metallic shimmer.

The passage begins with a dialogue between the blind Bringas and his little daughter, who is in the grip of a repetition compulsion. Isabelita's comic explanation for the marquesa's tears is an example of displacement, as defined by Freud: the disruption of logical meaning through linguistic deviance. It is typical of the way messages circulate in the novel: compulsively, yet in an eccentric or deviant form. The insistence on the day of the month, lamented by Milagros, points to the calendar as yet another example of a material, signifying system which at once situates and alienates the subject: Milagros cannot choose to move outside the calendar; she must play her part within it. In just the same way, she is 'placed' by her debt, forced to take up a subordinate role in a financial system from which women are alienated. The reference to her 'stroke' is also significant. Like Milagros's other *crises de nerfs*, whether real or feigned, the symptom is (in Lacan's terms) a metaphor, physical testimony to a mental condition. The woman's body is thus made to 'speak' of her trauma. The two women are isolated from the man, and Milagros can thus indulge her infinite passion for speech. But even here the trace of Bringas lingers. He has imposed darkness throughout the home as an extension of his own blindness. The absence of light, then, does not entail the absence of male surveillance. Indeed, the phallus is merely veiled by darkness, its tyranny all the more insidious when its nominal possessor is an invalid. The narrator drifts from reported speech into free indirect style: the consolation Milagros finds in the stars may derive from the metallic light they cast on her innermost soul. This association of the celestial and the mundane is plainly ironic, directed by the narrator against the unknowing character. But it is also heuristic, revealing that the 'depths' of Milagros's interiority are wholly superficial: there is no transcendent truth to be illuminated here. What is more, the sentence points unknowingly at the hidden complicity between woman and the divine: her desire is for the absolute Other, not the particular object which might gratify her needs.

Yet to claim that the passage raises such questions as the power of language, the function of patriarchy, and the nature of woman's desire is not to deny its humour. Indeed the satirical tone of the passage confirms the intersubjectivity already suggested by the fluidity of narrative perspective. For humour relies on a community of like-minded persons to whom it is directed. The text might seem offensive in its depiction of the foolish triviality of women. But in its minute attention to their conversation (typical of the book as a whole) it offers an implicit revaluation of their position. Why, asks one critic, blame the women for the decadence of contemporary society, when it is the men who have the power?[16] One answer would seem to be that it is precisely because they are marginal that woman are exemplary: as the supplement which resists assimilation they are compelled to embody the contradictions

---

[16] Stephen Gilman, *Galdós and the Art of the European Novel* (Princeton, 1981), 142.

of capitalism in all their extremity, to oscillate between the material and the abstract (between gold and the stars). A further objection might be that these are not women, but a male author imitating them. But, as we shall see, it is Lacan's contentious claim that the role of women is precisely that of imitating men. And Juan Valera's *Juanita la Larga* is a particularly extreme case of this 'female impersonation'.

3. *JUANITA LA LARGA*: THE INSISTENCE OF MEANING

Juanita la Larga may seem a curious choice for my second novel in this chapter. Compared to Galdós, Valera is held to be a novelist of second rank, and the work I have chosen is a late one, often considered to be less successful than others. *Juanita la Larga* does however share a number of characteristics with *La de Bringas*: the male interest in female psychology; the attention to language, clothes, and money as social determinants; the theme (frequent in the period) of frustrated desire: 'quiero y no puedo'. Hence the question posed to the psychoanalytic critic by *Juanita la Larga* is that of discrimination or evaluation. Is the difference between the value ascribed each of these texts merely conventional or does it correspond to textual strategies which submit to a Lacanian analysis? I shall argue that it is by paying attention to the 'worst' moments of Valera's text (to those points at which it is contradictory or deficient) that the critic can sketch out a reassessment of its value as a compulsive repetition of the psychoanalytic drama. As we shall see, Juanita is a highly narcissistic text, one in which letters are invariably returned to their senders. This 'circulation of the same' is veiled in Galdós; in Valera its very obtrusiveness serves to undermine phallic prestige, to introduce a discord into the hom(m)osexual harmony.

Until recently criticism of Valera often confined itself to the imaginary register: that is, it served to facilitate a sense of illusory identity, or immediate recognition, between writer and reader in which the text figured (if at all) as a transparent medium, mere vehicle of this narcissistic affect. Thus Luis González López couches his pieces on 'Valera's women' in the form of letters to a friend, and playfully treats the fictional characters as if they were real acquaintances of himself and his addressee.[17] Or again, for Rafael Porlán,[18] Valera's Andalucía is the proud and 'difficult' young lass ('mocita') who invites the traditional Spanish compliment ('piropo') (p. 172). The male sense of regional identity, then, is dependent on the setting-up of woman as Other, both embodiment of essential value and stimulus to the discourse which defines that value, which she cannot speak herself. Early critics sometimes hint at a contradiction here which they dare not make explicit. Thus Jean Krynen[19] notes first that Valera's quest for truth is always frustrated, and second that he sets up woman as the figure of inspiration, the unconscious possessor of a force which provokes desire (pp. 34, 48–9). I would suggest (and this is to follow Lacan in *Encore*) that there is an intimate connection between these two statements of which the critic himself is unaware. For it is precisely the establishment of woman as enigmatic figure of truth which both calls into being the male discourse on aesthetics and prevents that discourse from reaching a conclusion. Valera's 'woman of Córdoba' is at once specific and universal, and it is this (unacknowledged) paradox which ensures the interminability of the epistemophilia she provokes. It is thus no accident that a critic such as José F. Montesinos,[20] who praises Valera's 'disinterest' and 'objectivity' in *Juanita la Larga*, should also praise the novel's heroine as the 'essence of feminity' (pp. 162, 167). The prestige of the male perspective can only be ensured if woman is held to be fixed, unchanging. I shall argue that the curious instability of Juanita's character corresponds to similar fluctuations in narrative perspective and representational codes.

Later critics, less credulous than their predecessors, stress the intrusiveness of Valera's persona and deny his objectivity. Thus Pérez de Ayala had already claimed that the text constructs an implied reader identical to its author;[21] and Santiago Montoto notes Valera's pride in his grammatical mistakes, which the author took to be proof of the natural

[17] *Las mujeres de Juan Valera* (Madrid, 1934).
[18] *La Andalucía de Valera* (Seville, 1980).
[19] *L'Esthétisme de Juan Valera* (Salamanca, 1946).
[20] *Valera o la ficción libre* (Madrid, 1957).
[21] *Amistades y recuerdos* (Barcelona, 1961), 41.

spontaneity of his style.[22] Cyrus DeCoster cites Pardo Bazán's claim that Valera's heroines, for all their assertions of independence, speak only with the voice of the male author.[23] An excellent essay by Enrique Tierno Galván goes further in teasing out contradictions in Valera's texts, contradictions which are determined, finally, by Valera's class position.[24] The novels offer the reader an uneasy combination of brutality and refinement, pragmatism and idealism, prurience and prudery. What Valera calls 'the natural order of things' is in fact the bourgeois order interpreted by a would-be aristocrat (p. 117). His curious conflation of spiritual and monetary values points up distortions in the Spanish economy of the period, when a traditional rural capitalism was being displaced by a new financial capitalism (p. 129). Arturo García Cruz also derives Valera's oscillation between Platonism and physicality (abstraction and realism) from his unstable, indeed precarious, class position.[25]

As in the case of *La de Bringas*, then, the most acute critical readings are those derived very broadly from a Marxist tradition. It should be noted however that in spite of recent changes in Valera criticism the latest editor of the text[26] still proclaims Valera's objectivity (p. 18) and is happy to rehearse the themes and 'sources' of the novel as if these were self-explanatory. And it is no modern critic, but a contemporary of Valera (Clarín) whose comments remain the most acute.[27] For Clarín, Valera is 'the sphinx of current literature': to speak of him is always to err ('no acertar', p. 257); Valera's dramatic works resist classification: Clarín can name them only 'things' ('cosas de Valera', p. 326); Valera is the ideal academician: he knows a great number of words ('sabe *mucho diccionario*', p. 329). Here in each case Clarín offers ironic praise of Valera's defects. First, Valera is not the confident male, but a sphinx or female enigma; second, his work is not pleasantly varied, but a homogeneous mass, 'things' peculiar to him;

---

[22] *Valera al natural* (Madrid, 1962), 31.

[23] *Juan Valera* (New York, 1974), 101.

[24] 'Don Juan Valera o el buen sentido', in *Idealismo y pragmatismo en el siglo xix español* (Madrid, 1977), 95–129.

[25] *Ideología y vivencias en la obra de Juan Valera* (Salamanca, 1978), 178–9.

[26] *Juanita la Larga*, ed. Enrique Rubio (Madrid, 1986).

[27] *Solos de Clarín* (Madrid, 1891).

third, his extensive lexicon is no rich resource, but an intrusive and artificial display. Clarín's deadpan humour suggests both critical rejection and indulgent acceptance of an inferior. He implies that Valera's idiosyncrasies are to be valued for their own sake, especially where language is concerned, that 'cosas de Valera' inspire a particular affection, even a love, which suspends the critical faculties (p. 314).

I have already suggested that *Juanita la Larga* coincides with *La de Bringas* in its attention to language, clothes, and money as social determinants. It differs, however, in social milieu and geographical setting. *Juanita la Larga* takes place in Villalegre, the fictional composite of two towns known to Valera from his childhood in the province of Córdoba. The eponymous heroine, illegitimate daughter of an industrious mother, is courted by a respected elderly gentleman, don Paco. Before the novel can end in the inevitable marriage Paco must face a series of obstacles: Juanita's initial resistance; the hostility of his daughter, the strait-laced 'mystic' doña Inés; the disparity in age, social class, and financial status between him and his beloved. As in *La de Bringas* letters play an important role in the narrative structure. Paco sends a grave epistle to Juana la Larga, asking for her daughter's hand in marriage (xx; 159). Juanita returns it, with a letter she has dictated to her mother refusing him. Paco hides both documents in a secret drawer in his desk (xxi; 163). The redundant circulation revealed here (the coincidence of sender and recipient) is repeated in the structure of the novel's plot, its relation to the reader, and its depiction of the relation between the sexes. To take a typical episode as an example: when the lovesick Paco abandons Villalegre his wanderings bring him back to the place from which he had started (narrative structure) (xxx; 216); the appetizing food he consumes is wrapped in a copy of *El imparcial*, the paper which first published *Juanita la Larga* in serial form in 1895 (relation to reader) (xxix; 209); Paco is confronted outside the town with the only rival for Juanita's affections he has encountered within it, the youth Antoñuelo (relation between the sexes) (xxxi; 222). I shall argue later that this insistent, even oppressive, circularity and homogeneity confirm Lacan's dictum that 'there is no sexual relation'. Before treating the question of gender, however, I shall begin (as in the case of *La de Bringas*) with the question of language, and in particular the determining force of the signifier.

The main presupposition of 'L'Instance de la lettre' is the same as that of the seminar on *The Purloined Letter*: the dominance of language over the subject. Even at the moment of birth language has 'inscribed' the place of subjects through the proper name they are obliged to adopt. The signifier thus precedes the signified (the name precedes the identity). For Lacan the model of language is not a picture of a tree with the word 'tree' printed beneath it, but a picture of two identical doors with the words 'ladies' and 'gentlemen' printed beneath them. Language is thus arbitrary and can be traced back to gender as conventional marker of difference. Meaning, then, does not so much consist, as insist. The ceaseless movement of linguistic structure (metaphor and metonym) precludes the achievement of any definitive or self-sufficient meaning. But if it is the letter (the material specificity of language) which produces 'the effect of truth' then there can be no possibility of authentic self-knowledge, no possibility of reaching what Freud calls the 'kernel' or 'essence' (*Kern*) of our being. Identity, like meaning, is thus ever precarious. Our (spurious) sense of self is a compromise formation between ego and Other. In other words, identity is necessarily intersubjective. Indeed, for Lacan, Freud's achievement is to have introduced the subject-object relation (which marked the limit of previous sciences) into the centre of his investigation. The conventional distinction between observing intelligence and observed nature is thus called into question.[28]

Valera (like Galdós to some extent) mimics the insistence of the letter by branding his characters and even places with emblematic names. Villalegre is the happy village where no one can come to real harm; Francisco López (like his namesake Bringas) is a straightforward, rather unimaginative man; Juana and Juanita are defined by the connotations of their nickname 'Larga': they are tall, generous, and sharp-witted. Juanita is ostentatiously deprived of her father's name and is thus endowed by the author with an illusory independence.[29]

[28] *Écrits*, i. 255–6, 260–7, 277, 288.
[29] See Paul Smith, 'Juan Valera and the Illegitimacy Motif', *Hispania*, 51 (1968), 804–11.

Only this loss of name can qualify her for the fantastic game of reciprocity she is to play out with don Paco: a woman already branded with another's name would have to change it by adopting that of her husband, thus making explicit her subordinate status as object of exchange between men. The name of the father is conspicuous by its absence, by the author's transparent act of denial. Juanita's definite article (unlike that of Rosalía) cannot signify male property; but it must be made to signify something; and in this case it is a fantasy of female autonomy. However, the action of the novel reveals at every step the illusory nature of this autonomy, for as Juanita gains independence, the repressed father (a soldier who fell in battle) keeps returning in the insistent references to a 'martial' blood and spirit reproduced in the daughter.

Genealogy, then, is one example of a material inscription (a 'letter') which Valera's idyll seeks in vain to erase. At a climactic moment in the novel (to which we shall return later) Juanita asks the local *cacique* Andrés if her name must be an indelible stain on her character. Here she is forced to proclaim the very dishonour she seeks to transcend: signifier anticipates signified. Women's gestures towards autonomy are always assimilated: when Paco offers Juanita a gift of silk to make herself a dazzling new dress, she and her mother reciprocate by giving him a new frock coat. But they are unable to escape the gendered position allotted them by the system of fashion: the man who exhibits new clothing is relatively invisible; the woman who does so is highly conspicuous, flagrantly significant. The determining force of the letter (of names, of clothing) is also betrayed by contradictions in the novel's dialogue: Juanita, in spite of her rudimentary education, is accustomed to discourse with rhetorical formality. Yet she also employs the archaism 'tamaño' for 'tan grande', the ostentatious sign of rustic traditionalism. When Valera attempts, intermittently, to reproduce local dialect he fixes, fetishistically, on a single detail: the gutturalization of /j/ for /h/: 'jierro'; 'jumeones'. This is the insistence of the letter with a vengeance. A single consonant bears the weight of multiple polarities: national/regional; popular/educated; urban/rural. It is telling that the narrative itself is inconsistent in the spelling of words with /j/ or /g/: incorrectly given are 'heregía', 'emperegilada', 'mujidos' (pp. 138, 140, 213). The intrusive guttural becomes pandemic, jumping intersubjectively from particular speech to general narrative. Language is thus a battlefield on which social conflict is joined.

Villalegre itself is the place with a surfeit of words, with 'mucho diccionario'. Valera offers extensive lists of groceries, garden flowers, songbirds, and wild plants (pp. 103, 117, 130, 208). These lists suggest a locus of absolute knowledge, of encyclopaedic extension. In Villalegre, as the narrator repeatedly tells us, nothing can be kept secret. And the curiosity of the characters is mimicked by the narrator who can leave no item unnamed. It is not enough to say that such catalogues are 'evocative' or that they are examples of 'costumbrismo'. The very obtrusiveness of the lists suggests that Villalegre is not 'natural' and cannot be 'taken for granted', even by the narrator. It is an entity composed entirely of language, in which nothing can be assumed to exist, everything must be called into existence through naming. The rustic idyll also relies on sophisticated cultural precedent. Villalegre is dense with literary reminiscence: the *fuente* at which Paco watches Juanita is the well at which Eliezer meets Rebecca (iv; 89); Juanita is as fair as the nymph Nausicaa (x; 106) and as virginal as Diana (xviii; 151). Her lover will follow her like the cow follows the cowherd in a sonnet by Lope (xxvi; 194). Already in these examples dissonant associations intrude: Juanita is too often active and male, Paco passive and female. Elsewhere Valera's exempla seem almost perversely inappropriate: Paco is likened to Corydon, Virgil's homosexual lover (viii; 98); a rustic feast is compared on the same page to both the *Beatus ille* and the feast of Trimalchio (pastoral abstinence and urban gluttony) (xiii; 118). When Valera cites Garcilaso in comparing the 'sweet tokens' of the poet's lady ('dulces prendas') to the cooked meats prepared by Juanita's mother, the effect is one of wilful irony. (It is a well-known phrase which also occurs, unattributed, in *La de Bringas*.) But when in a reference unnoticed by the editor he praises Juana's skill in midwifery by alluding to the 'duros trances de Lucina' (iii; 82), the scholarly allusion to Garcilaso's first *Eclogue* is redundant, even pedantic. Indeed the modern editor, while failing to recognize citations such as the one above, seems determined to emulate Valera's redundant erudition: Valera's reference to the 'son of Anchises' gives rise to a biography of the father which is irrelevant to the passage to which Valera alludes (Aeneas' encounter with Venus in *Aeneid* I (x; 106)), of which the editor is ignorant; when Valera refers to Fabius Cunctator the editor claims incorrectly that the Roman was so called because of his 'parsimonia' (the name derives, of course, from his use of delaying tactics) (xxiii; 197); when the author cites Plato's prohibition of poets in the *Republic* the editor stresses Valera's attachment to the Platonic love of the ideal (derived from texts such as the *Symposium*) (xi; 108). Such careless annotation reveals in spite of itself the wayward insistence of the letter: even the professional reader will be led astray by the endless play of association. But it also raises the general question of intertextuality: at what point do associations become irrelevant? The more we attempt to fix the space of representation, to define its limits through appeal to authority, the more it eludes our grasp and slips into displacement. This is the case both with Valera's citational Utopia and the editor's ever-expanding frames of knowledge. Nature is displaced by culture, and love stands revealed as the compulsive repetition of gestures lost in a mythical past. Love is always already written.

This attention to the insistence of the letter (to its tendency towards autonomy) renders visible the intersubjectivity of the text: it is a compromise formation between the writer, language, and a community of readers. The belief in stable, individual identity is also called into question. As we shall see this is particularly true of Juanita, who is radically discontinuous. But it is also true of the narrator. The ostensible mouthpiece is a new *diputado* for the area, who is introduced in a rather cursory way at the start of the novel (i; 71). The device is abandoned early on (iii; 81) and is invoked only intermittently afterwards. Little attempt is made to offer a plausible motive for the *diputado's* exhaustive knowledge. Indeed, when Valera does call attention to the narrative perspective it is in an ironically obtrusive way. Thus Juanita's internal monologue is 'very similar if not identical' to the words offered the reader by the narrator (xxi; 165); the reader must believe the narrator's hyperbolic praise of Juanita's dressmaking skill: the narrator has been to Villalegre to see for himself (xxiii; 174). This humorous profession of reliability is similar to that of Galdós: there can, of course, be no absolute fidelity *à la lettre* in fiction. Truth is the result of intersubjective compromise, not literal reproduction. The difference between the texts is that in Valera this intermittence is subject to an uncontrolled proliferation. At times the subject of the main verb drifts between third and first person: in successive sentences, Inés 'became aware' of Juanita's virginal beauty; the narrator 'is unwilling and unable' to say more than that her beauty is angelic; and Inés 'attributed' to Juanita almost as many good qualities as she did to herself ('llegó a notar'; 'no quiero ni puedo'; '[ella] ponía') (xxiv; 181). This wholly random failure to observe the conventional distinction between narrator and character is perhaps more disturbing than Galdós's masterful use of the free indirect style which can safely be labelled as just another weapon in the author's literary arsenal. When Valera intrudes so blatantly into the thoughts of his characters (when he abolishes the difference between him and them) he unwittingly calls into question the possibility of authentic self-knowledge, of any centre of identity innocent of external influence. The 'kernel of our being' (as narrator, as character) is dispersed or decentred. The relation between subject and object thus becomes itself an object of the critic's attention. Where in Galdós the narrator's ambiguity is wilful and his intermittence coolly ironic, in *Juanita* the same techniques, less skilfully handled, become so obtrusive as to be self-defeating. I shall argue in a moment that in a rather similar way Valera creates obstacles to prevent the narrative reaching a premature conclusion, but which serve to subvert the narrative through their very obtrusiveness.

Another device unpopular with many critics is the interpolation of *costumbrista* passages of description, which Valera often fails to relate to the main body of the narrative. The main examples of this occur in the fiesta of the town's patron saint in chapter xv and the celebrations for Holy Week in chapter xxxvi. But these apparently marginal scenes point to truths repressed in more 'central' episodes. At festival time village life is a *mascarade*, the whole population is dressed in fancy clothes (xv; 128). Triumphal arches of greenery are erected: Nature is bent to the whim of Culture (xv, 130). The Virgin and Child are carried through the streets, a ritual circulation which concludes, inevitably, at the place at which it began: the church (xv; 131). The narrator praises the 'prosopopeya' of the parish priest (xv; 132), using the word in its sense of affected gravity and pomp. But the rhetorical meaning of the term could serve as a description of the narrator's strategy here: he attempts to frame speech and action to figures who remain stubbornly inanimate, reified by the picturesque regionalism of their language and dress. The inhabitants of Villalegre are as wooden as the images they parade through the streets. At Easter too, village life is a spectacle, the whole town described as a 'theatre' for the celebration of divine mystery (xxxvi; 237). The townspeople parade once more, this time wearing grotesque masks in supposed emulation of Jewish features; their mask-faces are immobile, and the identities of the Biblical characters they represent can only be learned from the names inscribed on the haloes above their head (xxxvi; 240). In just such a way Valera's characters rely on an original inscription or letter always already in place: their claim to natural spontaneity depends on the reader's recognition of cultural codes.

In such passages *Juanita la Larga* exemplifies (much more plainly than *La de Bringas*) the oppressive homogeneity and obsessive insistence of the phallic function: like the 'siempretiesos' on sale at the festival (toys whose name means literally 'always stiff'), Valera is ever ready for inflation and disproportion, always swollen with language and desire. *Juanita la Larga* thus confirms the ubiquity of the phallus, but also the corollary of this, treated in *Encore*, that 'there is no sexual relation'. Paco addresses Valera familiarly as 'tú'; she replies formally with 'Vd'. But while Paco is above Juanita, her other suitor (Antoñuelo) is far beneath her, described repeatedly as a 'dog' (xxii; 170). The relation between the sexes is always asymmetrical. When Inés takes a fancy to Juanita she permits her to call her 'tú' in private (xxiii; 177). But even this is no ideal female reciprocity: Inés is grooming Juanita for submission to the absolute Other of the religious order. In a final climactic scene Juanita humiliates the local *cacique* don Andrés (xlii), punishing him for his sexual aggression by holding him down quite literally beneath her. The disparity between the sexes, repressed in the Utopian relation between Juanita and Paco, thus recurs with violent irrationality in an inverted form (with the woman 'on top'). This neurotic repetition of the lack of 'rapport sexuel' is called a farce ('sainete') by the narrator. And it ends with Juanita offering her hand in friendship to the vanquished patriarch, an example of the fantasy of reciprocity identical to that enacted by Juanita and Paco.

Lacan claims that the male compensates for this lack of genuine 'heterosexuality' by inventing obstacles which prevent him from confronting the fact that reciprocity cannot be attained. This process cannot of course be openly acknowledged in a novel founded on the myth of true love, but it recurs insistently none the less. Thus Paco, having conceived his passion, claims he will jump all 'obstáculos' in his path like a racehorse (vii; 100). Some twenty chapters later he is still rehearsing in his mind the same obstacles: the hostility of his daughter Inés, his dependence on his boss Andrés, his reputation in the village (xxix; 208). Like the son of Anchises, Valera shoulders the burden of patriarchy and carries it wherever he goes. But like Fabius Cunctator, his mission is constantly deferred, and the final victory cannot be won before time has run its course. Thus Valera strives to prevent the inevitable conclusion at the same time as he is driven on towards it. This causes asymmetries or disproportions in the structure of the novel. Thus after Juanita declares her new-found love for Paco in chapter xxxiv the narrative proper has come to an end. But, as we have seen, the forbidden knowledge of the lack of reciprocity between the sexes (now repressed in the central relationship) returns with unexpected violence in the scene of physical conflict between Juanita and the minor character don Andrés some ten chapters later. There is thus a structural conflict in the narrative which reproduces the contradiction in the narration between the fulfilment of fantasy and the repression of forbidden knowledge (between the imaginary and the symbolic). The novel is expanded or inflated to encompass a paradox which it dare not acknowledge in an overt manner.

But if the novel can be read as a sequence of obstacles,

erected and erased by the guiding male hand, then it also
reminds us (and this is a further contradiction) that the
phallic function is not identical to biological sex. By the end of
the novel most of the male characters have suffered symbolic
castration: the haughty Andrés is humbled; the lecherous
aristocrat don Alvaro reduced to imbecility; the satanic
chemist don Policarpo has had his 'electric' finger nail cut by
his new wife. As Paco becomes feminized, weak and fearful
with love, Juanita is virilized, wilful, even martial (xxvi; 192).
This fluid sense of identity is connected with Valera's lack of
concern for psychological motivation: all of the characters
previously hostile to Paco and Juanita undergo implausible
transformations by the final chapter. But it is also related
more specifically to the representation of desire in the novel.
For Paco, Juanita is the perfect object of desire, the endlessly
mobile, labile object caught in the field of his own affect: in
Lacanian terms, the *objet petit a*. Juanita is a narcissistic
inversion of himself. Young, female, and natural, she is the
mirror image of his own self-conscious maturity, and her role is
to reproduce those qualities which he lacks. The 'complexity'
of her character (frequently proclaimed by the narrator) is
thus the effect of the male desire which claims that same
complexity as its origin. This strategy is even more transparent
in the case of doña Inés: the narrator tells us she is an
'enigma', that her true feelings can never be known (xl; 258).
But this new-found depth of character responds to the
imperatives of the plot, rather than to those of female
psychology: unless Inés is made to drop her resistance to her
father's marriage the requisite happy ending cannot be
achieved.

Man, then, relates to the *objet a*, mirror image of his own
self-absorption. Woman, on the other hand, relates to the
Autre, the ultimate discourse of which she has no knowledge.
Thus the womanly love of Inés for Juanita is always mediated
by God: even as she caresses the young girl's hair she thinks of
how it will be shorn in the convent. And Juanita's intuition is
a sudden, almost mystical, revelation. Indeed, the narrator
draws attention to the swiftness of this volte-face in her
affections (xxvi; 192). For all her virilization, Juanita is
repeatedly described as 'unknowing': she proclaims her own

'ignorance' to Paco at the same time as she professes to hide nothing she knows (xii; 113, 115). She is at once excluded from language and forced to voice the truth, namely those things which (as Lacan says) emerge into visibility. She, quite literally, does not know what she is saying: her coquettish looks are a 'mysterious writing' read by don Andrés, but unintelligible to their author (xxvii; 195). In her soliloquies (moments of personal authenticity) Juanita parrots the commonplaces of Catholic misogyny: woman provokes lust and must therefore take pains to live a blameless life (xxi; 164). Juanita, then, takes her *jouissance* without knowledge. But the transcendent Other from which she is excluded is dependent on that *jouissance* for its own authority. Thus Juanita figures an unknowing Nature which is both the origin and the object of male observation; Inés figures a rapturous devotion which both exemplifies and falls short of the theological discourse she can never herself master. Woman is *pas-tout*, incomplete even in so far as she embodies abstractions. She is not a complement to the man, but an irreducible supplement to him.

Woman's particularity (her definite article) must be made to signify. But the meaning of the 'la' resists generalization. Hence the final contradiction of *Juanita la Larga* is that between particular and universal, a distinction which corresponds in Lacan's terms to need and demand. Juanita is at once and alternately the essence of womanhood ('the woman') and the vehicle of regionalism ('the woman of Córdoba'). Her language veers between occasional *andalucismos* and a neutral 'purity' of diction. In a rather similar way, the novel shifts between need and demand: the indulgent, even gluttonous, evocations of food alternate with abstract passages of Platonic idealism. As I have already suggested, for Lacan the space which opens up between need and demand is that of desire; and that between particular and general is that of woman. What is peculiar to Valera is the extremity of the difference between the two sides of the paradigm, the unwillingness to fill in the furrows in the narrative field, to smooth out the folds in the textual fabric.

One passage in *Juanita la Larga* displays these contradictions in a particularly heightened form. It is the meeting between

Juanita and Paco at which the former at last confesses her 'true feelings':

—No estés enfurruñado conmigo—dijo Juanita tuteándole por primera vez . . . provoqué a don Andrés sin reflexionar lo que hacía . . . Vengo a decírtelo para que me perdones, porque te amo.

¿Qué había de hacer don Paco sino ufanarse, enternecerse, derretirse, y perdonarlo todo al oír tan dulces y apasionadas frases en tan linda y fresca boca?

—Apenas puedo creer—dijo—que no repares ya en mi vejez, que no pienses en que puedo ser tu abuelo . . .

—No vida mía . . . Yo quiero darte la felicidad, si juzgas felicidad el que yo sea tuya. (xxxiv; 228)

'Don't be angry with me', said Juanita, calling him 'tú' for the first time . . . I encouraged don Andrés without thinking about what I was doing . . . I've come to tell you about it so you'll forgive me, because I love you.'

What could don Paco do except feel proud, feel moved, feel quite overcome, and forgive everything when he heard such sweet and passionate words from such pretty, youthful lips?

'I can hardly believe', he said, 'that you're no longer concerned about my age, and that you've forgotten that I could be your grandfather. . .'

'No, my darling . . . I want to make you happy, if it would indeed make you happy for me to be yours.'

The fantasy of reciprocity between the sexes (postponed until this moment) begins with Juanita's use of the intimate pronoun to address Paco, a pointer to the determining force of language in social relations. Her speech is typically vigorous, especially when she reiterates the misogynist commonplace that a woman is responsible for any reaction she provokes in a man, even when she is unaware she is doing so. Her change of heart is expressed baldly and without 'psychological' motivation: intermittence is woman's nature. Paco's response to these words is not unexpected: if they flatter and move him it is because they are contrived to be the perfect complement to his lack, the return of the message he sent himself when he fell in love with Juanita. Paco rehearses for the last time the catalogue of obstacles placed by Valera in the path of his characters, and his speech thus serves to reaffirm the artificiality of their nature and the implausibility with which they are erected only to be erased at the last moment. The abolition of these obstacles is ensured by Juanita's definition of her love as desire of the Other: her aim is to make Paco happy by making herself his property. Male desire is thus narcissistic, and woman's altruistic: there is no symmetry between the two. The meeting between the lovers re-enacts the charade of the sexual relation. It is based on a double act of female impersonation: the author mimics those 'feminine' qualities (naturalness, subservience) conventionally attributed to women; but those qualities are themselves projections of male fantasy, internalized by women. Hence Juanita is not simply a doll dressed by a male hand: she is a subject whose innermost essence is constructed under patriarchy. It is in the insistence of this circulation of the same, the persistence of this female impersonation, that the value of Valera's text lies. In his lack of pretence to heterogeneity (to 'heterosexuality') Valera reveals, quite unintentionally, that truth is to be found not in the spirit, but in the letter.

4. A LETTER OF LOVE

Most readers would consider *La de Bringas* to be a 'better' novel than *Juanita la Larga*. A reading of Lacan would suggest a more technical answer. Galdós presents the symbolic as an object of representation: the crypto-linguistic system of money and clothes is carefully offered the reader for his or her observation. This process tends, ironically, to veil or occlude the imaginary contribution of the reader to the text. Having been shown all too clearly the cruelty of alienation in the 'case-study' of Rosalía we are blinded to our complicity with the narrator. Indeed, this complicity is all the more insidious because Galdós has made us aware of the unreliability of his narrator. Galdós tells the truth of fictional language by disclosing that it relies on convention and intersubjectivity. The reader is thus (in Lacan's phrase) 'véritablement trompé': that is, truly tricked and tricked by the truth. As Lacan says in the seminar on *The Purloined Letter* there is no subtler trick than to lay one's cards face up on the table (to lay bare one's own devices).[30] Valera, on the other hand, offers a

[30] *Écrits*, i. 29, 31.

discourse wholly in the imaginary register. He presents a sequence of perfect symmetries in which subject is made to complement object; woman, man; and writer, reader. This untrammelled narcissism leads inevitably, however, to a return of the repressed symbolic in the form of persistent contradictions or 'faults' in the texture of the narrative and language. Thus Villalegre is at once Nature and Culture, Juanita both masculine and feminine, and the dialogue alternatively simple and mannered. I would suggest that 'realism' in the novel is precisely a compromise between imaginary and symbolic. Galdós is more 'realistic' because he negotiates that compromise with wit and irony: the very implausibilities and anti-climaxes of his text reinforce the illusion of the real for a knowing audience, too sophisticated to accept a form of mimesis which claims for itself a pure transparency. Valera fails to suture the gap which opens between imaginary and symbolic, and thus seems less 'realistic', more 'idealistic'. The play of identification and alienation skilfully directed by Galdós seems in Valera random and idiosyncratic. An illusion of the real can only be salvaged by a wholesale capitulation to what Clarín called Valera's 'appetite'. Critics of an earlier time were only too willing to make this capitulation; a critical awareness of the primacy of the symbolic (of the impossibility of unalienated communion in language) makes such a reading seem ingenuous today.

The aim of Lacanian analysis as a clinical practice is also for the patient to acknowledge the symbolic. The subject should attempt to elude the imaginary dyad (the timeless continuum of the mother-child relationship) and assume his or her 'castration' (the historical event by which each of us was deprived of plenitude and projected into the realm of the Father, of language, of society) (see Gallop, *The Daughter's Seduction* p. 36). This continuing quest for the symbolic would include, then, an attention to historical detail such as that we have seen in Marxist readings of the nineteenth-century novel. It would also preclude the lures of psychologism: archetypical characters, prescriptive analyses, allegorical interpretations. For Gallop this attention to materiality is also the feminist psychoanalytical approach:

The gesture of paying attention to small details is not simply some external methodological device, but is the very stuff of . . . a psychoanalytic, feminist reading. Lacan would call it attention to the letter. Feminists might call it attention to context, to materiality, which refuses the imperialistic, idealizing reductions that have been solidary with a denigration of the feminine—material, localized, at home, *in situ*—in favour of the masculine —active, ideal, in movement, away from the home. (*Feminism*, pp. 92–3)

The obtrusive details of Valera's text might be significant in this context: in his minute attention to the particular, the phallocrat feminizes himself, quits the broad highways of the ideal for the little home of the material. The lesson of psycho-analysis would then coincide with that of *costumbrismo*: that we should attend not to abstract totalities but to material specificities.

I shall end with two such apparently irrelevant details, one from each novel. Critics have been dazzled by the picture made of human hair described at length in the opening chapter of *La de Bringas*: it is an image which presents itself all too easily as an opportunity for 'significant' interpretation. One unnoticed detail from near the beginning of the text is a slip of the tongue attributed to a nonentity who does not appear in the novel: doña Tula's late husband. He refers mistakenly to 'the sword of Demosthenes', an error which, we are told, is repeated throughout the Court and savoured by the Queen herself (vi; 78–9). The phrase is an example of what Freud calls 'condensation', which Lacan derives from the linguistic function of metaphor. In its crazy contraction the example hints at a truth generally repressed: that language, the weapon of the orator, must always have precedence over him; that the linguistic tool wielded by the male carries within itself the seeds of death and castration. Demosthenes and Damocles (oration and annihilation) slip and slide under one another. This interpretation of language, desire, and death is precisely 'the signification of the phallus'. My second detail comes from the final paragraph of *Juanita la Larga*. Antoñuelo, Juanita's rejected suitor, marries a black woman in Cuba and emigrates with her to the United States, where she learns English. The image of the English-speaking black woman seems to be offered as an example of exotic curiosity. It is certainly marginal to the novel, introduced only at the very end and with no preparation. Yet the tardy emergence of this insubstantial character suggests a contradiction inherent in the figure of woman throughout the novel. For Antoñuelo's wife embodies both nature and knowledge. She fills a lack in the male (the wayward prick) asserting a linguistic potency of which her husband is always denied and with which Juanita herself is only intermittently endowed. She thus poses with particular urgency the question of woman's exile from language, a question which lies at the heart of Lacan's *Encore*.

Perhaps my version of Lacan seems paralysing: subjects (especially those who place themselves on the side of the woman) are always disabled or alienated by language. But the model is not wholly passive, because the movement of the signifier is always deviant and its dominance imperfect. Thus in *Encore* (again) Lacan identifies 'meaning' with 'direction': both in French are denoted by the word 'sens'. Meaning can only point towards the goal it always fails to reach. Thus for Lacan language is a letter of love: 'une lettre d'Âmour'.[31] The condensation of love ('amour') and soul ('âme') called into being by the circumflex accent suggests once more the hidden complicity of desire, language, and a grand abstraction or Other which can never be attained. This (untranslatable) letter of love is a love without essence, a love within language: the passion of the signifier as it works (on) the body. And it points the way to a new 'heterosexuality' which does not insist on the erasure of difference and on the reproduction of the subject in the object. It it towards this inaccessible goal that psychoanalytic criticism sends out its message, a message which may yet return to its sender in a wholly unexpected form.

[31] *Encore*, 73–82 (pp. 74, 78).

4

LORCA AND FOUCAULT

I. AGAINST HUMANISM

FOUCAULT begins *Les Mots et les choses* (Paris, 1966) with two examples taken from Hispanic sources. The first is Borges's Chinese encyclopaedia. It contains a list of animals: belonging to the Emperor; embalmed; fabulous; included in the present classification; drawn with a fine camel hair brush; et cetera (p. 7). For Foucault the humour of the list derives not so much from the placing of incongruous items next to one another as from the impossibility of assigning all of the items to a common field of reference or 'operating table' (pp. 8–9). Borges's 'heterotopia' is disquieting because it disrupts the familiar discursive framework within which knowledge finds its place in our culture: the history of the 'order of things' in the West is the history of the Same. When this order is challenged (when knowledge breaks down or mutates) then the very earth seems to move beneath our feet (pp. 15–16).

Foucault's second example is Velázquez's *Las meninas*. For Foucault this painting exemplifies the order of knowledge in what he dubs the Classical period. Velázquez spreads out before the spectator the material evidence of depiction: the painter's look, his brush, palette, and canvas (p. 27). The spectator is assigned a privileged, yet inescapable, position 'outside' the frame: he or she is superimposed on that inaccessible space where the logic of the picture dictates that the royal couple should stand (p. 29). But this spectacle of or in the look ('spectacle-en-regard') does not serve to demystify the artistic process. As a representation of representation it offers itself as pure transparency. In the empty space in front of the picture a transcendental figure can emerge: Man as both subject and object of the look, founding father and active agent of discourse.

The Chinese encyclopaedia stages the dissolution of knowledge; *Las meninas* its construction in the figure of Man. What is implied by both examples is that knowledge is always historically loaded, and never neutral. Thus the common belief in the primacy of an unexamined human nature is at once the effect and the instrument of the order of discourse we inhabit. Foucault's anti-humanism is radical. On the last page of *Les Mots et les choses* he predicts that if the configurations of knowledge on which we depend were to disappear, then Man himself would be erased, like a face traced in the sand at the edge of the sea (p. 398).

One particularly revealing example of the function of Man in discourse is the author. In an article first published in 1969 Foucault asks the question 'What is an author?'[1] He begins conventionally enough, by linking the rise of the phenomenon of proprietorial authorship (so different from the habitual anonymity of medieval literary texts) to the increasing sense of individualization in Europe. Even today the cult of the individual remains pervasive. The 'death of the author' proclaimed by theorists in the 1960s merely substitutes one unexamined concept for another: the empirical subject gives way to the unity of the 'work' or the transcendent anonymity of 'writing' ('écriture') (pp. 103–4). Rather than simply denying the power of the author, Foucault (typically) seeks to trace its particular configuration. For Foucault the author is not a person but a function, which operates under a number of conditions. First, the author is associated with legal and institutional systems: the author's name began to be indissoluble from his work only when texts became routinely subject to surveillance and their writers capable of transgression. Second, the author-function does not affect all discourses in the same way at all times. For example, in the modern period (unlike in earlier times) the authorship of a scientific text does not serve to prove its validity. The convention by which the proper name is the guarantor of value has passed to the literary text. Third, the author is not spontaneous but constructed by the reader: 'those aspects of an individual which we designate as making him an author are only a projection . . . of the operations we force texts to undergo . . .'.

---

[1] Reprinted in Paul Rabinow (ed.), *The Foucault Reader* (Harmondsworth, 1986), 101–20. The best intro. to Foucault remains Alan Sheridan, *Michel Foucault: The Will to Truth* (London and New York, 1982).

These operations derive ultimately from Christian exegesis, according to which the saintliness of the author served to prove the worth of the text. They are: consistency of value; conceptual coherence; stylistic unity; historical specificity. The fourth and final condition of the author-function is that it refers not to a single individual but to a multiple subjectivity. For example, in the first-person novel the author is neither the fictitious speaker, nor the empirical writer, but the gap or 'scission' between the two, a difference which is constantly shifting and mutating (pp. 108–12).

These points may seem unnecessarily complex. What is clear to Foucault, however, is that the author should be deprived of his role as originator. For he is not, as traditional critics claim, an inexhaustible source of meaning but rather 'the principle of thrift in the proliferation of meaning . . . by which . . . one limits, excludes and chooses; in short by which one impedes the free circulation, the free manipulation, the free composition, decomposition and recomposition of fiction' (p. 119). Foucault frames his essay with a quote from Beckett: 'What difference does it make who is speaking?', and suggests we pay attention to the differences between speakers and not abstract them into a single monolithic unity.

García Lorca is perhaps the most extreme case of proprietorial authorship in Spanish literature: it seems impossible to approach his texts without acknowledging his person, and it is almost an article of faith amongst critics that in Lorca literature and life are one. It is thus particularly important to ask of Lorca the questions raised by Foucault: what difference does it make that Lorca is speaking?; how is the author-function made to operate in relation to his texts? The vast bulk of the criticism shares a number of preconceptions. First, Lorca is often presented as being at once universal and particular: the great man transcends his socio-historical limitations but must be called to account, none the less, for his political and sexual convictions. Second, this juridical assessment is historically specific: the anti-fascism and homosexuality repressed or condemned by early critics are proclaimed and celebrated by later ones.[2] Third, the image of Lorca as author

[2] In his programme notes to a production of *Bernarda Alba* directed by Nuria Espert (London, 1986), José Monleón reiterates the traditional view of an author who is able

does not arise spontaneously, but is actively constructed by critics. An author must be equipped with an *œuvre* whose value is consistent, whose conceptual field is coherent, whose style is unified.[3] Hence the lack of attention paid to an early, experimental work such as *El público*: as an incomplete work, aesthetic evaluation is problematic; as a play explicitly concerned with homosexuality, its subject matter is disturbing; as a text whose language is complex, even hermetic, it seems far indeed from the relative naturalism of, say, *La casa de Bernarda Alba*. Critics have indeed managed to incorporate *El público* into the *œuvre*, by stressing the formality of its construction, the presence of familiar Lorcan themes beneath the surrealist 'surface', the 'poetic' quality of its language, different in degree but not in kind from that of other less complex plays. But this is more a tribute to the ingenuity of the critics than to the consistency of the author: they see it as their role to construct an operating table which will reduce the most disparate catalogue of items to order. Once this table has been established, it may be projected back on to the writer as historically specific figure. As in the case of the Christian saint, this retrospective biography will serve both to resolve contradictions in the work and to guarantee its authenticity. To read Lorca in a Foucauldian way would be to resist the compulsion to erase difference and to make visible the multiple subjectivity confined with the single 'individual'. This would not be to invert traditional criticism and claim that the writing subject is wholly absent from the text. Rather, it would be to suggest (and this is the fourth of Foucault's operations) that the proper name 'Lorca' arises in the gap or scission between mouthpiece and writer, in the variable space which always separates the two. The ruthless selectivity of the

'to speak universally without going outside the particular four walls of Bernarda's house.' But in her own notes to the poster-programme for the revival of Víctor García's 1971 production of *Yerma* (Madrid, 1986) Espert calls attention to the value of theatre in helping a nation to remember its political history. Knowledge of Lorca's own political engagement has become more widespread. See e.g. the text recently ed. by Manuel Fernández Montesinos and Andrés Soria Olmedo, *Alocución al pueblo de Fuentevaqueros* (Granada, 1986).

  [3] See e.g. the intro. by Allen Josephs and Juan Caballero to their edn. of *Bernarda Alba* (Madrid, 1986) in which they cite Francisco García Lorca's claim that his brother's 'obra' is as organically unified as a tree (p. 15).

author-function might then give way to a (freer) circulation of meaning.

It seems only fair to give a specific example. The inextricable relations between Man, author, and discursive operations are clear in the preface to a well-known study of the drama, Gwynne Edward's *Theatre beneath the Sand* (London and Boston, 1980). Edwards stresses the 'unity' of Lorca's vision which reflects 'issues that haunted him throughout his life' (consistency is validated by biography); he praises the 'universality' of the plays which offer us 'mirrors' in which we see ourselves (artistic transparency guarantees the transcendental subject); he claims Lorca exposes 'human nature' behind the 'masks' of civilization (univocal consciousness displaces multiple subjectivity).[4] To take another example at random, Manuel Durán claims that the measure of Lorca as a great author is that he can 'tell us something about man'; that he enables us 'to catch a glimpse of something permanent and solid, while talking about what is evanescent and frail'.[5] Durán here points unknowingly to the central contradiction of humanism: that it is at once idealist and empiricist. The author is said both to achieve transcendence and to remain faithful to a local and specific experience. Critics frequently appeal to 'mystery' in their evocations of Lorca. I would suggest that this mystery is not so much an essential quality of the author, as a projection of inconsistencies unresolved in their own critical discourse. The fact that Lorca himself appeals in his prose to the 'mystery' of lyric and defines drama as 'poetry made human' need not mean that the commonplaces of ultimate meaning and essential nature go unchallenged in the plays themselves. Indeed, it is a curious convention of authorialism that a writer's explicit pronouncements on his work can take precedence over that work itself. I will argue that Lorca's dramatic discourse is transparent: that there are no hidden secrets or transcendent meanings, because there is no absolute subject to have created them.

To be very schematic once more, there are three modes of Lorca criticism, corresponding to three models of interpretation.

---

[4] See pp. 2, 22.
[5] In the intro. to his edn., *Lorca: A Collection of Critical Essays* (Englewood Cliffs, NJ, 1963), p. 15.

Each of them assumes the author as originating subject. The first is allegorical. It treats the text as 'surface' and claims to discover a 'deeper' meaning beneath it. This meaning may be single or multiple; but the multiple meaning is no less authorialist than the single, since it is assigned to the controlling influence of the writer and permits little or no contribution from the reader. The second mode of criticism is euhemerist.[6] It treats the text as 'information' and seeks evidence in it for historical circumstance and personal confession. Thus the rural tragedies are held to 'reflect' aspects of Andalusian life in the period and to reproduce Lorca's presumed attitude to such issues as the position of women and the condition of agriculture. The third mode is elegiac. It treats the text as an unfinished monument to a life cut short, as a theatre in which future death is at once anticipated and commemorated, Francesca Colecchia's bibliography of Lorca criticism (New York and London, 1979) contains no fewer than 26 pages in which elegies and homages are listed. It would be easy to dismiss elegiac criticism for its supposed *naïveté*. Rather, it draws our attention (as Foucault would also) to the continuing potency of the author-function: elegiac criticism is not (or not merely) evidence for the role of affective displacement in reading. It is also a frank acknowledgement of the insistence of the humanist order, an insistence which the modern theorist cannot simply erase.

These three modes of criticism can be re-read in the light of the author's sexuality. For example, allegorical critics might claim that the rebellious heroines of Lorca's drama are 'really' men, disguised or displaced figures of the author's own sexual oppression. The euhemerist reading is rather similar: the (unexamined) 'fact' of homosexuality serves to 'explain' Lorca's supposed empathy with women and his understanding of the female predicament. Transposed to the sexual register, elegiac criticism will see the death of Lorca not so much as the loss of a universal genius, but as the final confrontation of deviance and violence. In the sexual register the control of the author seems to slip away and that of the critic is consolidated. The innermost 'secret' of sexual preference marks that still

---

[6] I borrow this term from Bernard McGuirk in an article on Vallejo to be cited in the next chapter.

point at the heart of Foucault's author-function 'where incompatible elements are at last tied together or organized around a fundamental or originating contradiction' (p. 111). Whether the attitude adopted is positive or negative makes no (theoretical) difference: both conservatives and libertarians take it for granted that sex is the kernel of our being, the essence of Man, the driving force of the author. The appeal to sexuality serves as a final principle of limitation and exclusion. As Lacan said of women, homosexuals 'do not know what they are saying', they require the critic to emend or supplement their work, to make it more 'authentic'. It is significant that just such a strategy was used against Foucault himself by commentators who claimed that his sexual preference made him incapable of undertaking a general history of sexuality.[7]

Not surprisingly, this quest for the hidden knowledge thought to be secreted in sexuality is a common strategy in biography. For example, the first volume of Ian Gibson's monumental *Federico García Lorca* (Barcelona, 1985) begins with an aetiology of sex. Lorca's homosexuality is the cause of a founding contradiction in his career: the conflict between rebellion against conventional mores and the anguish of erotic frustration. Now the truth need no longer be hidden; we must know Lorca in his entirety ('a cuerpo entero') (pp. 21–2). In his critical review of Gibson's work Luis Fernández Cifuentes relates this search for totality ('the whole body') to the historical method implied throughout the biography.[8] Gibson has a reverence for 'facts', for discrete pieces of information. These can be assembled to form a truth which is single and transparent. What he cannot tolerate is the detail, the random specificity which speaks only of the author's likes or dislikes and which betrays the role of chance in history (pp. 226–7). Fernández attacks Gibson for the unreflective positivism of his method, which dare not acknowledge that the categories of 'fact' and 'truth' have been called into question; and he implies that the real body of the author is to be found not in

---

[7] See Mark Poster, 'Foucault and the Tyranny of Greece', in David Couzens Hoy (ed.), *Foucault: A Critical Reader* (Oxford, 1986), 205–20 (p. 207). This is a sympathetic essay in a collection often hostile to its subject's work.
[8] *NRFH* 34 (1985–6), 224–32.

the hermetic abstraction of the fact but in the resonant
materiality of the detail.

As we shall see, Foucault's political anatomy of the body is
also one of detail rather than of fact; and his later work is a
critique of that 'will to knowledge' which forces sexuality to
speak the truth of the subject. But Foucault also offers a method
(or anti-method) which can be used to displace the traditional
positivism of scholars such as Gibson. In 'Nietzsche, Genealogy,
History' (first published in 1971) Foucault attempts to
account for historical change without succumbing to that
nostalgia for lost origins we have seen in critics' attitudes to
the author.[9] Why is Foucault against the origin (*Ursprung*)?
Because origin presupposes essence or primordial truth: 'the
removal of every mask to ultimately disclose an original
identity' (p. 78). At the beginning of things is found not
identity but disparity: 'the dissension of other things'. In
Nietzsche's phrase the modern period is 'the time of the
shortest shadow' when humanity no longer believes, as it did
at the dawn of history, that truth flows like light from a single
source (pp. 79–80). Foucault proposes two Nietzschean terms
to take the place of origin: descent (*Herkunft*) and emergence
(*Entstehung*). The random nature of descent (of an individual,
of a culture) reveals that truth adheres not to essences but to
accidents; hence descent is attached to the body (pp. 81–2).
The violent nature of emergence reveals that there can be no
suprahistorical perspective or objectivity (pp. 86–7). The
naïve faith in continuity (the belief that Man always remains
the same) inspires a 'consoling play of recognitions' between
past and present (p. 88). For the genealogist such recognitions
are to be avoided. Now that Europe has become an immense
'spectacle' or 'theatre' his role is to 'push the masquerade to
its limit and prepare the great carnival of time where masks
are constantly reappearing' (p. 94).

I shall argue later that Lorca's *El público*, with its radical
stress on parody and dissociation, can be studied only by
means of the genealogical method. What my quotes from the
above essay confirm, however, is the drama, even theatricality
of Foucault's prose style, a style inherited to some extent from

---

[9] Reprinted in Rabinow, 76–100.

Nietzsche. This is no affectation: it serves rather to remind us constantly of one of Foucault's most important insights: that discourse is not objective but strategic. The insistence of Foucault's recourse to theatrical metaphors suggests that his work may be of value for the study of drama as a genre even when it takes prose or philosophy as its object. Thus in the early book on *Raymond Roussel* (Paris, 1963) one chapter focuses on the role of metamorphic exchange in Roussel's 'theatrical spectacle' (pp. 96–124). The dramatic quality of Roussel's language means that it hides no silent secret: it presents only a shining surface which covers a central void or target ('blanc') (p. 19). I will suggest that the stress on metamorphosis in Lorca's drama also implies the lack of an authentic origin, and that the shimmering epidermis of his language conceals no hidden essence. Another of Foucault's texts on a favourite author also invokes the model of the theatre. '*Theatrum philosophicum*' is a review of Deleuze's *Différence et répétition*, first published in 1970.[10] What Foucault finds in Deleuze is a theory of thought freed from the tyranny of a knowing subject (Man) and a unified object (the world). For Deleuze, the anti-Platonist (as for Nietzsche), difference precedes essence: there can be no founding identity. Philosophy is a theatre because it cannot engage directly with the real but can only mimic or reproduce differences. The old category of 'concept' is displaced by the new one of 'event'. The event is an effect of pure difference, which disrupts the continuity of the same. It is as a parade of events (rather than a continuing revelation of concepts or essences) that I will read Lorca's theatre.

In this introduction I have made Foucault's thought seem very abstract. In fact, it is remarkably attached to the physical. More perhaps than any other thinker, Foucault is the theorist of the body. Hence knowledge is not autonomous: it is always bound up with power and pleasure. In the rest of this chapter I will suggest that the relation between knowledge and power is acted out in *La casa de Bernarda Alba*, and that between knowledge and pleasure in *El público*. Traditional critics have claimed that these plays reveal the opposition

[10] In *Critique*, 26 (1970), 885–908.

between vitality and repression and between nature and Law:
the daughters in the first play seek release from their
tyrannical mother; the multiple characters of the second
proclaim the naturalness of a desire which takes precedence
over social convention. My own strategy will be to call into
question these received dichotomies. And in doing so I shall
focus on two disputed areas of desire: female and homosexual.
As we shall see, the main theme of Foucault's history of
sexuality is that we should attempt to conceive of sex without
reference to a transcendent Law or monolithic authority. For
Foucault power and pleasure are so closely intertwined that
the very idea of 'liberation' may well be a mirage. A very early
text (first published in 1963) anticipates many of these points
which are made much later and at much greater length in the
three published volumes of his unfinished history of sexuality.
The text is called 'Preface to Transgression',[11] a term Foucault
views as critically as 'liberation':

Sexuality points to nothing beyond itself . . . We have not in the least
liberated sexuality, though we have, to be exact, carried it to its
limits: the limit of consciousness, because it ultimately dictates the
only possible reading of our unconscious; the limit of the law, since it
seems the whole substance of universal taboos; the limit of language
since it traces that line of foam showing just how far speech may
advance upon the sands of silence. (p. 30)

The image of the beach reminds us of the 'face traced in sand'
which is erased by the waves at the end of *Les Mots et les choses*.
For Foucault (and, I shall argue, for Lorca) Man is a fragile
construct indeed. And if his sexuality is not to be liberated,
then his attempts at resistance are equally problematic:
'Transgression, then, is not related to the limit as black to
white, the prohibited to the lawful, the outside to the inside, or
as the open area of a building to its enclosed spaces. Rather,
their relationship takes the form of a spiral which no simple
infraction can exhaust' (p. 35).
    When applied to Lorca's heroines, this knowledge may
appear perverse, even irrelevant. For they are confronted with
the darkness of night, the full force of prohibition, and the

---

[11] Reprinted in *Language, Counter-Memory, Practice*, ed. Donald F. Bouchard and
Sherry Simon (Oxford, 1977), 29–52.

oppressive materiality of enclosure. Yet I shall argue that the model of their revolt (and hence of the dramatic structure of the play) is to be found not in the simple opposition of contraries but in the more complex action of the spiral. Foucault's example of transgression is the flash of lightning. Brilliant, fragile, and violent, it denotes the articulation of space and time in an instant of pure difference. It is a fitting image of both the theatrical event and the dark *éclat* of sexuality.

2. *BERNARDA ALBA*: POWER AND KNOWLEDGE

In the third and final act of *La casa de Bernarda Alba* the youngest daughter, Adela, asks her mother why St Barbara is invoked when a shooting star or a flash of lightning are seen.[12] Adela loves to watch the flash of movement in the sky. Her sisters (the embittered Amelia and the hypocritical Martirio) prefer not to see such phenomena or to consider what they might mean. Bernarda herself states that it is better not to think about such things (p. 76). It would be easy to read this scene allegorically as part of the wider conflict in the play between vitality and repression: the mother seeks to repress her daughter's innate sexual energy, thus creating a tension which must finally seek release in transgression. However, as I suggested earlier, the humanist appeal to transgression (based as it is on the supposed autonomy of the subject and the imperative that she liberate her sexuality) is insufficient for the analysis of a work as complex as that of Lorca. Adela's 'revolt' may lead only to a new and more subtle kind of oppression, her compulsion to confess may itself be an effect of power. My thesis is that what is revealed by the action of *Bernarda Alba* is not the monolithic authority of repression but the multiple flexibility of subjection.

I also suggested in the introduction that 'conservative' critics have much in common with 'radical' ones where the sexual register is concerned. This is certainly the case with *Bernarda Alba*. We can take three critics as examples. H. Ramsden (editor of a popular annotated text) offers a series of

---

[12] My refs. are to the edn. by H. Ramsden (Manchester, 1983).

oppositions as the basis of the play, oppositions artfully created and exploited by the author. At the level of the characters we find vitality versus repression; at the level of the language we find realism versus poetry. Ramsden takes it for granted that the twin virtues of drama are verisimilitude and psychological complexity: the spectator must ask 'whether the characters appear as real-life persons who respond convincingly to real-life situations in a real-life context' (p. xxxv). As in all humanist criticism the category of 'person' remains unexamined. At times the author cannot fulfil the tasks required of him by the critic and fails to conform to the (Foucauldian) discursive operations by which he is normally recognized. Thus Ramsden attacks the maid's speech on social deprivation in Act I and the scene with the neighbour Prudencia in Act III: the first compromises the conceptual coherence of the work by hinting at inescapably political issues; the second compromises the stylistic unity of the work by introducing a character that plays no essential part in the action (p. lvi). Both call into question, for an instant at least, the consistency of value which is the necessary hallmark of the great writer's *œuvre*. The role of the author-function as 'principle of thrift' in the text's economy is very plain here: it enables the critic to exclude or repress any elements that he finds unpalatable.

What the humanist critic stresses, then, is the opposition between a knowing subject (Man) and a unified object (the world). Unlike Foucault (or Nietzsche or Deleuze) he cannot tolerate the notion that difference precedes essence. As so often, the role of the author-function is precisely that of neutralizing differences: thus Ramsden defers to Lorca as historical originator of the play, but he dare not acknowledge Lorca's sexuality; and he takes it for granted that drama reflects humanity, but cannot admit that it can speak for or of women in their specificity. Gwynne Edwards's position is rather similar when he remarks that Lorca's women 'are essentially *no different from the rest of us*, their anguish is ours too' (p. 265; my emphasis). It is by no means clear who 'we' are. Does it include the woman reader? Would it have included Lorca himself? Material differences of gender and sexuality are dissolved into the complacent abstraction of

'Man', a Man who is outside politics. When Ramsden remarks with irritation that 'ideological commitment is currently playing havoc with dispassionate criticism' (p. xlv) it is because the intrusion of 'ideology' into criticism disrupts the consoling play of recognition by which his own subjectivity finds a narcissistic mirror in the text.

This traditional politics of omission has as its counterpart a radical politics of assertion, which calls attention to itself as strategic agent. Thus Julianne Burton and Paul Binding have read *Bernarda Alba* in terms of women's and gay studies respectively.[13] Their lack of pretence to objective commentary and open acknowledgement of polemic is much preferable to the bland homogenization of the traditionalists. They realize (as Foucault does) that knowledge is made not for understanding but for cutting ('Nietzsche', p. 88). However the incision they make in the critical corpus is not as clean a break as they might imagine. Burton claims that Lorca sought to destroy the violent hierarchy which subordinated women to men: '[Lorca saw] a sociosexual code which privileged men at the expense of women's autonomy, participation, and self-realization . . . [He made] a concerted attempt to expose and denounce the social system which gives rise to such irreconcilable and untenable contradictions' (p. 260). In doing so he re-enacts the rebellion of his women characters, in their struggle for liberation: 'The distinguishing characteristic of Lorca's tragic heroines is their refusal to resign themselves to the fate society has decreed for them' (p. 276). Binding unites women and gays in their common struggle against oppression, a reading ratified, once more, by appeal to the controlling will and experience of the author: 'In his rage at the malformation of life to which the women of his drama are subjected Lorca must have been thinking of the denial of natural impulses and feelings to homosexuals in the conservative Spanish countryside . . . The sensibility that informs the last play he wrote and makes it so powerful a cry against all injustices must have ultimately been nurtured by his membership of a class which knew what rejection and denial meant, the homosexual'

---

[13] 'The Greatest Punishment: Female and Male in Lorca's Tragedies', in *Women in Hispanic Literature* (Berkeley, 1983), 259–79; *Lorca: The Gay Imagination* (London, 1985).

(pp. 189–90). Here we see the allegorical mode of criticism: beneath the supposed surface of the text Lorca's women are really men. Moreover the use of the term 'class' implies the existence of a collective solidarity uniting women, gays, and proletariat, a solidarity which it might be possible to theorize but cannot simply be assumed to exist. Once more differences are erased. My objection to this kind of sexual politics is not that it is biased; on the contrary it marks an important strategic and critical intervention. Nor is it that these critics sink to the level of the biographical fallacy. Indeed, Paul Binding is scrupulous in avoiding such banalities. However by failing to theorize notions such as woman and homosexuality (by assuming that they are always the same) they tend to reiterate a new kind of humanism, a new kind of deference to the author.

Burton and Binding also fall prey to the mirage of liberation. If the opposition could only be reversed (if women and gays could take power over their oppressors) then a new realm of authentic action and natural impulse would emerge. This liberationist model raises a pair of theoretical and practical questions which the critics themselves cannot answer. The theoretical question is: if our culture is overwhelmingly patriarchal or heterosexist what space is left for an 'authentic' minority or oppositional discourse uncompromised by the dominant forces? The practical question is: if Lorca believes in this essential nature or metalanguage of the minority then why does his drama make so little attempt to reproduce it? For example, the women of the rural tragedies are portrayed in ways which come uncomfortably close to reconfirming patriarchal priorities: the *novia* of *Bodas de sangre* is defined by her marital status, Yerma by her childlessness. In *Bernarda Alba* Poncia states quite bluntly that 'a man is a man' and that the daughters' problem is that they are 'women without men' (pp. 80–1). Of course it would be naïve to take any single statement within a play as exemplary of its inner truth. The fact remains however that it is not only the minor characters but the heroines themselves who perceive women in the traditional (even reified) manner as a hole which must be filled, a lack seeking a supplement. What women want, in these plays at least, is a man or a child.

One way out of this impasse is the empirical model: Lorca offers his heroines no prospect of genuine autonomy or real satisfaction beyond the world of men because, at that moment of history, none was available to them. The alternative view however (and this is the Foucauldian one) is that there is no essential self to liberate in any period, because knowledge and pleasure are always bound up with power and institutions.[14] This would help to explain the intermittent individualization of the characters. If, in the course of the play, we become aware that Angustias is old and withered, Magdalena relatively sympathetic, and Martirio devious and hypocritical, it is often difficult clearly to distinguish each sister from the other, particularly in performance where they are dressed identically much of the time. Amelia especially remains a shadowy figure. For psychologically biased critics this would be a fault in the play to be decried or refuted. I would suggest however that the discontinuous naturalism of the play reveals that the characters should be read not as psychologically complex individuals but as subjects, only individualized in so far as their bodies are animated and constituted by power.

For Foucault power operates not by oppression or repression but by subjection. He traces the work of subjection in the material conditions of a number of linked institutions: the asylum, the prison, the family. For example *Le Désordre des familles* (Paris, 1982) demonstrates the willingness with which families in eighteenth-century Paris invited the state within the walls of their homes to settle private squabbles. Isolated in its own house, each family is subject to surveillance from neighbours ('le regard des autres') which heightens the intensity of the 'drama' played out within (p. 35). Foucault discovers that the notorious 'lettre de cachet', once thought to be the instrument of alien oppression by the state, is in fact an intervention often requested by the family itself, ashamed at its own disorder. The circumstance is different from that of *Bernarda Alba*, but the structuring principle is the same: the

---

[14] For (non-Foucaldian) accounts of power and history see José Ortega, 'Conciencia social en los tres dramas rurales de García Lorca', *GLR* 9 (1981), 64–90; Carolyn Galerstein, 'The Political Power of Bernarda Alba', in *Drama, Sex, and Politics* (Cambridge, 1985), 183–90; Linda C. Fox, 'Power in the Family and Beyond: Doña Perfecta and Bernarda Alba as Manipulators of their Destinies', *Hispanófila*, 29 (1985), 57–65.

supposed opposition between private and public (domestic and civic) is untenable. The drama of family disorder is played out on the 'threshold' where the micro-unit intersects with macro-institutions of law and morality. In another text Foucault recalls the role of the 'eye of power' in constituting the family unit.[15] The very disposition of rooms in the house (where spaces are specified for parents and children, boys and girls) should be seen not only as a matter of space but also one of power (p. 149). Likewise, in *Bernarda Alba* it is precisely the division between contingent spaces (between the various bedrooms of the daughters; between the house, the patio, and the street) which provokes and elicits the inexhaustible appetite for surveillance and transgression. Martirio's quest to discover Adela's secret love is at once inspired and facilitated by the contiguity of their rooms (Act II; p. 40); relations between women and men are objectified in the 'reja' or grille, which never ceases to incite desire and deny gratification. The logic of the threshold or grille dictates that there is no simple opposition between outside and inside, between the open area of a building and its enclosed spaces. The outside is in the inside: the neighbours' observation of the family is re-enacted by each member of the family in relation to the others and even by individual members in relation to themselves. The inside is in the outside: the family's secret drama is re-enacted in the stories of the wanton Paca la Roseta and the pregnant daughter of la Librada performed in the street for the audience within the house.

The family, then, is a primary example of those disciplinary institutions which reproduce in their tiniest details a political anatomy of the body (its investment with power and knowledge). One related model is the asylum. For Foucault the history of madness in modern times[16] is marked not so much by the mass confinement of patients but the replacement of naked cruelty by more ingenious principles of subjection: silence, recognition by mirror, perpetual judgement (pp. 483–530). These are the same techniques used by Bernarda: the play opens and closes with her call for silence; she constantly

[15] In *Power/Knowledge*, ed. Colin Gordon (Brighton, 1980), 146–65.
[16] *Histoire de la folie à l'âge classique* (Paris, 1972).

confronts her daughters with images of their own poverty and
undesirability; she holds them in perpetual judgement by
continuous observation. Of course this is not to deny the
material reality of confinement (and of punishment). Rather,
it is to suggest that the techniques of subjection are more
insidious because they are more easily internalized by those to
whom they are applied. The sisters do not beat or confine
themselves; but they can and do make themselves silent, remind
themselves of their physical and financial inadequacies, and
judge themselves by their own uncompromising standards. If
the family home is reminiscent of an asylum than it also
contains one woman held to be insane: Bernarda's mother
María Josefa. It is clearly ironic that the madwoman's desires
are identical to those of her granddaughters: she wishes to go
outside; to possess a man who will fill her lack; to reach that
liminary place of transgression, the seashore (Act I; pp. 32–
3). The figure of María Josefa confirms Foucault's judgement
on madness: that it does not offer unique access to the
unchanging truth of the human predicament; that rather it
denotes the threshold where power polices its own boundaries.
Thus María Josefa seeks release from confinement; but even
madness cannot offer her escape from the tyranny of the
Same, from the codes of subjection which women have made
their own.

Foucault's most sustained treatment of the rise of subjection
is *Surveiller et punir* (Paris, 1975), published in English as
Discipline and Punish. As a history of the prison as a model for
modern society, *Surveiller et punir* traces the same movement of
'leniency' we saw in the history of madness. The spectacular
tortures of the *ancien régime* represent the acting-out of absolute
power on the body of the offender and the search for the *éclat*
(release of tension, flash of light) in which truth will be made
visible. The carceral regime of the Enlightenment on the other
hand relies on discipline rather than punishment, and on self-
regulation as much as external intervention. Discipline aims,
in its relentless attachment to detail, to correct not the body
but the soul. But this 'soul' (a perfect socialized humanity to
be liberated by the state) is itself an effect of power, a mirage
drawn from the depths of the subject in his subjection. Hence

Foucault's paradoxical dictum: the soul is the prison of the body (p. 34). The soul is that transcendent subject which always remains to be abstracted from the chaotic and specific materiality of the body and its pleasures.

I will suggest in a moment that this ever-retreating self-realization is the motive of Adela's impossible revolt. But first it remains to be shown how the disciplinary techniques associated with the prison recur (like those of the asylum) in Lorca's family cell. One means by which discipline integrates space and vision is the panopticon (pp. 197–229). The panopticon is a circular building set around a central observation tower. It is divided into little cells in which each subject (each madman, patient, worker, or prisoner) is isolated from all the others. Every tiny cell is a 'theatre' (p. 202) in which the subject is caught in the 'trap of visibility'. Bernarda's house, in which each daughter is constantly observed and subject to discipline, aspires to this Utopian carceral regime. And it shares the most unexpected of its characteristics: the effects of the panopticon are positive as well as negative. Surveillance produces increasing individualization, and a spiralling demand for resistance. But there can be no escape except into ever increasing visibility. The brightness of Bernarda's walls and the brilliance of the noonday sun (the time of the shortest shadow) suggest a space of perfect visibility both inside and outside. But Adela's first act of revolt is to make herself visible even in the darkness of night, to stand almost naked in the lamplight at her window where Pepe can see her. Her pleasure (her 'transgression') derives from a sense of self which continues to be defined as the object, not the subject, of the look. As Foucault says, discipline always promotes asymmetry, lack of reciprocity (p. 225): Adela can be seen but cannot see. And the prison succeeds even where it seems to have failed (p. 281): Bernarda's regime ensures that any delinquency must finally expose itself and make itself visible in full light. But if the panopticon is a theatre (in which transgression is elicited and isolated) then the theatre is a panopticon (in which transgression is re-enacted for the eyes of an invisible, anonymous audience). In the necessary conditions of its dramatic form *Bernarda Alba* reproduces the reversibility of the relation it takes as its object:

the collusion between power and pleasure in the presentation of the visible body.[17]

We are now in a position to re-read Adela's final revolt in Act III. Martirio has just confessed her own love for Pepe:

ADELA. Pepe el Romano es mío. El me lleva a los juncos de la orilla . . . Ya no aguanto el horror de estos techos después de haber probado el sabor de su boca. Seré lo que él quiera que sea. Todo el pueblo contra mí, quemándome con sus dedos de lumbre . . . y me pondré delante de todos la corona de espinas que tienen las que son queridas de algún hombre casado . . . yo me iré a una casita sola donde él me verá cuando quiera, cuando le venga en gana. (p. 87)

ADELA. Pepe el Romano is mine. He takes me to the reeds on the river bank . . . I can't stand the horror of these roofs anymore now that I've experienced the taste of his mouth. I'll be what he wants me to be. The whole village against me, burning me with their fingers of fire . . . and I'll place on my head in front of them all the crown of thorns which is given to those who are loved by a married man . . . I'll go off to a little house on my own where he'll see me when he wishes, when he feels like it.

Traditional humanist critics would read this passage as the climactic moment in the conflict between vitality and repression. On the one hand, there is deadly captivity (the horror of the roofs); on the other, vibrant sensuality (the taste of Pepe's mouth). Or again, on the one hand, there is the oppressive weight of convention (the whole village); on the other, the lone stand of the individual (the many against the one). The passage seems to obey the criteria of verisimilitude and psychology: Adela's new-found strength (she could control a wild horse with her little finger) derives from the authentic revelation of her sexual being. The question of formal unity is more difficult: how can Adela claim that Pepe takes her to the river when we are told elsewhere in the play that this is a village of wells with no running water? In general, however, the passage reveals quite clearly the essential nature of (ungendered) individuals: they seek freedom and sexual

[17] For an example of traditional criticism as the drawing into visibility of that which remains obscure in the text see Robert G. Havard, 'The Hidden Parts of Bernarda Alba', *RN* 26 (1985), 102–8. For the relationship between visibility, technology, and the body see David Green, 'On Foucault: Disciplinary Power and Photography', *Camerawork*, 32 (Summer 1985), 6–9.

gratification. This knowledge is held to be universal and, hence, apolitical.

The radical critics will emphasize the same oppositions to very different purpose: the passage reveals the oppression of women (and perhaps, by implication, of gays) in an over-whelmingly hostile society. Once more nature and the individual are set against repression and society, but this time with overtly political intent. The radical critic will praise Adela's rebelliousness but lament her adoption of a new subordinate position: she continues to define herself in patriarchal terms as the fallen woman, the mistress. She takes control of her body, but only to surrender it immediately to a man. However it is possible to resolve this problem empirically by appealing to the historical limits on women's expectations in Spain in the period, or perhaps to the gay writer's inability to conceive the possibility of his own freedom at that time and in that country.

The Foucauldian reading would suggest that Adela's new-found sense of self is no spontaneous revelation of internal essence, but the effect of a material process of surveillance and punishment which originates outside herself. At the final moment of her confession she invokes the whole village as witness to her pleasure. The attention of the village (its observation and gossip) serves as a panopticon: a multiple, anonymous device which heightens the intensity of the disciplinary drama. But the regime is also internalized: there is no life for her outside the village, outside patriarchy. The compulsion to confess is thus not the affirmation of authentic self-knowledge but the confirmation of an acquired docility. Adela will make her delinquency both visible and audible (and hence betray the possibility of success for her escape). Her pleasure cannot be separated from the power inscribed in her body: extremity of subjection provokes extremity of eroticism in a spiral that cannot be exhausted by mere transgression. That the place of the rebel is already dictated to her by social convention makes no difference to her pleasure: transgression can approach no place of absolute alterity; pleasure can have no meaning in a Utopian 'external' order of knowledge. And power is so pervasive that it cannot be localized in a single place or object: by breaking Bernarda's stick Adela confronts oppression but not subjection. But this is a revolt none the less. Adela cannot transcend her position, but resistance is to be found not in transcendental imperatives but in bodies and their very particular pleasures.

We can read Adela's revolt, then, not as the revelation of a coherent identity, but as the emergence of a discrete event. It takes its place in a moment of difference: on the threshold of home and society, in the mutation between girl and woman. Difference precedes essence. And if *Bernarda Alba* hints that there is no transcendence (no nature, no Man) then it also exhibits a hopeless nostalgia for the place where such concepts were once to be found: Adela on the river bank, María Josefa on the sea-shore. And this curious combination of critical scepticism and idealist nostalgia is also to be found in Lorca's most complex and uncompromising play, *El público*.

3. *EL PÚBLICO*: POWER AND PLEASURE

In the first volume of his unfinished history of sexuality, *La Volonté de savoir* (Paris, 1976), Foucault appeals once again to the figure of the spiral. One passage may serve to describe not only the 'will to knowledge' inherent in sexuality but also the fluid, reversible movement of capture and seduction typical of the Lorcan theatrical event in *Bernarda Alba*:

The pleasure that comes from exercising a power that questions, observes, watches, spies, searches out, palpates, brings to light; and, on the other hand, the pleasure that is aroused at having to evade, flee, mislead or travesty this power . . . These appeals, these evasions, these circular incitements have traced around sexes and bodies not closed frontiers, but *perpetual spirals of power and pleasure*. (p. 62; trans. Sheridan, p. 175)

If power, knowledge, and pleasure are so closely intertwined then we can no longer imagine an absolute authority in either politics or sexuality from which subjects can be liberated. That is, we must abandon the concepts of oppression and repression. In Foucault's formula we must attempt to conceive 'le sexe sans la loi, et le pouvoir sans le roi' (p. 120). Power elicits a desire for knowledge of others (surveillance), but it also provokes a desire for knowledge of the self (subjectification). And it is this incipient 'souci de soi' (sense of or concern for the self) that Foucault explores in the second and third volumes of his history which treat Greek and Hellenistic conceptions of pleasure.[18]

Lorca's treatment of sexuality has also been called 'classical' or 'pagan': it is no accident that one scene of *El público* (a scene which I will examine in detail later) takes place in a Roman ruin. However, for Lorca (as for Foucault) there can be no question of return to the supposedly innocent hedonism of Antiquity. Rather, Antiquity is a founding moment of difference for the West, and a warning that the essential truth of the subject need not lie in his or her practice of pleasure. The relative unpopularity of *El público* must also lie in its difference, and more particularly in the inability of critics to tolerate that difference. In the introduction I suggested that *El público* did not readily fulfil those criteria necessary to admit it to the great author's *œuvre*. What is more radical is that it also violates those rules within its own dramatic body: it maintains no constant level of value (some scenes are sketchy and unrealized); it contains no consistent field of conceptual coherence (the 'theme' can be taken to be either theatre or love); it lacks stylistic unity (the language oscillates between the crude and the lyrical); it unsettles historical specificity (classical motifs are juxtaposed with modern elements). As might be expected, those critics who have treated *El público* after its (much-delayed) publication, have attempted to smooth out or erase these differences.[19] For Gwynne Edwards (whose reading owes much to Martínez Nadal) the play has a unified subject: 'the revelation of love in its different forms', and a conceptual coherence: 'the logic and consistency of themes and ideas in the process of constant elaboration' (pp. 65, 77). Lorca's love of metamorphosis (at its most extreme in this play) is here curtailed by an essential human truth (love) located within the body: the X-rays which form the backdrop in Scene 1 demonstrate 'the play's intention to expose the truth that lies beneath appearances or façades'

---

[18] *L'Usage des plaisirs* (Paris, 1984); *Le Souci de soi* (Paris, 1984).

[19] For a study which finds thematic unity in sexual deviation see Suzanne Byrd, 'Panerotism: A Progressive Concept in the Final Trilogy of García Lorca', *GLR* 3 (1975), 53–6. My refs. are to *El público*, ed. Rafael Martínez Nadal (Oxford, 1976).

(pp. 68–9). Likewise for Paul Binding the screen behind which the characters pass in Scene 1 (and from behind which they emerge in changed costumes) is 'revelatory of the profoundest sexual needs/identities' (p. 154). What neither critic can admit is that the essential truth of sex 'beyond' or 'inside' the text (under the skin, behind the screen) may be an effect of the sexual quest for knowledge, rather than the object which precedes it and for which it searches. I shall argue that traditional criticism (whatever its attitude to the play's homosexual theme) is unable to address a play which is profoundly sceptical of identity and truth in the realms of both theatre and sexuality.

Two problems we met in *Bernarda Alba* recur with greater urgency in *El público*. The first is the problem of the status of the characters. The characters in *El público* are in constant flux and mutation: they change names, roles, and costumes with bewildering rapidity. It seems evident that a traditional psychological criticism is inappropriate here, and I will read them (as I did Bernarda's daughters) as examples of *mise-en-discours*: the focus or locus of discursive warfare, rather than the witness to authentic experience. The question I shall ask of them is not 'who?', or 'why?', but 'how?' (not identity, or causality, but genealogy). That is, I shall analyse the way in which they function in the discrete dramatic 'events' of each scene. The second question is that of an authentic minority voice for the oppressed. Critics tend to see in the play a definitive statement (albeit coded and disguised) on the truth of homosexuality. I shall suggest myself that the action of the play reveals that sexuality hides no essence within itself and that the minority voice is always dependent or parasitic on the majority. *El público* is structured around a constant metamorphosis which has no primary or originary term, and a shimmering linguistic surface which conceals no hidden meanings or motives. And this is because both theatre and sexuality are based (as we shall see) on a founding moment of difference.

In the opening moments of *El público* the Director bids the audience enter the theatre. Thus from the very beginning the play presents itself as a representation of representation: as in *Las meninas*, the artist's means of depiction are also objects

depicted for the spectator. How can we read this reflexivity?
For the traditional critic it merely continues to ensure that
circulation of the same held to be the universal condition of
Art: 'In *The Public* there is no separation between its action
and its audience. The playgoer . . . is made aware that he is
looking at an actor who is, in fact, himself, and that the play is
merely a reflection of the larger stage of life' (Edwards, p. 68).
Once more we find the consoling play of recognition. I would
suggest however that *El público* stages not the (re)unification of
the individual but the splitting of the subject. The process is
similar to that described by Foucault in his little book on
Magritte's *Ceci n'est pas une pipe* (Montpellier, 1973). In
Magritte's picture the combination of image and text unsettles
the old oppositions: showing and telling; figuring and speaking;
imitating and signifying (p. 28). What the picture contradicts
is the convention by which the work of art is unable
simultaneously to refer directly to the world and to represent
it (make something else stand in its place). This distinction is
implicit, but repressed, in any piece of theatre: the actor's
body serves both as direct reference (the material presence of
the real) and indirect representation (the abstract imitation of
Art). Lorca's play, like Magritte's picture, collapses the two
modes of reference and representation which Classical art must
keep rigorously separate. We can never be sure if the public or
audience invoked is a historical community (ourselves) or a
fictional construct (a character). Hence by making theatre
itself one of the main concerns of his play Lorca does not
simply denaturalize convention or lay bare the fictional
device. Rather, he suggests the split between presence and
performance in all human action.

    Let us take a specific example, a sequence of events from
Scene III. The First White Horse invokes the 'beautiful apples
made of ashes' which grow near the Dead Sea. Juliet says that
ashes are not good, but the Horse replies that he speaks not of
ashes but of ashes which have the form of an apple (p. 95).
The motif has a long history: in the Renaissance Dead Sea
apples served as emblems of the bitter truth of human
mortality hidden beneath the seductive forms of sensual
pleasure. In *El público*, on the other hand, the comforting
opposition of inside and outside (form and content) is

dissolved. No 'allegorical' reading is possible; the apples betray their substance on their surface. Death is not a hidden secret, but open knowledge: as the Black Horse says, the dead keep speaking and the living use the lancet. A little later the Black Horse speaks of stripping off 'the last garment of blood' ('traje de sangre') to reveal the truth within. Here the body itself is inauthentic: its innermost fluid is merely a cover or surface, and cannot serve its habitual function as guarantor of essence. The discussion of masks which follows develops the motif of surface. The First Man claims not to have a mask; but the Director contradicts him by stating that there is nothing but mask. Even when we explore the hollows of our bodies (the nostrils or anus) the plaster of the mask presses down on the face. The First Man says he has struggled with the mask until he has seen the Director naked. But this hint of authentic interiority is rejected by the First White Horse who states, mockingly, that 'a lake is a surface' (p. 105). The First Man replies that it is a volume; but the Horse laughingly caps him: a volume is a thousand surfaces. This rather abstract (indeed topographic) repartee serves as a commentary on the main action, generally taken to be the struggle of the Director and the First Man to acknowledge their true feelings for one another. If all is surface however (if there is no inner essence or experience) then the quest for depth or volume will be interminable. The Director complains that the First Man's love for him lives only in the presence of witnesses (p. 107). But this is the constant condition of homosexual relations, subject as they are to continual surveillance by a dominant society. The First Man wishes to 'strip [the Director's] skeleton'; but he will never reach the authentic kernel of sexual experience, because that very experience is at once forced into concealment and summoned into visibility by the inescapable mechanism of sexuality itself. As Foucault argues in *La Volonté de savoir* the language of homosexuality must be a 'reverse discourse' ('discours en retour'), an attempt by the minority to speak back from the position to which it has been assigned by the majority (p. 134).

What we find in *El público*, then, is not an essential or original state of homosexuality, but a critique of its descent and emergence in relation to its divergence from other terms.

In Foucault's sense of the word, *El público* is a 'genealogical' text. The dramatic techniques used by Lorca also coincide with those borrowed by Foucault from Nietzsche. First, Lorca uses parody to undermine our received sense of the 'real', and thus forbids us a sense of recognition in his theatre of puppets. There is no opportunity for the complacent veneration of cultural monuments in Lorca's Roman ruin. Second, Lorca uses dissociation to undermine our faith in human identity, and mocks our respect for psychic or historical continuity. Third, he sacrifices the subject presumed to know in a struggle against the belief in disinterested truth, and thus prevents us taking his work as the product of authoritative knowledge. Hence the stress on masks in *El público*. Masks serve in Lorca's text to parody the real, to dissociate the spectators from fixed identities, and to disabuse them of the faith in absolute knowledge.[20] *El público* is the work of a genealogist who will 'push the masquerade to its limit and prepare the great carnival of time where masks are constantly reappearing' ('Nietzsche', p. 94). This is not to suggest that Lorca had a coherent intellectual programme which he carried out in the play. Rather, it is to acknowledge that the extreme difficulty of his text raises broadly philosophical questions which cannot be answered by the psychological models of humanist critics.

However, to say that homosexuality has no absolute origin or ultimate meaning is not to deprive it of all significance. On the contrary, Lorca offers a sophisticated commentary on the value of homosexual relations, a commentary which tends to coincide with Foucault's narrative of sexual ethics in Antiquity. Thus Lorca, like the Greeks, shows little concern for a code of prescription or prohibition guaranteed by a transcendent being. As critics have remarked, he invokes no general 'law' of nature to differentiate between desires. Love between women and men (between Juliet and the First White Horse) is as riven by 'engaño' or deception as love between men (p. 89): the difference in object choice does not imply a difference in subjectivity. For Lorca (as for the Greeks once more) neither sex nor power is based on a monolithic authority: the First Man promises to bring the Director the Emperor's head (III; p. 81).

[20] For a recent reading which retains the classic humanist binarism of 'truth' and 'mask' see María Clementa Millán's intro. to her edn. of the text (Madrid, 1987), 47–52.

However, as we shall see, this decapitation is unnecessary: the Emperor has no more power in the sexual regime than anyone else. Lorca is concerned, then, not with absolute morals but with ethical pragmatism, with the relation of the subject not to God or the King but to other subjects and to the self. We have noted that Lorca does not seem to distinguish between different kinds of desire. The radical student in Scene v does not care whether Juliet is a woman or a man: love is the same (p. 131). However two questions are posed more urgently by homosexuality than by heterosexuality: the question of reciprocity and that of the Other. Foucault's shows in *L'Usage des plaisirs* (Paris, 1984) that the Greeks were not concerned with desire as such, that they felt no compulsion to reveal 'the insidious presence of a power [*puissance*] whose limits are uncertain and masks multiple' (p. 47). Sex begins to become an ethical problem only in the specific area of relations between men and boys. While the relation between men and women is one of simple dominance (master to slave) the boy who is the object of desire must also become a respected citizen, an autonomous agent. The problem, then, is how to respect the 'freedom of the other' and how to ensure the transformation of 'the object of pleasure into the subject who is master of his pleasures' (pp. 219, 248). This disturbing reversibility uniquely applicable to relations between males points forward to a time when symmetry and reciprocity will become the aims of (heterosexual) 'true love', when love is addressed to the inner truth of the individual and provokes 'the interrogation of man by himself as subject of desire' (p. 269).

This interrogation of the self, however, is not yet linked (as is that of the Christian) to transcendent Law. And it is at this point that Greek 'love of boys' (so different from modern homosexuality) coincides with one aspect at least of the modern condition. As Foucault asks in a late interview: 'Are we able to have an ethics of acts and their pleasures which would be able to take into account the pleasure of the other? Is the pleasure of the other something which can be integrated in our pleasure, without reference either to law, to marriage . . .?' (Rabinow, p. 364). I would suggest that this is also the question asked of homosexuality by Lorca in *El público*. Lorca

takes it for granted that relations between men need no
legitimation from natural or human law. But power structures
within those relations do indeed pose an ethical (rather than a
moral) problem. Thus in Scene III the Director proclaims as
he struggles with the First Man: 'I will transform myself into
whatever you want' (p. 83). This is very similar to Adela's
proclamation of identity through subjection: 'My body
belongs to whomever I wish'. From the subject who is master
(indeed 'Director') of his pleasures, the male lover makes
himself object of another's pleasure. Yet (and this is the
paradox) it is to ensure his own pleasure that he does so.
Love presents itself as an interminable process of reversibility.
As the Director and the First Man struggle, the Second Man
and the Third Man also treat the question of dominance. If
the Third Man possesses a slave it is because the Second Man
is a slave; but if both were slaves together then they could
break their chains in different ways. The symmetry of
relations between men provokes an interrogation of the self,
which in turn suggests the possibility of liberation in the
attainment of reciprocity. However the farcical register of the
scene and the bewildering rapidity of the characters' transformations suggest that any stable integration of ethics into
pleasure (any continuous recognition of self in the other) is at
best a mirage, a chimera.

We can now study in detail the best-known passage of
homosexual metamorphosis in the play, the dialogue between
the Figure of Bells and the Figure of Vine Leaves which takes
place in the Roman ruin:

FIGURA DE CASCABELES: ¿Si yo me convirtiera en nube?
FIGURA DE PÁMPANOS: Yo me convertiría en ojo.
FC: ¿Si yo me convirtiera en caca?
FP: Yo me convertiría en mosca.
FC: ¿Si yo me convirtiera en manzana?
FP: Yo me convertiría en beso . . .
FC: ¿Y si yo me convirtiera en pez luna?
FP: Yo me convertiría en cuchillo.
FC: [*Dejando de danzar*].   Pero, ¿por qué? ¿por qué me atormentas?
. . . Te gozas en interrumpir mi danza y danzando es la única
manera que tengo de amarte. (p. 57)

FIGURE OF BELLS: If I turned into a cloud?

FIGURE OF VINE LEAVIES: I'd turn into an eye.
FB: If I turned into shit?
FVL: I'd turn into a fly.
FB: If I turned into an apple?
FVL: I'd turn into a kiss . . .
FB: If I turned into a moonfish?
FVL: I'd turn into a knife.
FB: [*No longer dancing*]. But why? Why do you torture me? . . . You enjoy interrupting my dance and dancing is the only way I have of loving you.

The passage stages quite literally a 'dance' of reciprocity between male subjects. It unfolds in a Roman ruin, the desecrated remains of the cultural monument, the 'theatre' of Nietzsche's decadent Europe. Lorca's intermittent and parodic references to Antiquity (the vine leaves of Bacchus, the flute of the classical shepherd) deny us the chance to recognize ourselves in his characters and undermine our sense of the reality of history. We are dissociated from the Figures, whose identities are wholly provisional, and whose perpetual changes preclude any illusion of psychic continuity. Parody and dissociation lead to sacrifice: the sacrifice of a univocal truth (of a subject presumed to know) in the violent struggle of the will to knowledge. The Figures' spiral of autoaffection (autointerrogation) reveals a master and slave dialectic which precludes the survival of absolute knowledge. Cloud to eye; shit to fly; apple to kiss: the relation is one of passivity to activity, which culminates in the contrast between the soft, yielding moonfish and the sharp incisions of the knife. The dance stops: the pleasure of the other is no longer assured; the object can no longer aspire to mastery within the knowledge of its own subjection. But which is the subject and which the object? The roles will be reversed in the next exchange, and even these provisional identities exist only through autoaffection: to dance is the only way to love, but it is a dance without a leading partner.

The possibility of reciprocity thus requires the problematization of the subject as moral agent. At what point does mastery of the self preclude the autonomy of the other? The radical knowledge of the scene is that sexual relations are (precisely) relational: they conceal no essence, imply no founding identity. The Figure of Vine Leaves claims to be all man; but he wants his partner to be even more of a man than he is. The question of homosexuality, then, is (as for the Greeks) the question of activity and passivity. And as for the Greeks once more, the unease to which the question gives rise is related to the reversible status of the male citizen, alternately subject and object of pleasure. Lorca asks himself 'What is a man?', but can offer only a relational definition: he is the one who sees himself seeing (who interrogates himself as an ethical subject).

In *El público* this 'sense of self' is ontological rather than psychological. The characters do not seek the 'real root' of their desire or indulge in the hermeneutic work of deciphering it. As Foucault says in the interview, it is this lack of concern for the origin of desire which distinguishes Greek awareness of subjectification ('assujettissement') from the 'Californian' cult of the self, from the search for an essential identity (p. 361). When Plato asks 'How can the eye see itself?' he replies that it is only through looking into another eye, using another pupil as a mirror of one's own (p. 367). It is a fitting image of the reflexive model of sexuality proposed by Foucault and implied by Lorca. The final scene of *El público* is played with an enormous eye on the stage wall and the closing moment of the play is one of brilliant, white light. However, just as metamorphosis implies not Platonic essence but anti-Platonic difference, so visibility implies not ultimate revelation but material observation or reflexivity. The 'theatre beneath the sand' (once proposed as the 'true' theatre of authentic experience) now stands revealed as a theatre of death and confinement, a tomb for the Director. Indeed, there has been a certain asymmetry in the references to this image throughout the play. The theatre beneath the sand suggests interiority, hermeneutic process, and the struggle for hidden essence; but it also implies concealment, inauthenticity, and the deadly repression of life. The Director's open-air theatre is a charade: that which is visible cannot be authentic; but the underground theatre is no real alternative: invisibility is death. Hence the final knowledge of *El público* is that of *Bernarda Alba*: even on the sea-shore or under the sand there can be no escape into freedom. As the Director's mother discovers (p. 161) there is no way out of the theatre, no way out of the sexual fix. To escape into visibility is to follow the rules already dictated by power.

4. A SENSE OF SELF

If *El público* offers a flash of insight or revelation, it is the sceptical, critical knowledge that homosexual desire, as such, does not exist:[21] Lorca acknowledges the specificity of relations between men without implying an inherent 'nature' for those who participate in them. Lorca offers no positive role models for gay men, just as he offers none for feminist women. It is difficult to abstract from the plays a coherent awareness of sexual community or class. This is not to say, however, that it is illegitimate to enlist his works in a programme of oppositional sexual politics. There can be no neutral approach to the author's sexual object choice: to repress it is to collude with the oppressive 'universal' subject of humanism; to diagnose it as homosexual or to proclaim it as gay is to insert the author into medical and political discourses which assume (like humanism) that sex is the essence of subjectivity. If the ultimate force of the theoretical argument is to question that assumption, then this is not to deny the reality of actually existing power struggles in the sexual arena: we can question but not transcend the subject positions allotted us. This is the work of the reverse discourse.

The popular image of Lorca seems to be the result of the multiple restrictions of the author-function: as a Spaniard, and more particularly an Andalusian, he has often been regarded as a 'natural' genius, a child of instinct and passion. His popularity outside Spain seems directly related to his apparent reconfirmation of such commonplace definitions of the 'Latin' temperament. It would be ironic if an increased awareness of the homosexual theme in his writings were to intensify the reductive focus on supposedly determinative origins (whether geographic or erotic). A reading of *El público* contradicts any notion of emotionalism or *naïveté* in relation to either the treatment of the sexual theme or the conception of

---

[21] This is the paradoxical thesis of Guy Hocquenghem in *Homosexual Desire* (London, 1978).

dramatic form. A recently published thesis speaks of the 'silenced voice' of Lorca's homosexuality.[22] This is very true. However a reading of Foucault suggests a more complex model of subjection and reveals that to give voice to one's identity (to confess) may bring negative as well as positive results.[23] Lorca's work will no doubt be exposed to patronizing psychosexual studies. And if he is to be seen as representative of a 'gay imagination' then this term should not be derived from (and projected back on to) a historically invariable constituency. Foucault's actual advocacy of minority rights assumed no necessary or consistent identity of oppositional groups, no 'we' (Rabinow, p. 385); the assumption of a community of interest may not be the most productive way to introduce a knowledge of sexual variety into an Academy which tends, still, to repress that knowledge.

Foucault warns us that power is ubiquitous. He does not attempt to explain how it achieved that position. Rigorously sceptical of origins, he no doubt considered the question metaphysical: he is concerned with the material techniques of power, not its ideal cause or nature. In just such a way Lorca fails to provide the spectator with a convincing motive for Bernarda's tyranny, which has always begun and is never ended: he shows us how her regime functions, but not why. When power is so radically dispersed, then resistance becomes problematic indeed. We saw this in the analysis of Adela's impossible revolt. The epigraph to the last volumes of the history of sexuality asks us to speak against ('contredire') the historical repetition of the Same. But that same history, with its apparent return to a stress on the determining function of discourse in the creation of the self (even the perverse self) makes any attempt at contradiction seem puny, even absurd. Perhaps the answer lies in a continuing critique of our own

[22] Angel Sahuquillo, *Federico García Lorca y la cultura de la homosexualidad* (Stockholm, 1986). For a psychoanalytic reading of the life (which is not Lacanian, in spite of its title) see Michèle Ramond, *Psychotextes: La Question de l'Autre dans Federico García Lorca* (Toulouse, 1986). For the latest scholarly account of Lorca's loves and friendships see Agustín Sánchez Vidal's best-selling *Buñuel, Lorca, Dalí: El enigma sin fin* (Barcelona, 1988).

[23] Jonathan Dollimore contrasts one gay writer who embraces the per/in-version of the 'essential' self with another who seeks liberation in authentic self-knowledge: 'Different Desires: Subjectivity and Transgression in Wilde and Gide', *TP* 1 (1987), 48–67. A Foucaldian account of Lorca would be closer to Dollimore's Wilde than to his Gide.

position, rather than a disabling absorption with that of the Other. Indeed, in an essay published posthumously, Foucault, the celebrated scourge of the Enlightenment, claims Kant as a precursor of his own method: 'work on our limits . . . a patient labour giving form to our impatience for liberty' (Rabinow, p. 50). This critical activity would transform the academic from the subject presumed to know to the sacrificial victim of the will to knowledge; and would change our conception of the author from a unified function of delimitation to a multiple body of association. It would also correspond to a new (post-Christian) definition of sexuality: the abandonment of desire as absolute; of legitimation by divine law; of self-examination as moral imperative. The title of Foucault's last book refers to the avowals or confessions of the flesh,[24] and in Lorca the body is often made to speak of its desire: Adela is said to have a lizard between her breasts (II; p. 34); the Third Man has tiny branches of grapes hanging down his shoulders (III; p. 79). Both are visible testimony to invisible love. But this speaking body needs no interpretation: its meaning is transparent, wholly 'superficial'. As the critic disclaims authority and the author is stripped of transcendence, so the body is emptied of volume or depth.

Once the body is evacuated (humanism defeated) *El público* can be seen as an entry in the Chinese encyclopaedia: no operating table is flexible enough to encompass the variety of its elements, a variety which should be respected. *Bernarda Alba* can be seen as an analogue of *Las meninas*: it offers a more integrated mode of depiction which permits the recognition of identity. But perhaps a truly critical spectator of the work should refuse to take up the transcendent position it offers in front of the stage, and leave the place of the King vacant before the allegory of representation. For both Lorca and Foucault are hostile to transcendence. One slogan of May 1968 was 'Beneath the pavement is the beach.' But as María Josefa's sea-shore and the Director's theatre beneath the sand reveal, power has no outside, civilization no underneath. The pleasure of Lorca's theatre is that it gives voice to these necessary revelations of freedom. The power of Lorca's theatre is that it denies the possibility of their existence.

[24] *Les Aveux de la Chair* (on sexuality in the early Christian period) is still to be published.

5

NERUDA, VALLEJO, MARX

I. MARXIAN SEXUALITY

MARXIST literary theory is currently unfashionable in Europe and the United States. This is partly the result of the critiques it has suffered at the hands of such thinkers as Foucault and the apostles of post-modernism. But perhaps the most damaging charge made against orthodox Marxism is that it cannot provide an adequate answer to the questions raised by gender and sexuality. Typical of recent criticism is Toril Moi's claim that while Marxism has proved valuable as a precedent for the (feminist) study of significant gaps or absences in hegemonic texts, there is now no coherent body of Marxist–feminist theory to challenge the dominance of the French and North American schools (*Sexual/Textual Politics*, pp. 93–4). In the seventies a number of mainly British women did indeed attempt syntheses of Marxism and feminism. Thus Ann Foreman, for example, compares the position of woman to that of the proletariat in *Femininity as Alienation* (London, 1977): the product of woman's labour is expropriated; her social relations are displaced by monetary relations, and the use value of her labour is reduced to exchange value (pp. 70–1). But Foreman begins her book by condemning the continuing separation of sexuality and economics in Marxist theory and suggesting that 'the problem of developing a theory of women's oppression [is] not one of adding to the existing body of socialist and marxist [*sic*] thought . . . but of questioning its whole tradition' (pp. 7–8). The editors of *Feminism and Materialism* (London, 1978) also attack the 'additive' strategy (p. 2), which makes of gender just another item to be added to the theoretical shopping list. For Annette Kuhn and Ann Marie Wolpe, a materialist analysis of women's position in the relations of production and reproduction (an analysis based on productivity, history, and the sexual division of labour) must lead to the transformation of Marxism itself. This is because orthodox approaches to woman and the family have foundered on the rock of 'domestic labour' (pp. 7–8). As one contributor to their volume confirms, housework cannot be slotted neatly into Marx's labour theory of value, for the latter takes as its starting-point productive male labour outside the home (p. 200). Women's work thus has an additional or supplementary status, which serves to destabilize the edifice of 'male-stream' theory. Kuhn and Wolpe would agree with Rosalind Coward whose thesis in *Patriarchal Precedents* (London, 1983) is that the blind spots in Marxist theory are not accidental; and that there must be a realignment in the whole field of Marxism before women can emerge into full visibility. To sum up, then, even at the height of feminist interest in Marxism there is a sense of unease or anxiety which becomes increasingly evident. This unease seems to derive from the awareness of an untenable contradiction: that the theory which claimed to give voice to the 'unsaid' in the literary or cultural text was itself deaf to the unspoken preconceptions on which its own method was based. But if the orthodox claim to scientific objectivity is no longer tenable, I would argue myself that this need not spell the end of materialism as a critical discourse. What is required is a historicization of Marxism which would strip it of the spurious universalism which the logic of its own method must surely deny. Marxism may thus be subjected to a Marxist analysis.

In a rather similar spirit Kuhn and Wolpe argue strongly in favour of a properly critical theory and against another false universalism, that of the humanists who appeal to subjective 'experience':

Criticism of theoretical work on the grounds that it does not immediately relate to 'reality' may be seen as an assertion of the impossibility of describing, let alone of analysing, situations which are not open to experiential observation. What must follow from the demand for making sense of the everyday world is not a rejection of *all* theory *per se*. Because such a demand is located within an epistemological base (largely unrecognized in this instance), the rejection is of specific theoretical positions . . . (p. 5)

The anti-theoretical position is itself theoretical, based on the erroneous assumption that 'the world is reducible to . . . terms of subjective meanings produced and deployed by actors in concrete situations of face-to-face interaction.' What Marxism would suggest, however, is that 'experience' is itself a historical construct, and that it is the nature of capitalism to repress the process by which it is constructed, to present culture as nature.

But if the adoption of a self-consciously theoretical stance is seen as essential (indeed inevitable) by these British women, the positions adopted by women outside Europe can be very different. Latin Americans have rarely contributed to the recent debates on sexual difference (although Jean Franco has suggested that this is not the case in Brazil).[1] The material conditions of scholarship are of course very different from those in the North. For example, in the first essay in a collection on women in Chile, Lucía Santa Cruz stresses the difficulties involved in even attempting to salvage women's lost history.[2] The first obstacle is the difficulty in isolating woman from the social and familial complexes in which she is so profoundly implicated. The second is quite simply the lack of documentation available to the researcher in women's studies (p. 15). Similarly, in the introduction to their collection of interviews with women in Peru, Esther Andradi and Ana María Portugal stress the rigid controls to which women are still subject in their country, which lead them 'implacably' to marriage and children.[3] Women are not free 'to be themselves' (p. 9). This stress on emancipation and on the quest for authentic identity recurs in (male) versions of Marxism in Latin America, which often promote a Utopian promise of liberation through revolution. But, as Sheldon B. Liss notes at the end of his survey *Marxist Thought in Latin America* (Berkeley, 1984), there has been a lack of women political theorists in the continent and a marked neglect by male writers of such questions as alienation in the sexual relation, the materialism of sex, and the exploitation of women (pp. 274–5). If the problems of gender and sexuality have not

[1] 'Gender, Death, and Resistance: Facing the Ethical Vacuum', unpublished paper read in New York, 1985.
[2] *Tres ensayos sobre la mujer chilena* (Santiago, 1978).
[3] *Ser mujer en el Perú* (Lima, 1978).

been solved by theorists in Europe, they have rarely been raised by the diverse Marxisms of Latin America.

A more fruitful approach is to examine the position of Latin America itself in Marxist theory. José Aricó's excellent *Marx y América Latina* (Lima, 1980) traces the emergence of the continent as a historical subject in Marx and Engels and their commentators. He begins by claiming that Latin America is a place of marginality which problematizes the very limits of Marxist theory: the question of what it means to be a Marxist *in* Latin America is itself problematic (pp. 43, 45). Marx's neglect of the continent cannot be explained away by ignorant Eurocentrism. On the contrary, he had ample access to material and, indeed, a knowledge of Latin America had played an important, if contradictory, role in European thought from the Enlightenment onwards: it served on the one hand to justify a general science of man (even 'savages' could be redeemed by progress), and on the other to justify cultural relativism (the vastness and multiplicity of the continent could not be reduced to a European perspective) (p. 54). Marx and Engels did produce subtle analyses of other subject nations. Thus, with the development of the world market, they saw that Britain had become dependent on its colonies as both source of raw materials and market for manufacturing goods (p. 55). And according to Marx's analysis of the Irish question, the emancipation of the English proletariat was now dependent on the emancipation of the nation held subject by the British government (p. 67). In the prologue to the first edition of *Capital*, Marx had held up Britain as a mirror to the other nations, an anticipation of their own stories, citing a Latin tag: *de te fabula narratur* (p. 77). But in the later Marx the image is turned on its head and, by a movement of reverse colonialism, the revolutionary focus shifts from Europe to the colonies, and the oppressors become dependent on the oppressed. What were the obstacles which prevented Marx from applying this dialectical method to Latin America, the blind spots which prevented him from seeing what he should have seen (p. 79)? Perhaps the most important is an unexamined Hegelian residue: Latin America was seen as an immense emptiness, the echo or reflection of Europe. For Marx and Engels it existed only as pure exteriority, in its

relation with the outside world (p. 98–9). Like Hegel's
Asiatics, Latin Americans were a people without a history,
lacking autonomous potency and expansive virility (p. 120),
and their political culture was arbitrary and irrational. A
Marxian treatment of this Hegelian residue must therefore be
based on that which is 'unsaid' by Marx himself (p. 136).

Like woman, then, Latin America marks that threshold of
marginality beyond which theory fears to tread. To admit it
into the conceptual field would mean redrawing the boundaries
and remapping the ground. Defined by Marx himself as
invisible, empty, ahistorical, and irrational, Latin America
exemplifies the point at which Marxism is no longer Marxist,
but idealist. By staking its claim, none the less, to autonomous
agency and identity the continent calls into question one tenet
taken for granted by many Marxists: the claim of dialectical
materialism to universal applicability. In the case of both
woman and Latin America, the subject term speaks back to
the dominant order using the language it has inherited from
that order. This is Marx's reverse colonialism, rather similar
to Foucault's reverse discourse.

In the rest of this chapter I consider two Latin American
poets: the Chilean Pablo Neruda and the Peruvian César
Vallejo. In his *Odas elementales* Neruda sets out to reproduce
natural objects in their essential materiality, but can only do
so by appeal to 'naturalization', that is, the passing off of
culture as nature. I oppose to this naturalizing strategy the
antidote of 'defamiliarization', the recuperation of the cultural
labour partially erased by the text itself. In his *Poemas humanos*
Vallejo proposes an implicit model of Man which cannot elude
ideology, that is, the passing off of a particular perspective as a
universal law. To this ideological residue I oppose the
antidote of 'reproduction', an attention to the enabling
conditions of literary discourse as material practice. Neruda's
collection is overtly political, Vallejo's more problematic, but
the materialist method is equally applicable in both cases. For
it serves to submit the unacknowledged idealism of both
writers to a double specification: first, the historicization of the
transcendental subject, who can no longer claim the privilege
of the abstract 'individual'; second, the gendering of that
subject, who can no longer claim the status of sexual neutrality.

2. NATURE IN THE *ODAS ELEMENTALES*

Neruda is the poet of politics and of nature. That is, he offers both a vision of society renewed and reintegrated by socialism, and a heightened experience of the materiality of the world, of the physicality of the concrete object. Politics and nature unite in the ostensible aims of the *Odas elementales*, which are well-known: to speak simply to a general audience in a voice which is their own and on everyday topics of direct concern to them.[4] Early critics seem to have accepted this ambition at face value. For Rodríguez Monegal, Neruda (like Whitman) is the vehicle for the direct mirroring of poet and reader, for an unmediated communication at once ideal and material, for if Neruda's voice says 'I', this 'I' is also 'you', and when he celebrates himself (his love, his objects, his elemental experiences, his land, and his faith) the poet is celebrating all men.[5] Neruda is not merely a poet in these poems, but a 'person', at once individual and universal.

But, as Robert Pring-Mill has shown by publishing the manuscripts of some of these poems, the *Odas* are by no means the natural effusion which the poet claims them to be, but are rather the artificial products of a meticulous labour process, of selection, correction, and substitution.[6] For Pring-Mill, however, the question of a natural aesthetics remains unexamined: the virtue of the poem lies in its status as objective correlative of the essential and quotidian beauty of the onion, say, which it has reproduced directly through the transparency of its language. Jean Franco, on the other hand, has hinted at flaws in this supposed transparency. While acknowledging Neruda's claim to have made a poetry 'as natural as song', she states that he is 'disingenuous' in claiming to reject the Book (in the Ode of the same name) as an alienation of authentic experience (p. 19). She notes also that the 'ordinary people' embraced by Neruda in these poems are subject to a kind of arrested economic development, and remain innocent of the

---

[4] See e.g. Jean Franco's intro. to *Pablo Neruda: Selected Poems*, ed. Nathaniel Tarn (Harmondsworth, 1975), 13.

[5] *El viajero inmóvil: Introducción a Pablo Neruda* (Buenos Aires, 1966), 280.

[6] 'La elaboración de la cebolla', in *Actas del iii congreso internacional de hispanistas* (Mexico, 1970), 739–51.

assembly line and commodity capitalism: 'They are sailors, bricklayers, miners, carpenters, or bakers—all those whose work involves the handling of primary materials' (p. 20). Neruda's workers are not the modern industrial proletariat, but the small-town craftspeople of his own childhood. More recently, Enrico Mario Santí has suggested that the apparent suppression of self proposed by the *Odas* is in fact a 'poetics of self-effacement' which carries within itself an ironic reading or misreading.[7] That is, the poet's dissolution of self before the plenitude of the object is in fact a rhetorical posture, which serves merely to reinstate authorial authority at the centre of the poetic universe, more obliquely perhaps, yet no less thoroughly.

The surface contradictions of the *Odas*, then, are quite apparent to the critical gaze. Neruda's aims seem to go unfulfilled: the simple is constantly displaced by the complex, the universal by the individual, and the transparent by the opaque. These contradictions seem to arise from Neruda's attempt to present his own very partial and culturally specific experience as natural and universal, as the imaging of the cosmos and of history. The *Odas*, then, are in part and necessarily a labour of naturalization. I will suggest in this section that it is not where Neruda succeeds in his aims, but rather where he fails that he gives contemporary readers the material for a (Marxist) critique of his attractive yet deficient critique of capitalism. I will be mainly concerned with three areas of cultural practice: language, subjectivity, and politics. My thesis is that Neruda's language, far from being transparent, tends inevitably towards excess and lyric superfluity; and that this (unintended) excess highlights contradictions in the commodity and the subject under capitalism. The principal contradiction (and one which has not to my knowledge been treated before) is that of gender: Neruda's naturalization of male as universal subject of language and vision and his consequent deprived representation of female as passive object of this vital male force. Explicit in the *Odas* is a 'political

---

[7] *Pablo Neruda: The Poetics of Prophesy* (Ithaca and London, 1982), 211. For a bibliography of recent articles on the *Odas* see Santí's note on the same page. For prophesy as ideological link between Marx and the Neruda of the *Canto General* see pp. 179–81.

nature' in which objects testify to the authentic (economic) reality of social relations distorted by a corrupt and corrupting dominant ideology. Implicit in them, and underlying their overt oppositional mission, we may find a 'natural politics' which is unexamined by the poet himself, a deeper stratum of cultural relations ideologically determined, yet perceived and represented as natural and unchanging. More generally, I shall argue that this naturalization of gender roles is endemic even in 'scientific' Marxism, and indeed may be traced back to *Capital*. And more widely still, I shall treat the question of a politically progressive or oppositional poetry: what are the conditions of its existence and the qualities required for its production? This question is acute in the case of the *Odas* in which transparency vies with linguistic innovation, and conceptual clarity with formal difficulty. In the final instance, can Neruda's odes escape the play of naturalization? How can the materialist critic rescue them from the recuperative ruses of the complacent bourgeois reader?[8]

As critics have often noted, surface contradictions in the language and matter of the *Odas* are overtly displayed to the reader in the introductory or liminary poem 'El hombre invisible'. Thus Neruda attacks the old lyric poetry for its use of the first person pronoun ('yo'), while constantly deploying it himself. The old poets celebrate the (female) love object ('la dulce que aman'), blind to the realities of social and economic production which surround them; but Neruda himself ironically picks up the same reference later in the poem ('la dulce que amo'). This 'acknowledgement of self-indulgence' (Santí, p. 210) demonstrates how in these poems denial leads inevitably to assertion and the synthetic or vatic voice attains an emphatic if ambiguous prominence in the very act of proclaiming its transparency. The status of 'El hombre invisible' is also ambivalent. It is both outside the main body of poems, denied participation in them, and anterior to the Odes proper, implicitly claiming by its position a certain precedence and authority over them. From this uncertain position (both inside and outside the book as a whole) it

---

[8] For materialist and feminist approaches to Spanish American literature see Jean Franco, 'Trends and Priorities for Research in Latin American Literature', *IL* 16 (1983), 107–20.

initiates a dialectic which will be developed throughout the
rest of the work: that between nature and culture. Thus the
'ancient', sentimental poet has a certain affection for nature,
for the land and the sea ('sus sentimientos | son marinos') but
is denied access to the authenticating culture of the labour
process which supplements deficient primary materials and
which is celebrated by the 'modern' political poet. The latter
seeks plenitude in the specificities of material production, in
the factory not the country, and in the baker's union, not the
commodity they produce: 'bread' as universal and natural
cipher. Yet this overt stress on a material culture is displaced
by the ideal communion of the final couplet: 'the song of the
invisible man | who sings with all men.'[9] In this opening
poem, then, Neruda both proposes to reveal the invisible
labour secreted in the capitalist commodity and yet aspires
himself to the condition of invisibility, to the elimination of
those social and economic relations which necessarily mediate
between a poet and his audience. In other words, he reassigns
the myth of a 'natural production' from alienated labour to
authenticated utterance, concealing his own work as he
reveals that of others. And in doing so, he raises the question
of the place of female labour in this ideal poetic economy. For
while the 'men' of the poet's audience may be taken perhaps
as generic, the poet himself is specifically and eternally male,
and woman the object and recipient of the poet's amorous
discourse, whether ancient or modern.

   This unexamined appeal to gender as natural principle of
differentiation recurs in various forms when the poet seeks to
highlight the invisible (male) labour which confers value on
the commodity. It is perhaps implicit in the first Ode in which
the poet calls on the air to become material (he claims to be
happy that it has abandoned its transparency) and begs it not
to submit to the promiscuous exchange of the market-place
(urging it not to sell itself). The air must reject the
propositions of the capitalist in his automobile, and join the
poet instead in his dance of liberation: they will go dancing
together through the world (pp. 14–16). The transparency of

---

   [9] The collected Odes are published as *El libro de las odas* (Buenos Aires, 1972). I
restrict myself to the first book, cited in the following edn.: *Odas elementales* (Barcelona,
1983).

nature is thus compromised by the materiality of culture distorted by capitalism, but subordinated by the poet to the rites of heterosexual courtship. The air (in spite of its masculine gender in Spanish) is a woman and partakes of those qualities 'natural' to her sex: she may be bought by the money of one suitor or seduced by the song of another. This movement is more explicit in the ode to the onion. The poet begins with an evocation of the 'birth' of the onion, its formation under the ground. On being thrust above the earth it reveals its 'naked transparency' (like the air once more), lifting up its breasts ('senos') like Venus emerging from the surf. This female object, described with bantering yet affectionate humour by the poet, offers itself nobly to the fiery embrace of the saucepan, adds its 'fecund influence' to the salad, and sates the hunger of the journeyman on his way. The onion, then, has all the female virtues. Chaste, generous, and fertile in turn, it is the Holy Virgin of the vegetables, distant yet accessible, 'naturally' productive, yet dependent for its generative capacity on the (male) subject it exists to serve.

Descriptions of cooking or the preparation of food are frequent in the *Odas*, and there can be no doubt that they tend to serve a political function, in their attempt to confer a heightened poetic value on a domestic labour invisible or neglected in the traditional lyric canon. Thus the reader is offered directions for the making of a typical Chilean fish stew ('caldillo del congrio'), but the success of the recipe is guaranteed by its ability to 'marry' the flavours of sea and land (p. 45). Cultural practice (a particular dish) is dignified by association with natural elements, which are themselves underwritten by implicitly gendered relations. This process is more obvious in the ode to bread, the commodity whose material conditions old poets were said to ignore. We begin with the ingredients, the necessary condition of production: bread rises with the help of flour, water, and fire. Like the growth of the onion, the rising of the loaf recreates the movement of the female generative principle, the swelling of the woman's body, with its waist, mouth, and breasts. The virgin bread is the object of male labour: she is 'intact' or 'untouched', the 'product of man'. If she flees his house ('la casa del hombre') she is exposed, like the air before her, to the perverted propositions of the male capitalist, and risks being prostituted by the miser or grabbed by the rich man (pp. 190–2).

Hence, if the commodity is a woman, then woman is a commodity. As the capitalist naturalizes the economic relations inherent yet invisible in the products he consumes, so the socialist naturalizes those sexual relations which perpetuate the conventional supremacy of gender he unwittingly enjoys. And if woman is a commodity, object of male Culture, she is also Nature itself, passive matter designed to receive the dominant male form. Thus in 'Oda a la fertilidad de la tierra' the poet inseminates the womb of mother earth, which in turn brings forth the harvest of his words: she must allow his song to fall into the earth so his words will rise every spring (p. 88). Or again and more explicitly in the 'Oda a la tierra' where the poet's song is the necessary supplement to a deficient female earth: he sings to her because 'man' will make her give birth, will fill her with fruits (p. 246). The poet idly caresses the earth with his hands, finding in it the breast and thigh of the beloved ('la que amo'), and finishes the poem locked in primal embrace with the telluric woman, sowing the deepest of kisses (pp. 246–7). Hence if woman is natural she is by no means integrated. She requires the masculine labour of tilling and reaping ('culture' in the etymological sense of the word) to perform the generative mission essential to her existence. And if woman is deficient as both cultural commodity and natural element it is because of an essential and disabling gap in Neruda's labour theory of value: the elision of women's work as economic reality and the consequent inability to formulate and reproduce a coherent subject position which the woman reader may adopt.

In *Capital*, as in the *Odas*, the object is often personified. Marx enlivens the somewhat abstract and technical exposition of the evolution of value forms with comic moments in which spindles, lengths of linen, or coats speak or perform actions. The commodity is promiscuous, jumping in and out of bed in its eagerness to exchange with its mates like the wanton Maritornes in the inn in *Don Quijote*.[10] Women themselves

---

[10] *Capital*, i (Harmondsworth, 1976), 179.

('femmes folles de leurs corps') are jokingly included in a list of commodities commonly used for exchange in the medieval period.[11] The commodity cannot resist its owner ('man') who must if necessary take possession of it, force it to comply to his will. The appeal to woman as metaphor is only half erased. Or again 'labour is the father of material wealth, the earth is its mother.' The female earth (Nature) is lacking and inadequate, requiring the male principle to complete it. The 'scientific' theorist is as gender-blind as the poet and woman has the same dual status in both: at once objectified and naturalized.

In Neruda this failure to examine the terms of sexual politics leads to a gross sentimentalism exemplified in 'Oda a la pareja', in which the association of woman and man is represented in ideal and absolute terms, free from all social or economic restraint: 'Together quite simply, | a man and a woman.' The poet offers himself as universal marriage partner for any woman left incomplete by her lack of a man (pp. 195–7). What Neruda fails to see is that relations between the sexes have no natural simplicity, and that marriage itself is a cultural institution as specific as any economic or political relation. The nineteenth century had falsely specified and restricted authentic experience to the 'personal' space of family and marriage. Neruda generalizes and expands this same space to encompass social relations as a whole, without, however, questioning that initial, founding specification. If the growth of the private as an asylum of bourgeois sentiment may be seen as a response to a new and radically alienating mechanical labour process, then Neruda's privileging of the private is bought only at the cost of eclipsing those economic and political relations which are the initial motive of the Odes. His universal naturalizing mission is here revealed as a persuasive but Utopian fantasy—in Marx's derisive term, a *Robinsonade*. Neruda's siren ('sirena reina de las islas') invokes the dream of individual production possible only on a desert island (free of cultural determinants) and for a man (free of sexual subjection).

Yet it could be argued that Neruda's conspicuous failure to

[11] Page 178. This example and those that follow are cited by Julia Swindells in 'Falling Short with Marx: Some Glimpses of Nineteenth Century Ideology', *LTP* 3 (1984), 56–70.

represent a consistently objective aesthetic, his inability to prevent the intrusion of a highly particular subjectivity (of which the exclusion of woman is only the most prominent absence) tend in practice to draw attention to the naturalized conventions inscribed in the ideology he seeks to attack. In other words, Neruda reproduces with heightened (even exemplary) intensity the hidden cultural contradictions within the natural simplicity he claims as the zero-degree of experience and of writing. The moral of the *Odas* is that there is no *tabula rasa*, whether existential or literary, no primal origin immune to and ignorant of cultural coercion. And this dispiriting truth both underwrites the language of the Odes themselves and engages them once more in the continuing and ambivalent dialectic between Nature and Culture. Thus in 'Oda a la crítica' the natural and material plenitude of the verse is alienated by critics who appropriate it from the working people to whom it properly belongs. Or again, in 'Oda a la sencillez' the poet and his companion 'simplicity' are refused admission to 'the cafés of the most exquisite pederasts' (p. 233). This is not merely a gratuitous insult to the gay reader. It is the logical consequence of a theory of value based implicitly (like that of Marx) on gendered notions of matter and form. The gay man (like the critic) is excessive and unproductive, denied access to the natural integration of poet and simple reader. As in the 'Oda al hombre sencillo' it is not woman but man who now represents Nature, no longer deprived and material, but abstract and disembodied: 'you are as transparent | as water | and so am I'. And once more, this transparency is completed by possession of woman: the poet holds his girl in his arms as the reader does his (p. 115). Woman as ever is ancillary, marginal, magically elided from the ideal mirroring of subject and object which mesmerizes male poet and reader.

Yet, of course, Neruda's language strays constantly from the simplicity he has dictated for it, and thus betrays the constrictive and reductive nature of this avowedly libertarian mode. There are heroic, even epic, odes to the cities and countries of Latin America, the catalogue of birds in the 'Oda a las aves de Chile' reminiscent of the hunting scene in Góngora's second *Soledad*, and the echoes of Garcilaso and

perhaps even of Horace in the poet's claim that his voice will
continue its song after his own death ('Oda a la envidia',
p. 81). Surrealist incantations, more proper to the poet of the
Residencias, break through in the 'Oda al mar' which invokes
the sea's 'seven green tongues | of seven green dogs, | of seven
green tigers, | of seven green seas . . .' (p. 158). Language here
displays a rhetorical redundancy, a rhythmic and metaphorical
excess which denies all attempts to reduce it to transparency.

But what of the poems in which Neruda does indeed employ
a 'simple' syntax and vocabulary? 'Oda al día feliz' is overtly
conversational in tone:

> Esta vez dejadme
> ser feliz,
> nada ha pasado a nadie,
> no estoy en parte alguna,
> sucede solamente
> que soy feliz   (p. 68);

This time let me | be happy | nothing is up with anyone, | I'm not
anywhere, | it's just | that I'm happy.

Here the transparency, even banality, of diction and sentiment
tends to yield to a sense of the materiality of language, of the
physical presence of the word on the page, enclosed and
enhanced by 'white space'. Semantic fixity gives way to
phonetic virtuality: the repeated 'a's of the third line, or the
sibilants of the fifth and sixth are emphasized by the absence
of conceptual or metaphorical competition. In other words it
could be argued (in formalist fashion) that language itself is
denaturalized by the antilyrical posture, revealed at its most
basic level as an arbitrary system of phonemes. And of course,
in its wilful deprivation of lyric resource, Neruda's 'natural'
poetics is as self-conscious (perhaps more so) as his mock-epic
invocations.

Compare the opening of 'Oda a la flor', a more conventionally lyric motif:

> Flores
> de pobre
> en las
> ventanas
> pobres

pétalos
de sol pobre . . .   (p. 89)

Poor people's | flowers | in the | poor | windows | petals | of poor
sun . . .

Once more the phonetic is emphasized: the 'o–e' assonance of
the first two lines; the 'e–a' assonance of the next two; the
highly emphatic initial 'p's of the following lines, all would
have been 'invisible' and repressed if the lines were written as
prose. The brevity of line and the lack of punctuation, here as
elsewhere, suggest that the poem offers itself as natural
effusion, language unbound from cultural convention and
confinement. Yet the isolation and repetition of the single
word ('pobre') promotes a new and defamiliarized perception
of its specificity. No longer transparent but opaque, the word
invites the reader to meditate on its new-found linguistic and
material substantiality.

Thus the extreme brevity of line throughout the *Odas*,
explicitly proclaiming a 'natural' simplicity of tone, tends in
fact to disrupt the habitual conditions of everyday, naturalized
language: its continuity and closure. Like the extravagant
metaphors in other poems, the short line form promotes
'vertical' association, at the expense of 'horizontal' juxtaposition.
In the 'Oda al hilo' the thread invoked is that of poetry itself:
events follow one another like sheep loaded with wool
(p. 108). In the *Odas* as a whole, however, the linguistic
process is rarely so docile. The metonymic chain of word-
objects is constantly disrupted by metaphoric transcendence
or paradigmatic interference. The linguistic assembly-line
(the goal of a natural or neutral series without paradigm) is
revealed as an impossibility.

And if metaphor is the privileged trope, then apostrophe is
the dominant figure. Neruda constantly addresses the object
or reader in an overt attempt to discover and reveal the
essence of each. Yet, as Jonathan Culler has suggested,
apostrophe is the most self-conscious and artificial mode in
the lyric canon, not so much the figure of invocation as of
vocation.[12] That is, rhetorical address promotes not the
precipitation of the inherent qualities of the object, but the

---

[12] See 'Apostrophe' in *The Pursuit of Signs* (London, 1981), 135–54.

valorization of the contingencies of the subject. The vocative case 'rebounds' as the nominative (the representation of self as privileged source of the oration) and address becomes exposition (the revelation of self as deficient projection on to world). We might compare Neruda's choice of alphabetical order in his presentation of the Odes. The conventional sequence is ostensibly neutral, 'objective'. In fact, of course, it serves as the sign of the poet's ostentatious abdication of authority, of a conspicuous, even mannered, representation of absence.

This complex subjectivity, at once present and absent, recurs in Neruda's poetic performance, in his recreation of a relationship with the (male) reader. At some points, communication is presented as immediate and reciprocal: the poet speaks and the 'invisible man' replies. But at others (and more habitually) communication is deferred, the poet declaims and no response is required from his represented audience. The poet as subject is thus both commensurate with and completed by the reader. Like the female nature to which he also appeals, the poet is (intermittently, at least) deficient and disabled, unable to perform the universalizing mission he presents as essential. And I would suggest that this repressed indeterminacy, this projection of self across a plurality of discourses, derives from an equivalent inability to fix writing within the shifting boundaries of nature and culture. Thus in the first 'Oda al libro', the book is shown as an alienating force, an absence between poet and the direct experience of natural labour: when the poet closes the book he opens life (p. 138). Yet in the second, the book is equated with Nature itself (it is 'a tiny forest') and with the instrument of a primal, authenticating Culture: the peasant 'ploughs with a book' (p. 144). Thus writing is both a substitute for and a supplement to the Nature it claims to reflect.

It may be, then, that if Neruda strives for a transparency of language, the poems themselves tend (even at their 'simplest') to divulge like a guilty secret the inevitable yet repressed opacity and materiality of words; and that if Neruda seeks to represent a unified, universalizing subject, it is frequently revealed, again by the poems, to be particular and deficient, dispersed across a plurality of stylistic and ideological registers. Yet these (inadvertent) textual effects may be quite properly enlisted for an oppositional reading by the materialist critic: Neruda's linguistic and subjective discontinuities testify more strongly than any naturalizing transparency to the historical determinacy of human utterance and consciousness. It is Neruda's failure to achieve the totalizing clarity he seeks which should alert us to the pervasiveness of the ideology he fails in part to disclose. For the will to transparency and to universalism is itself ideological, effect and instrument of state apparatuses which call the subject into being by appearing to address him or her as an 'individual', that is, at once uniquely particular and of general significance. Neruda's nomadic language and persona are merely heightened examples of the general process by which socialization is achieved, and the subject alienated at the very moment of its emergence from the discourse and psyche it experiences as its own. The *Odas* reveal in spite of themselves that even under socialism, ideology will continue (does continue) to exist. The supposed reconciliation of 'man' and 'Nature' leads instead to new modes of subjection, new sets of received and naturalized 'facts'.

Yet, ironically, it is in these inadvertent characteristics that the poems most closely approximate to the popular texts they proclaim themselves to be. For the language of orality is excessive and redundant. It abounds (like Neruda's more rhetorical odes) in extravagant metaphor, archaism, repetition, and phonetic effect.[13] The popular text rarely communicates a transparent meaning. Rather, it takes its pleasure in linguistic play, emphasizes the materiality of the word in its love of unmotivated rhythm and alliteration. What is more, the popular text (such as the ballad) tends not to offer a unitary, vatic perspective but rather to unfix reified subject positions.[14] It is generally a communal production, and the status of individual author is ambiguous and frequently irrelevant. Finally, (and this is a characteristic which the *Odas* do not share), the popular text offers space for a female subjectivity, in its intermittent celebration of women's play ('nonsense' skipping rhymes) and women's labour (the songs of spinners

---

[13] See Walter J. Ong, *Orality and Literacy, passim.*
[14] See Antony Easthope, *Poetry as Discourse* (London, 1983), 78–93.

and washerwomen). When 'ordinary people' turn to poetry, they seek not the self-conscious simplicity beloved of literatcs, but the rhetorical display characteristic of orality. That is, they enjoy not the prosaic linguistic 'bread' that Neruda offers to give them, but the effusively lyric 'cake' that he tends in fact to deliver.[15] Paradoxically, Neruda's deviation from the course he sets himself brings him closer to achieving his original aim.

Neruda, then, is the type of the twentieth-century individual. He is at once productive and subjected; indeed, productive because subjected. His fluency derives from his blindness, and the prestige of his (male) perspective from its habitual repression of a divergent (female) point of view. His appeal to the reader (like that of the State to its subjects) is both seductive and repressive, an 'interpellation' which seeks to recreate the addressee in its own image, to naturalize the cultural and to universalize the specific. Yet, like the individual in society, the dissident reader may attempt to demystify the dominant rhetoric, within which, none the less, his or her experience finds its historical meaning. The unintended or senseless[16] reader thus has a privileged role in the rejection or recuperation of the naturalizing text. He or she can refuse identification with the author.

The *Odas* stand revealed as deficient, partial productions of culture, not integrated, universal effusions of nature. Yet it is the very relativity of their perspective which provides the basis for a continuing critique of the social relations they claim to reproduce in their 'transparency'.[17] Their effect on the disabused reader remains potent. In so far as they continue to inspire an emotion experienced as authentic, they remind him or her that the ideology inscribed in them is not merely the distorted reproduction of social relations, but the very substance of those relations themselves, the exchange of

[15] Michael Hamburger makes this analogy in relation to Neruda and other poets of what he calls 'a new austerity' in *The Truth of Poetry* (Harmondsworth, 1972), 250.

[16] See Naomi Segal, *The Unintended Reader: Feminism and 'Manon Lescaut'* (Cambridge, 1986).

[17] For an excellent reading which also claims that Neruda's flagrant *machismo* subverts itself see Christopher Perriam, 'Metaphorical *Machismo*: Neruda's Love Poetry', *FMLS* 24 (1988), 58–77. For a reminder that some of the Odes violate the norms of their genre see David G. Anderson, 'Pablo Neruda's Non-celebratory Elementary Odes', *RN* 26 (1986), 226–31.

meanings by which women and men experience their lives and (mis)recognize themselves in the world. No individual (still less Neruda) can wholly transcend naturalization. There could be no social practice without signification which is conventional: that is, not random, but culturally specific. Neruda's silences and elisions 'speak' more loudly perhaps than his ingenuous eloquence. But to read them is to adopt an interrogative stance which we must surely be prepared to apply to our own (critical) discourse. Neruda's flagrant discontinuities, his most conspicuous absences, are offered ironically, even defiantly to the spectator. The *Odas* mark an incipient subversion of the speaker which grows more marked in Neruda's subsequent verse.[18] However, as Neruda himself suggested (but not quite in the way he believed), the practised and evasive ruses of the critic may prove to be the subtlest and most deceptive naturalizers of them all.

3. MAN IN THE *POEMAS HUMANOS*

In 1938 Neruda published a 'funeral eulogy' of Vallejo in the *Aurora de Chile*.[19] He begins by stressing Vallejo's foreignness in Paris: Vallejo was an Indo-American 'spectre' who never transcended exile (p. 217). He then proceeds to compare Vallejo to a 'palace of subterranean rock' in the depths of which there burns 'the fire of the implacable spirit'. He ends by saluting Vallejo, the great poet, as his brother (p. 218). The eulogy sets out a trajectory reproduced by many subsequent readers of Vallejo: it starts by stressing the specificity of the poet's position (an exile in Europe); goes on to invoke an idealist essence or interiority (the cave and fire), and concludes by claiming that interiority as a reflection of the critic's own self (he is the poet's brother). We shall return to the image of the cave, which is somewhat more complex in Vallejo's own poems. It is enough here to note that Neruda's recuperative reading (in which the poet's particularity is sublated into a bland universalism) is a frequent response by humanist critics when confronted by the challenge Vallejo's poetry makes to their unquestioning faith in linguistic

---

[18] See Santí, p. 213.
[19] Reprinted in Julio Ortega (ed.), *César Vallejo* (Madrid, 1975), 217–8.

transparency and subjective integrity. But I shall also suggest (and this is to read the blanks of Vallejo's text, to speak what is unsaid) that Vallejo's much-discussed concern for the universal alienation of humanity is dependent on the neglect or repression (by poet and critics) of a female subjectivity which stages a persistent and unexpected return. Critics have stressed Vallejo's status as exile. But they have not considered that there may be a term exiled from (or imperfectly assimilated to) Vallejo's verse itself: woman and her role in the relations of production.

The *Poemas humanos* are quite different from the *Odas elementales*. They are a complex, disparate collection, published posthumously, with the text often unrevised and the title unconfirmed. A few critics have attempted Marxist readings of the *Poemas*. The best-known remains that of Noel Salomon (reprinted in Ortega's *César Vallejo*, pp. 289–334). Salomon claims that the 'human' of the *Poemas humanos* is no metaphysical or aesthetic ideal, but rather the result of historical and political commitment (p. 299). The human is made concrete in and by unalienated labour and through the dialectical resolution of contradictions (pp. 322, 323). Vallejo believed for a time at least (1927–31) that it was possible to realize the full development of an integrated humanity in language by means of proletarian revolution. In the poems written at this time bourgeois individualism is thus replaced by proletarian solidarity, which is 'human' and thus 'universal' (pp. 328, 329). We can see from this last statement that Salomon's paean to Vallejo's supposed Utopian socialism carries within itself a submerged idealist residue: the faith in an essential subjectivity which transcends material differences (of culture, history, and gender). Although Salomon rightly attacks the bland homogeneity and universalism of humanist critics, in the final analysis he shares with those critics an unshakeable belief in the possibility of unalienated experience and the direct communication of that experience to others. As we shall see, developments in Marxist theory would tend to call into question this trust in the ability of the privileged subject to transcend false consciousness.

Later critics are also ambiguous in their attitude to Vallejo's politics. Thus R. K. Britton attacks with Salomon critics' suppression of Marxist influences on Vallejo.[20] But he goes on to claim the poems are the expression not of political engagement, but of a psychological trauma scarcely mediated by language: 'Far from being the deepening of Vallejo's humanitarian feelings for his fellow men . . . *Poemas humanos* is rather a record of the passion and despair of a mind often precariously balanced on the edge of disintegration' (p. 542). Critical disagreements of this kind derive in part from the heterogeneity of the collection and the continuing controversy over the dating of particular poems. What is more, it is known from Vallejo's prose that his political commitment fluctuated during the period of composition, passing through a number of different stages. However, the urge of critics to wholly erase or suppress the Marxist component in the poems remains persistent. The latest editor coolly conflates linguistic experiment and Marxist revolution,[21] and manages on the same page of his introduction both to quote Lenin on the revolutionary artist and to affirm that for the critic the only matter at stake is a purely literary revolt (pp. 52–3). Hence Marxist treatments of Vallejo's verse remain relatively few and uninfluential, when set beside the dominant 'apolitical' idealism.

The role of the body, on the other hand, has received increasing attention. Much of that attention is, however, superficial. Thus Roberto Paoli promises an 'anatomical map' of the *Poemas*,[22] but delivers only a facile identification of the body with a 'human condition' which remains unexamined and is communicated directly to the reader without the mediation of rational discourse (pp. 52–3). As Bernard

---

[20] 'The Political Dimension of César Vallejo's *Poemas humanos*', *MLR* 70 (1975), 539–49. For a political approach to the poetry see A. Sicard, 'Pensamiento y poesía en *Poemas humanos* de César Vallejo: La dialéctica como método poético', *Socialismo y participación*, 19 (1982), 97–103. For the question of Vallejo's political position see Stephen Hart, 'Was César Vallejo a Communist? A Fresh Look at an Old Problem', *Iberoromania*, 22 (1985), 106–33; and the same author's *Religión, política, y ciencia en la obra de César Vallejo* (London, 1987).

[21] *Poemas humanos*, ed. Francisco Martínez García (Madrid, 1987). I cite this edn. I have also referred to *The Complete Posthumous Poetry*, trans. Clayton Eshleman and José Rubia Barcia (Berkeley, 1978).

[22] 'Mapa anatómico de *Poemas humanos*', in *César Vallejo: Actas del Coloquio Internacional Freie Universität Berlin* (Tübingen, 1981), 41–53.

McGuirk[23] has suggested, this faith in the revelation of true meaning and identity exhibited by so many readers unites a number of apparently unrelated schools of Vallejo criticism. It persists even in readings which are philosophically informed. Thus Lorna Close,[24] for example, concludes an article by citing Vallejo's pun in *Trilce* on the homophone *rebelar/revelar*: 'Vallejo restores the word to its human function . . . In rebelling words have truly revealed themselves as they are' (p. 184). The faith in the essential nature of the subject (humanism) thus coincides with the faith in the authentic substance of language (logocentrism): each is (in McGuirk's reading) 'theological', that is to say dependent on authoritative fiat, not material evidence.

Gonzalo Sobejano was the first critic to pay close attention to the body in *Poemas humanos*.[25] For Sobejano, the theme of the body is a constant of the collection, and 'human' should be read as 'corporeal' (p. 181). Vallejo treats essential human drives such as pain and sex, but he does so with the ironic distance of an observer (pp. 186, 188). He also employs evolutionist images which contradict his 'Marxist humanism' (p. 189). By the time of *España, aparta de mi este cáliz*, however, there is no doubt: the poet has staged a secular resurrection of the flesh through the common will of everyone. César Vallejo is thus (the) man, each man (p. 190). In spite of his stress on the material, then, Sobejano still promotes the poet as the representative of humanity, rather than as a mouthpiece for a particular class or political position. The physical cedes to the metaphysical. And, what is more, there is a hint at least that Vallejo's 'body' cannot comprehend all citizens: Sobejano describes the soul as the 'female' of the body (p. 182), ideal complement to its continuing lack. Thus Vallejo's unrelenting emphasis on the specificity of the body's experience does not

[23] 'Undoing the Romantic Discourse: A Case-Study in Post-Structuralist Analysis. Vallejo's *Trilce* i', *RS* 5 (Winter 1984–5), 99–111.
[24] 'Vallejo, Heidegger, and Language', in *Words of Power: Essays in Honour of Alison Fairlie* (Glasgow, 1987), 163–86. For an excellent reading which draws on cultural theorists such as Benjamin see Christiane von Buelow, 'The Allegorical Gaze of César Vallejo', *MLN* 100 (1985), 298–329; and the same author's 'Vallejo's Venus de Milo and the Ruins of Language', forthcoming in *PMLA*.
[25] 'Poesía del cuerpo en *Poemas humanos*', in *Aproximaciones a César Vallejo*, ii (New York, 1971), 181–90.

lead the critic to abandon his faith in the universal subject, much less his belief in the male of the species as representative of humankind.

The subtlest treatment of the body remains Jean Franco's *César Vallejo* (Cambridge, 1976), a study which draws heavily and unselfconsciously on Marxist terms of reference. From the beginning Franco's aim is to demystify the poetic process and demythologize Vallejo. Unlike the writers of Vallejo's youth she is well aware that poetry is not ' "beyond ideology" and so must be either an adornment for the system or in conflict with it' (p. 8). She frequently contrasts Vallejo with Neruda, the latter a 'Marxist humanist' (p. 77), who believes in the presence of the human voice and its potential for immediate communication (pp. 191, 209). Vallejo's greater complexity is related to his preference for writing over speech, a preference itself linked to the body: 'Throughout Vallejo's poetry, the human body is presented as a text in which the history of the species has been documented' (p. 57). Franco's model of the body (unlike Sobejano's) is thus thoroughly materialist and historical. In his poems on miners and peasants Vallejo celebrates 'the production of man' as a political subject (p. 165), as opposed to the idealist mythology of a transcendent individual always already in place. Consciousness is thus not given, but is rather produced under material conditions and 'cannot be isolated from the body' (p. 175). Capitalism tends to produce 'the alienated individual and the reified products of modern society' (p. 178). Any sense of self, then, is not autonomous but dependent, dialectically, on economic reality. Hence Vallejo's anguish is not existential but material: 'in a world of reified objects man has no mirror in which to find a reflection of his dignity and work' (p. 193). The poet cannot therefore occupy the site of an authentic, primal identity: 'There is no possibility of getting back to origins in *Poemas humanos* because consciousness works through language which is never immediate' (p. 212).

Here the lost origin is linked to the questions of reflection or reproduction, the 'secondary' processes on which the 'primary' subject is dependent. Thus Franco claims that it is 'man's capacity for reflecting on his own condition and relating it to the other that makes him human' (p. 175). But from what position can 'he' carry out this work of self-definition? The promise of the miners in Vallejo's poem is of 'the future organic and unalienated men whose language itself is to be organic and natural' (p. 170). But, as we shall see, my own reading of this poem is not so sanguine; and in Marxist theory the ability of the proletariat to evade false consciousness is not always taken for granted. Franco herself rarely takes up the question of gender in this context. But in her discussion of one poem (*Trilce* no. 33) she stresses the role of the mother as both producer of food and reproducer of the work force: 'the vessel of the species and the source of individuation' (p. 73). And a few pages later she makes a link with the Marxist theory of 'reproduction' as that (often invisible) process which enables production to take place. Vallejo is exploring in such poems 'the genesis of individual consciousness, the priority of reproduction over the cultural superstructure, the formation of a false consciousness which conceals the true purpose of existence' (p. 76). There seems, once more, to be an idealist residue here in the appeal to a 'truth' which waits meekly for the poet to reveal it. But I would suggest that this stress on reproduction and its link with women's labour provides a point of entry into Marxist theory which will itself facilitate a new reading of the *Poemas humanos*. The quest for reproduction should make visible blind spots in Vallejo's ideological position. My thesis is that contradictions in Vallejo's poetry coincide with problems raised by such theorists as Lukács and Althusser, and that Vallejo shares with these theorists a neglect of women's position in economic relations which is dialectically implicated in those other problems. The reader might object that, unlike the *Odas elementales*, the *Poemas humanos* make no claim to speak on behalf of all people, that this claim is made by the critics not the poet. If Vallejo is mainly concerned with his own subjectivity and with the experiences of his fellow men, then he should not be criticized for failing to fulfil a criterion which is not his own. But we have learned from feminism that 'personal experience' cannot be taken for granted. And if Vallejo is indeed writing as a man (rather than as a nominally neuter human being), then the specificity of that gender position must itself be examined and cannot be simply assumed to exist.

Georg Lukács's early work *History and Class Consciousness* (first published in 1923) gives an influential account of a term already introduced by Jean Franco: reification.[26] The essay 'Reification and the Consciousness of the Proletariat' (pp. 83–222) begins with a definition of the phenomenon: 'a relation between people takes on the character of a thing and thus acquires . . . an autonomy that seems so strictly rational and all-embracing as to conceal every trace of its fundamental nature: the relation between people' (p. 83). This economic sleight of hand 'stamps its imprint on the whole consciousness of man; his qualities and abilities are no longer an organic part of his personality, they are things which he can "own" or "dispose of" like the various objects of the external world' (p. 100). This commodification of inner life is exemplified by Kant's definition of marriage as the mutual possession of sexual organs. The universality of the law of the market economy decrees that it 'may not even be fully and adequately knowable'; and the social fragmentation caused by the division of labour 'leads to the destruction of every image of the whole ' (pp. 102, 103). As Rodney Livingstone suggests,[27] the role of art for Lukács is thus to dereify reality: 'If under capitalism all consciousness is reified, then the immediate reflection of appearances can never transcend that reification' (p. 12). There are two problems here. First, the problem of positionality: in what space can the artist (or proletarian) stand if reification is ubiquitous? Second, the problem of reflection: how can the political artist imitate life when he has been deprived of that gold standard of authenticity (the proletarian) by which he can evaluate his relation to the real? I would suggest that many of the contradictions in Vallejo's poetry derive from a partial awareness of the unstable relative positions of poet and worker suggested here by Lukács: for Vallejo the poet is no longer the privileged individual of humanism; but nor is the proletarian the unequivocal embodiment of revolutionary consciousness. Through reproduction (rather than mere reflection) the poet can perhaps demystify the world for his readers; but if those readers are no longer the 'perfect subject-objects' who resolve all contradictions, how

---

[26] *History and Class Consciousness*, trans. Rodney Livingstone (London, 1968).
[27] In his edn. of Georg Lukács, *Essays on Realism* (London, 1980).

can he be sure they will recognize the revolutionary art for what it is? As Lukács's quote from Kant reveals, even the 'personal' space of sexual or marital relations is thoroughly colonized by capitalism.

The question of positionality makes itself felt even more urgently in the work of the structural Marxist Louis Althusser.[28] In his essay of 1968 'Ideology and Ideological State Apparatuses' (pp. 127–86), Althusser stresses that ideology is not (merely) false consciousness, but rather the actual substance of people's lives under capitalism. He states explicitly (p. 128) that ideology works at the level of reproduction: it silently creates those conditions under which the capitalist system will appear natural, reconciling the work force to their alienation. Like Lukács, Althusser pays little attention to gender or sexuality. But he does comment at one point (p. 180) on the function of such cults as that of the Holy Family. By a dialectical process of reflection the bourgeois family is confirmed in its belief in both the sanctity of its own condition and the humanity of the sacred original. Ideology thus serves, like reification, to facilitate a spectral play of reflection which enforces homogeneity and disarms resistance. The implications of Althusser's theory are relevant to my reading of Vallejo: it suggests that there is no authentic origin from which truth can be acquired and no stable position from which it can be spoken. The status of Marxism itself as revolutionary science is thus called into question. As Ted Benton[29] writes: 'If the "common sense" in which individual subjects "live" their lives is a "web of errors" . . . then how is an open and "living" relationship between science and popular struggles ever to be established?' (p. 29). As this quotation illustrates, the thicket of quotation marks favoured by Althusser and his commentators is testimony to their paralysing self-consciousness in the face of the gulf between ' "life" ' and ' "science" '. It is a self-consciousness shared by Vallejo in many of the *Poemas humanos*, and one which cannot be reduced to metaphysical *Angst* or romantic sensitivity. For Vallejo's alienation is material not existential, and it guarantees no privileged insight to the artist. For if reification and ideology have no

[28] See *Lenin and Philosophy* (London, 1971).
[29] *The Rise and Fall of Structural Marxism* (London, 1984).

outside, then the role of the revolutionary poet (like that of the scientific theorist) can no longer be taken for granted.

How do these theoretical questions leave their trace in Vallejo's text? First, with regard to the question of gender. In the prose poem 'El buen sentido' or 'Common sense' (*Complete Posthumous Poetry*, pp. 4–7) the poet restages the family romance between mother and son. The separation from the mother creates a lack which can only be filled by his return: when he comes back he 'closes her'. The mother's lack is also the son's, nostalgic for womb and breast. But it remains the case that the woman's reproductive function confines her to the little house of domesticity, while the man's worldly ambitions give him access to the great foreign city. Another prose poem begins 'Una mujer de senos apacibles' or 'A woman with peaceful breasts' (*Complete Posthumous Poetry*, pp. 52–3). Here mother, father, and child are glimpsed at church. The woman's role is to reproduce male language: she 'declines the word of man in her single case of woman'. The child attempts to return to the 'maternal point' between his mother's legs by playing with her skirt. Once more feminine sexuality is linked to the maternal function. But it is also complicit with religious practice: the child's hand makes the mother's pupils dilate as they do at the confessional. Vallejo's blasphemous parody of the Holy Family serves to reconfirm the cult of a (secular) Virgin Mother, naturally and spontaneously generative. If it is reproduction that defines woman's place in these two poems, it is reproduction in its traditional role as a secondary, marginal activity. As the poet's point of origin and the focus of his loss, woman can have no knowledge of her own condition.

Some of the verse poems do indeed move woman into the centre of the poetic stage. Thus 'Hoy le ha entrado una astilla' or 'Today a splinter has entered her' (Martínez García, pp. 200–1) dramatizes the repeated violation of a female body. 'She' is wounded by fate, the door, the binding around her waist ('faja'). Who, asks the poet, will keep her company on Saturday night? At the end of the poem her predicament can be expressed only through tautology and mechanical repetition: pain has pained her, the poor, poor thing ('le ha

dolido el dolor . . . | ¡La pobre pobrecita!'). As so often in
Vallejo, suffering is communicated through bodily detail: it is
'exactly there precisely' that she is hurt. However this
particularity cannot conceal the generalities which define 'her'
position in the poem. As was the case with the mothers in the
prose poems, the female role is one of passivity and interiority,
of wounded and unknowing acceptance. More complex is 'Un
hombre está mirando a una mujer' or 'A man is watching a
woman' (pp. 73–4). Here woman is the object of a male look
which precedes violent sexual activity. Once again the woman
takes the child as supplement to her lack ('constructor of her
sex') and her pregnancy is a generative mission ('augmentative
condition'). And once more Vallejo cites the Holy Family as
the problematic reflection of its secular counterpart. The
poem ends with a difficult reference to 'cascos delanteros'.
'Casco' can mean helmet, skull, and (in Peru) breast. These
ambivalent objects thrust in front ('delante') of the reader
thus combine the anticipation of death with the prominence of
woman's sex. In spite of his emphasis on reproduction, then,
in Vallejo the woman's body bears within it negativity and
death. Without a husband or child she is empty and invisible,
her subjectivity organized around the persistent threat of male
penetration. This is not to suggest that the male subject is
secure in his own identity. But Vallejo's (intermittent)
concern for women's reproductive function does not prevent
him from repressing that knowledge in the main body of his
poems, from offering his own subjectivity as an implicitly
neutral paradigm. His inability or unwillingness to present
woman as subject of primary labour (a gap we have already
seen in Marxist theory) thus reconfirms the overt subject of
these poems: the commodification of inner life, the reification
of familial and sexual relations.

   We can see this naturalization of the male at work in three
well-known poems. 'Un hombre pasa con un pan al hombro'
or 'A man passes with a loaf of bread on his shoulder'
(pp. 198–9) contrasts the materiality of economics and
politics with the lofty abstractions of art and culture. How can
one speak of psychoanalysis, when a man is picking lice from
his armpit, or weep in the theatre when a banker is falsifying
his accounts? Vallejo's chaotic enumeration of subjects

(cripples, masons, outcasts) stakes a claim through its very idiosyncrasy to be representative of society. But the formal symmetry of the poem (each verse has two contrasting lines) is mirrored in the sexual exclusivity of its cast of characters: all are male. Capitalists and socialists are thus presented to the reader as locked into a system of specular oppositions. It is no surprise that the translator gives the grammatically neuter line 'Alguién limpia un fusil en su cocina' in the gendered version 'Someone cleans a rifle in *his* kitchen' (p. 267; my emphasis). Even the woman's space of the kitchen is invaded by man. Hence for Vallejo any theory of the political subject is always appropriated to the masculine: the intrusion of the feminine as third term in this poem would sabotage both its formal coherence and its ideological rigour. Women are too compromised by interiority and abstraction to serve as the material base against which the cultural superstructure can be thrown into relief. This is a labour which can only be entrusted to men.

'Considerando en frío, imparcialmente' or 'Considering coldly, impartially' (pp. 121–2) is another rather more ambiguous poem on (male) subjectivity. Once more man's condition is historical and material: he coughs and combs his hair; he is made up of the days he has lived. This physicality is compared and contrasted with abstract categories in such phrases as 'fórmula famélica de masa', in which the shockingly physical 'starving' is juxtaposed with the polyvalent 'fórmula' (formula or recipe) and 'masa' (weight, number, or dough) (see Close, p. 179). In puns such as these the cool rationality of male discourse is called into question, shown to be wholly compromised by the slippery displacements of language and the body. The horror of alienated labour (the worker's attempt to 'erase his atrocious day') does not submit to lucid analysis. In a rather similar way, the possibility of communion between men (taken for granted elsewhere) is here problematized. The poet oscillates between love for and indifference to his fellow man, and if he ends the poem embracing him with emotion, he is declaring none the less 'So what!': '¡ Que más da! Emocionado . . . Emocionado . . .'. The final points of suspension signal a continuing process of interaction between the poet-subject and the worker-object. The pathos of the latter's position is the same as that of the woman's: unbearable suffering fails to bring him an awareness of the nature of his condition. There is no breaking out of the formula.

'Intensidad y altura' ('Intensity and height') (p. 138) is also motivated by the breakdown of rational discourse. The title might be taken as suggesting the conflict between sensation (the play of intensity) and abstraction (the height from which Man looks down on the world). The first line reads: 'Quiero escribir pero me sale espuma' ('I want to write but foam comes out of me'), and throughout the poem the difficulty of self-expression in language is contrasted with the involuntary performance of bodily functions such as coughing and weeping. However, the poem does not suggest that this alienation from the body is metaphysical. Rather, it is the inevitable effect of commodity fetishism, when even the soul is put into cans like fruit ('nuestra alma . . . en conserva'). The poet gives a final injunction to 'drink that which is already drunk' ('lo ya bebido') and exhorts the crow to go fertilize its mate. Here the impotence of the poetic subject is reconfirmed with the suggestion that the sexual relation can only be the compulsive repetition of a past experience which is itself always already subject to reification.

I would suggest that such poems can be read as reflections on the limits of male rationality.[30] But it is by no means obvious from what position the poet can make this critique. Thus his language is no transparent window from which the reader can look down loftily on free-floating 'themes', but rather in its very contradictions and paradoxes bears the trace of the impotent struggle to take up such a vertical, 'objective' position. Hence it is the material details of the language that the twists and turns of phallogocentrism are drawn into visibility. The frustrated symmetry of 'Un hombre pasa', the perverted puns of 'Considerando en frío', and the rigidly constrictive sonnet form of 'Intensidad y altura' betray a poetic language which cannot claim for itself the status of the vehicle of unmediated experience or the embodiment of idealist notions of pure self-expression. Rather, these poems confirm, in their very gaps and absences that language is a

[30] For rationality and masculinity see Margaret Whitford, 'Luce Irigaray's Critique of Rationality', in *Feminist Perspectives in Philosophy* (London, 1988), 109–30.

material practice inextricable from human labour. We shall thus go on to consider in more detail poems on three groups of men who are defined by their relationship to work: the unemployed, miners, and peasants.

'Parado en una piedra' ('Stopped/Unemployed on a stone') (pp. 127–9) reveals the process by which the worker internalizes external economic conditions when he is unemployed. Once he sweated 'towards the outside' in his work; now his 'refused blood' sweats 'towards the inside' in his frustration. The builder of pyramids, his body and his 'atrocious tool' have now been stopped. In its stupor at this tragedy, the earth itself has also come to a halt. The body of the unemployed man bears witness to his predicament: the motor screams in his ankle, the clock growls impatiently in his back. It is a body which is wholly reified, which presents itself as an arbitrary relation between objects, and can be reflected only in the random detritus of the city: scraps of paper, nails, and matches. What is at stake here is not so much the soul of man under capitalism, as the very ground on which he stands. Although seated firmly on a stone, his position is progressively undermined. Even at work he was the builder of mausolea (pyramids) and of triumphal disasters ('fracasos'). That is, his (alienated) labour brought him no authenticity and was always compromised by death and negativity. There can be no freedom from false consciousness under capitalism, for the entire social space is stamped with its reifying imprint. Thus if unemployment is symbolic castration (the checking of the tool), then labour is by no means authenticating (the carving out of a tomb for the poor, a mausoleum for the rich).

I would suggest that this is also the case in 'Los mineros salieron de la mina' ('The miners came out of the mine') (pp. 86–8). For Jean Franco this poem reveals 'the formation of consciousness through work' (p. 168). It is a process by which 'thought and behaviour are quite literally mined out of the earth through work'; or again, 'thought and labour, theory and practice are united when man changes nature and himself' (pp. 169, 170). In other words, the poem combines the materialist understanding of knowledge with the socialist understanding of the proletarian as synthesis of dialectical opposites. While this is true of much of the poem, there remains in it a persistent and troubling negativity which can be assimilated to this positive paradigm only with difficulty. For example, when the miners leave the mine, they 'close the shaft with their voices, in the form of a profound symptom'. Franco suggests of this image that they 'close the gulf between thought and action' (p. 169)) but the image is also reminiscent of the prose poem in which the mother is also 'closed' by the return of the son: the hollow space must be filled. And if the 'symptom' can be taken as an allusion to the revolutionary potential already implicit in the miners, then it also suggests that their labour carves out for itself an echoing void in blind, passive matter. An implicitly feminine Nature is thus cast as the complement to male labour, a complement which enables the man to achieve a coherent identity, to know and change himself, only at the cost of its own exclusion. However, technology has already infiltrated men's bodies and their sexual relations: their mouths are functions of anvils and machines ('yunques de boca', 'aparatos de boca'), their nuptial sheets are to be made of iron. Thus, while on the one hand the male is identified with a natural, productive labour, on the other, that very labour distances him from the natural world, reifying his body. In this curiously mobile male economy there is only one explicit reference to women '¡Mujeres hasta abajo, sus mujeres!': their wives are women 'through and through' or 'all the way down'. Here the poet reiterates the ancillary, reproductive role of women in a wholly conventional way. She is marginal to the economy, but demonstrates by her supposed authenticity the naturalness of the order which persists in excluding her. She embodies the passive materiality of the earth which must be penetrated 'all the way down' by aggressive male labour. At the end of the poem the miners open up the shaft they had previously closed with their voices and are hailed by the poet as 'creators of profundity'. But I would suggest that this illusion of depth is achieved only at the cost of the repression of femininity, that the poem reproduces (unknowingly) not the production of man, but the construction of masculinity. And that masculinity is stretched, perilously and ignorantly, over a hollow space which it dare not acknowledge.

The third poem on the theme of men at work is 'Gleba' or

'Clod', its title referring once again to the unstable relation between active man and passive nature. 'Gleba' is the soil turned over by the plough, but also the soil to which serfs are bound. Franco suggests that this poem reveals that 'the directness of the peasant comes from an unmediated relationship with nature' (p. 172). My own thesis is that what the poem reveals, intermittently at least, is that such a relationship is impossible. The first stanza is typically unresolved:

> Con efecto mundial de vela que se enciende,
> el prepucio directo, hombres a golpes,
> funcionan los labriegos a tiro de neblina,
> con alabadas barbas,
> pie práctico y reginas sinceras de los valles. (p. 94)

With the world-wide effect of a candle which is lit, | with foreskins straight, men made from blows, | the peasants work within shot of the mist, | with praised beards, | practical feet, and sincere queens of the valleys.

At first the depiction of the peasants seems wholly positive: their light illuminates the world, their foreskins are straight or immediate, and they are men carved out by blows. However a closer reading brings out dissonant connotations. The blows (from an axe?) may be castrating. It is in any case a passive, receptive model of the achievement of identity: it may be significant that the translator's version of 'prepucio directo' is 'prepuce right *off*' (p. 47, my emphasis), suggesting negativity rather than pure, masculine presence. The peasants are within range of the fog which is formless and insubstantial; and their praised beards seem incongruous when set so close to the feminine flowers, 'queens of the valley'.

The second stanza does indeed stage a scene of ideal communion between these men, in which they exchange ideas over the secular sacrament of a bottle. But in the third stanza their steps, gestures, and words are dependent on sticks; and in the fourth they shake their lacks ('faltas') in the form of ancient skulls and hoist their capital defects ('defectos') with ribbons. Free exchange thus gives way to rigid mechanization (the stick) and anxious negativity (the lack). A phantom erection is raised over the mother earth. And in the last lines the peasants cry 'Away with the whores, with Luis Taboada, with the English!' The list is typically opaque (Taboada is a nineteenth-century humorist of no obvious relevance in this context). But it confirms my suggestion that in the *Poemas humanos* masculinity is founded on the fantasy of male communion, erected over a fear of phallic loss, and supported by a gesture which excludes the Other (whether cultural or sexual). Hence, the evidence offered by 'Gleba' for the unmediated relation of the peasant to his land is by no means as firm as it might be. Indeed, it would be unlikely to 'stand up' in the court of critical interpretation. But it is precisely the refusal of the text to adopt a dominant vertical perspective ('altura'), the insistent fluctuations of its pulse or register ('intensidad'), which make of this poem a critique rather than a celebration of the role of masculine labour. In a movement of reverse colonialism, the femininity repressed by the poet stages a violently unpredictable return in the skull-shaped absences and fluttering defects of the male peasants.

The structural asymmetries of Vallejo's text seem to coincide with the idealist residue in much Marxist theory. At the end of his translation of *History and Class Consciousness* Rodney Livingstone gives an account of some concepts taken over by Lukács from Hegel. For both thinkers ' "immediate" sense perceptions are . . . the product of complicated mediations . . . [and] the truly concrete is not a particular, isolated phenomenon, but an aspect or "moment" of a "totality", while "abstract" is related to the partial and one-sided, the individual and unmediated' (p. 344). This is a crucial problem for Vallejo's political and poetic enterprise. On the one hand, he undertakes to reveal that perception is always mediated by language, economics, and perhaps gender: his 'yo' stakes no claim to transparent supremacy. On the other hand, he dare not allow his attention to those mediations to slip into individualist particularity: the detritus of the city (nails and matches) must be read as concrete evidence for the totality of the capitalist world. What Vallejo cannot wholly abandon, however, is the quest for the 'identical subject-object' beloved or idealism, which will reconcile subjective experience and objective fact (and indeed will create both these terms). But as some Marxist theorists have argued, this dualism can never be resolved under capitalism. What the *Poemas humanos* reveal is that when faith in the proletariat as synthesis of opposites is shaken, then a third term intrudes in all its violence: the irrational negativity of the feminine, hitherto excluded by the cool rationalism or fanciful idealism of the phallocrat.

4. A POLITICS OF THE BODY

In this chapter I have attempted to demonstrate the inadequacy of the 'additive strategy' in gender studies. It is not enough to consider sexuality as just another fashionable, socialist cause to which an unvarying critical 'method' may be applied. In both poets and theorists the exclusion of woman is no unhappy accident, but is rather the founding gesture which clears the space for the masculine discourse. When femininity remains fixed in the traditional mould (as passive, negative, and material) then contradictions must inevitably arise in any project which attributes to itself the goal of universal emancipation. Whether those contradictions are blatant (as in the case of Neruda) or more covert (as in the case of Vallejo) their origin is the same. However, it is Marx himself who proposes the search for contradictions as a critical method; and it is his followers who suggest that there are always deeper levels of false consciousness, invisible to writers themselves, but accessible to later critics. Thus Marxism provides a conceptual framework not only for the continuing critique of such literary phenomena as poetry, but also for the examination of its own analytic perspective. The murky space of reproduction (the invisible labour which enables production to take place) must be explored over and over again, continuously drawn into the realm of visibility.

Early socialist approaches to women's liberation bear a curious similarity to Marx's analyses of Latin America. In an essay in the recent collection *Feminism and Political Theory* (London, 1986), Ursula Vogel shows how the rights of women were vindicated in the name of both a rationalist conception of 'human nature' and a romantic fantasy of 'feminine identity'.[31] The first argument was based on the assumption of universality

[31] 'Rationalism and Romanticism: Strategies for Women's Liberation', in *Feminism and Political Theory* (London, 1986).

(people are all the same); the second on the acknowledgement of specificity (some people are essentially different from others). We have seen in the introduction to this chapter that the same twin contradictory arguments were also applied to Latin America: it was set upon the margins of a received global problematic, at once a pallid reflection of the Old World and a radical disjunction from it. A rather similar contradiction surrounds a third topic of Marxist interest, that of creative writing. The problem is whether literary production is primary or secondary labour, inside or outside capitalism. Thus at one point Marx claims that all writers are 'productive' only in so far as they generate surplus value for the owners of the book trade. But at another he contrasts the 'natural' production of a poet such as Milton, who creates poetry as a silkworm creates silk, with 'the literary proletarian of Leipzig who fabricates books under the direction of his publisher', books which are 'from the outset subsumed under capital'.[32] As David Laing suggests in his commentary on these passages 'Marx has here signalled a problem, rather than solved it' (p. 12). The labour of creative artists seems to share with that of women and Latin Americans a marginal status on the fringes of capitalism. It marks out the limits of a system which it may challenge but which it is unable to transcend. As we have seen, the question of the poet's position as mediator between aesthetics and politics is particularly acute in Latin America, where the contradictions at the heart of capitalism seem more blatant (even violent) than they do in Europe. The significance of that position, however, can be accounted for within Marxist theory. The critic need not rely on the idealist notions of eternal art, elemental nature, or essential humanity.

One Latin American woman writer who has attempted to address this constellation of gender, politics, and creativity is Luisa Valenzuela. In her essay 'The Other Face of the Phallus' she suggests we pay attention to the physicality of the position allotted woman, to the viscosity of her writing, and the pleasure she can take in that which disgusts.[33] She sees this

[32] From *Theories of Surplus Value*; cited by David Laing, *The Marxist Theory of Art* (Hassocks, Sussex, 1978), 12.

[33] In *Reinventing the Americas* (Cambridge, 1987), 242–8. For a very different attempt to address the possibility of pleasure in degradation see Angela Carter, *The Sadeian Woman* (London, 1979).

as a strategic weapon in the battle against phallocracy, pointing to a Utopia when 'women's language will not be held anymore in the outer, swampy and uncharted side of the symbolic phallus created by man's imaginary' (p. 248). This is a psychoanalytically inspired approach which would indeed provide an antidote to the crassly elemental role which men such as Neruda would have women play. But it is by no means incompatible with the most important insights of Marxism which we have seen in this chapter: the critique of nature; the attack on humanism; the rejection of any politics of the body which is founded on essence, biology, or evolution.

6

FUENTES, PUIG, LYOTARD

I. POSTMODERN CONDITIONS

WHAT is postmodernism? Recent collections of essays and papers have attempted empirical definitions of the area it encompasses or the object it treats.[1] This area or object is often held to be characterized by fragmentation, electicism, and reflexivity. A postmodern culture is one in which a formerly unified subject is split into his or her constituent parts; in which a single homogeneous style is superseded by a number of heterogeneous fashions; in which an artistic practice experienced as authentic or gestural gives way to one only too aware of its own status as art, as practice. These tendencies (fragmentation, eclecticism, reflexivity) seem to be most fully expressed in popular culture, particularly in such visual forms as television advertising and pop music promos. But these examples immediately raise the question of political allegiance. Is it inevitable that the superficial phenomena associated with postmodernism be compromised by the technological refinements of late capitalism? Is the function of these phenomena simply that of enhancing the value of the commodity in the eyes of an increasingly sophisticated consumer? Such negative accounts of postmodernism stress its similarity to the camp sensibility championed by Susan Sontag in the early sixties.[2] For Sontag, camp was the sign or symptom of the collapse of the moral or political into the aesthetic. Thus sexual object choice (for example) was removed from the sphere of ethics or religion and transplanted to a realm of pure affect, pure 'taste'. But if camp itself claimed to be apolitical, this did not mean it was 'outside' politics: just as Jewish liberalism was an act of prolepsis, an

---

[1] See e.g. Hal Foster (ed.), *Postmodern Culture* (London, 1985).
[2] 'Notes on Camp', in *Against Interpretation* (New York, 1967), 275–92. This essay was first published in 1964.

attempt to anticipate and disable the illiberalism of the gentiles, so the camp of the homosexuals served as self-defence against the attacks of the moralizers. Thus the very apoliticism of camp can be read as a political strategy, albeit of a highly oblique kind. The same may be true of the style known vulgarly as postmodernism.

Sontag's essay also suggests the inadequacy of empirical models of cultural phenomena. The characteristics of her sensibility are not absolute but relative: what was once camp, now is no longer (and vice versa). In a rather similar way, there is (and can be) no consensus as to the objective nature of the postmodern text or artefact, in spite of the list I gave above. If postmodernism must follow a presumed modernism then the time-lapse is a matter of debate: some scholars cite, conventionally enough, Adolf Loos and James Joyce as classical modernists; others shift the focus of interest back to Wagner or even the *philosophes* of the Enlightenment.[3] Thus I would suggest that postmodernism lies more in consumption than in production, in the acts of reading or viewing, not those of writing or creating. Hence the apparent paradox that the formal properties of postmodernism may be indistinguishable from their modernist antecedents: recent architects mimic the concrete and steel boxes of fifty years ago; the fragmentation of the subject so fashionable now is anticipated by Proust and Woolf. The difference between the two historical moments is one of finality: today's architect does not attribute to the skyscraper the moral and political significance with which it was once invested; today's writer may not share the serious concerns with time, memory, and human consciousness taken for granted by an earlier generation. And for the consumer, the modernist experiment (in form, in politics) may be just another style. But, once again, this apparently apolitical stance may turn out to be a rearticulation of political ends. For example, the most radical attack on the integrity of the subject is now that of feminists, some of whom use parody and eclecticism to decentre a consciousness compromised by patriarchy.[4] Thus the same techniques which serve to support

---

[3] See the various contributors to *ICA Documents, 4: Postmodernism* (London, 1986).
[4] Cf. the practice of women artists in the US such as Cindy Sherman and Sherrie Levine.

contemporary power structures can also be used with critical or oppositional intent.

The case of woman under patriarchy is rather similar in theoretical terms to that of the dependency of Latin America on a dominant First World. Like woman, Latin America has no language of her own. She is condemned to mimic or parody the discourse of the oppressor, to speak back to him in the fragments of speech delegated to her. Although excluded *en masse* from power, her very substance is torn by division: Mexico and Argentina, say, their histories and cultures very different, seem to have little in common save a history of oppression and colonialization. To speak of a generic Latin American culture is already to fall into the trap of exclusion and totalization implicit in such terms as 'the Third World'.[5] Any such culture must be fragmented (divided within itself); eclectic (composed of heterogeneous peoples and traditions); reflexive (concerned with the question of authentic or original articulation within such diversity). The postmodern re-reading of these same qualities thus offers the European reader the chance to re-evaluate the cultural productions of the continent in general, and the novel in particular. For the Latin American novel (or at least the novel that has found favour in Europe) in the novel of formal experiment and political engagement *par excellence*. It subscribes to the grand narrative of the Enlightenment, that of emancipation, and links this political concern to a formal imperative: the subversion of the traditional narrative form of bourgeois realism. The question to be asked today, then, is whether that political challenge is still potent, whether that experimentalism is still subversive. In Europe (and especially in France) the decline of the modernist project has coincided with a loss of faith in Marxism as an instrument of emancipation. Has Latin American experimentalism become just another style? And can it offer us a model of resistance to terror which avoids Marxism but does not fall back into liberal humanism?

---

[5] For the historical production of national 'identities' in post-colonial countries see Benedict Anderson, *Imagined Communities: Reflections on the Origin and Spread of Nationalism* (London, 1983). For a recent article which cites both Lyotard and Anderson see Simon During, 'Postmodernism or Post-colonialism Today', *TP* 1 (1987), 32–47.

One European philosopher concerned with just this question of non-Marxist resistance (and one of the few sensitive to the ravages of both colonialism and patriarchy) is Jean-François Lyotard. In *The Postmodern Condition* (first published in French in 1979)[6] Lyotard offers a genuine theory, rather than an empirical survey, of recent changes in the status of culture. His subject of enquiry is not aesthetics but epistemology. In the introduction Lyotard defines modern as 'any science that legitimates itself by reference to a metadiscourse . . . making an explicit appeal to some grand narrative' (p. xxiii). Lyotard's example is that of the Enlightenment hero struggling towards universal peace. 'Postmodernism' is defined quite simply as 'incredulity toward metanarratives' (p. xxiv). This lack of belief in any grand design outside the specificities of social practice is encouraged by such phenomena as the 'mercantilization of knowledge' (p. 5), that is to say, the subordination of knowledge to wholly economic ends, as in research sponsored by the multinationals. In such a climate, the old beliefs in capital, labour, or emancipation (in disinterested information) become increasingly difficult to sustain. But Lyotard suggests a new and more flexible mode of legitimation, borrowed from Wittgenstein, that of the language game (p. 10). Games have no formal properties in common; they are bound only by the social contract of the players, who agree to abide by rules which inevitably vary from one game to another (from one activity or area of knowledge to another). Hence, the breakup of the grand narratives does not lead, as other commentators have thought, to a helpless splintering of the subject; rather, it leads to an increasing complexification of the place of that subject within society: 'each [self] exists in a fabric of social relations . . . more complex and mobile than ever before' (p. 15). The multiplicity of language games thus relativizes knowledge (there is no single common denominator) but does not release it from the conditions of truth or justice (its legitimation is found within the various social contracts).

---

[6] I refer to the trans. by Geoff Bennington and Brian Massumi (Manchester, 1986). The only theoretical approach to postmodernism I have found which cites Fuentes and/or Puig is Linda Hutcheon, 'Beginning to Theorize Postmodernism', *TP* 1 (1987), 10–31. Hutcheon says that *Artemio Cruz* both installs and undercuts the traditional verifying third-person voice of History (p. 16); and that *La mujer araña* exhibits the subversive potential of irony and kitsch (p. 24).

Hence, unlike the Marxists, Lyotard does not dismiss certain areas of language or experience as 'false consciousness', but nor does he take refuge with the liberal humanists in the supposed autonomy of the individual and the absolute value of his or her intuitions.

For Lyotard the traditional form of knowledge is narrative (p. 19). The legitimation of narrative knowledge is immediate. For example, the tales of the ancestors recited in tribal societies require no external validation: it is enough that they be performed in time (pp. 20–2). But this pragmatics or agonistics of social competence is incompatible with Western 'scientific' knowledge, which relies on legitimation through enquiry, through metadiscourse (p. 23). The cultural imperialism of the West thus denies the status of narrative knowledge and restricts it to the powerless: women, children, 'savages'. Epistemological colonialism, unlike any other kind, thus derives from the demand for legitimation (p. 27). Ironically, knowledge in the West is now moving towards the small narratives of the South. Once there were two grand legitimizers of knowledge,: the political narrative of emancipation and the philosophical narrative of totalization (pp. 31–5). Both have collapsed: the State has too often invoked 'freedom' in its attacks on its citizens; the grand vision of totality led to the terror of Nazism. Lyotard turns to Wittgenstein's image of language as an ancient city surrounded by modern suburbs: in just such a way the 'fabric of society is formed by the intersection of . . . language games' (p. 40). There is no space for comprehensive town-planning in the linguistic or cultural city. Indeed, science now searches not for general principles of order, but for instabilities (pp. 53–60). Legitimation comes not through the logical abstraction of homology but the unpredictable deviations of paralogy (pp. 60–7). Again, the little narrative wins out.

It is not clear what political practice corresponds to Lyotard's vision of the radically heteromorphous and temporary culture which is forming: he suggests, somewhat weakly, that all citizens must have access to the data banks (p. 67). We may doubt whether Lyotard's proposed 'war on totality' (p. 82) can take place without just a little help from those master discourses he is so anxious to displace. Although there is amost no reference to art in this book, the stress on narrative as a privileged form of knowledge is valuable, especially in that it links tribal societies with the latest developments in Western culture. But one problem with *The Postmodern Condition* is its perspective or tone: Lyotard adopts the authoritative voice of the metadiscourse at the same time as he announces its death. No doubt he would reply that the language of scientific dispassion is just another game, and one must abide by the rules if one is to be heard at all. But in an earlier book Lyotard makes some rather similar points in a far more disturbing and uncompromising way. That book is *Economie libidinale*, published in Paris in 1974 and (significantly, perhaps) not yet translated into English. As its title suggests *Economie libidinale* juxtaposes two grand narratives, those of political economy and psychoanalysis. Lyotard seeks to read each master discourse in terms of the other, to find the traces of passion in economics and of economics in passion. Here, then, the hostility to metanarratives is played out, rather than simply stated. The peculiarly dense and allusive quality of this text is the result.

Lyotard's posture is always provocative, even shocking. The book opens with an extended address to the reader which begins: 'Open up the so-called body and spread out all its surfaces' (p. 9). As the limbs, membranes, and cortexes are dissected by our scissors and lancets, we are led to see our body and its pleasures as a Möbius strip, a single continuous surface in spite of its twists and turns: 'the endless strip . . . does not have two sides, but only one, and thus has no inside or outside' (p. 11). Lyotard's 'great ephemeral skin' ('pellicule') is thus a model of the body which permits neither absence nor alterity; unlike the topographies of Lacan, for example, in which lack and the Other play leading roles (p. 12). The theatrical metaphor is apposite: for Lyotard, the skin is like the 'theatre' of pagan worship in which a number of incompatible forces (divinities) lend their influence for the performance of a single action, such as a marriage (p. 17). The Christian theatre of exclusion, on the other hand, is based on a single absence, the great Zero of the one God. Lyotard claims that this bar of exclusion or disjunction which marks the difference between pagan intensity and Christian negativity also serves to create the master discourses and the colonialism which attends them: 'How we love them, these exteriorities! They bring with them travels, ethnology, psychiatry . . . It's theatre; the whiteness of the West in expansion . . . the bar of disjunction' (p. 24). Inversely, the pagan theatre of multiple libidinal intensity has no extrinsic reference beyond itself: its masks refer to no face beneath or within (p. 29). As for the polymorphously perverse child, for the pagan there is no hole (no negativity)—there is only skin (p. 32). Even psychoanalysis (a narrative of emancipation) conspires to reduce the intensity of libidinal charge: for Freud, the formation of the superego is like the installation of troops in an area which threatens to rebel (p. 39). Semiotics, too, is negative and colonialist by nature: the African must be made to signify, just as the voyage of conquest is a 'mise en signe', an enterprise of semiotic appropriation. The European seeks 'rapports': both reports on native culture and return on his investment (pp. 59–60). Knowledge, economics, and politics are inextricable.

Lyotard's vision of the libidinal skin or membrane does not signal a return to the infinite, indefinite pleasures of the infant or pagan. It is not an 'option' he offers us, nor is it 'good'. Rather, it serves as a model of the body (and hence of culture) which rejects both the negativity of psychoanalysis and semiotics and the pure presence of liberalism; that is, it is based neither on alienating difference, nor therapeutic unity. For if the band is single it is by no means unified, and varies constantly in intensity: where an area stretches or becomes tight (as in the rigidity of the hysteric) then Lyotard gives it the anatomical name of 'tensor'. He proposes that we attempt to conceive both linguistic and economic functions in terms of this intensity (p. 18). And just as the band cannot be reduced to a reassuring unity, so Lyotard's pagans and barbarians cannot be made to signify a lost origin or an exotic other. Rather, they embody a rejection of unitary faith (in the God of Augustine, in Marx or Freud), an acceptance of a more complex and dispersed mode of power, and the existence of a marginal viewpoint which lays no claim to privileged knowledge. In another text on the fall of the great narratives, cast in the form of a dialogue, Lyotard speaks in the person of a *metoikos* (French 'métèque'), used by him to denote the barbarian

dwelling in Greece, who has no right of citizenship.[7] This
position of 'resident alien' seems appropriate not just for the
subject of postmodern culture (suspicious of the master
discourse), but also for the Latin American writer and the
European reader. For the writer is often acutely aware of his
debt to Europe, and the reader is equally aware of the
inadequacy of his response to Latin American history. The
critical value of Lyotard's postmodernism is that it reduces (or
elevates) each of us to the status of resident alien.

   In the remainder of this chapter I treat two very different
novels in the light of the theories set out above. Of course, any
choice of text must be random to some extent: I do not claim
that these works are 'representative'. *La muerte de Artemio Cruz*
is a classic 'boom' novel of 1962 in which Carlos Fuentes takes
the life and death of a single man as exemplary of the history
of Mexico and the corruption of its culture.[8] Its style is
rigorously experimental, its narrative wilfully fragmented. *El
beso de la mujer araña* was published much later in 1976. Manuel
Puig gives us the dialogues of a homosexual and a Marxist in a
Buenos Aires prison, much of which are taken up with the
plots of popular films (both real and imaginary) as told by the
first prisoner to the second.[9] Although Puig's narrative is
equally fragmented, his tone is quite different from that of
Fuentes, and the ambitions of his work less easy to define.
According to vulgar conceptions of postmodernism, Fuentes
should be the serious modernist and Puig the 'campy'
postmodernist. This is reflected in the jackets of the paperback
editions I have used: *Artemio Cruz* is given a heroic mural of
the Mexican revolution, in which men brandish guns and
flags; *La mujer araña* a kitsch print of a Victorian girl on a
mountain top, her hair and tunic billowing improbably around
here. Here, then, is the difference, the bar of disjunction:
politics versus aesthetics; authentic art versus commercialism;
'masculine' potency versus 'feminine' sensibility. In my
appeal to Lyotard, however, I shall argue for a strategic
reversal of these dichotomies, one which is not 'objectively' in

[7] *Instructions païennes* (Paris, 1977). Lyotard does not use the word in the modern
racist meaning.
   [8] I cite the edn. pub. in Madrid, 1983.
   [9] I cite the edn. pub. in Barcelona, 1986.

the texts themselves but is produced by my reading of them. For the fundamental question posed by postmodernism is whether changes in the economy of knowledge have affected the way in which we read even texts which are quite recent historically. And the question I would add to it is how the postmodern changes of emphasis relate to the questions of gender and sexuality.

2. *ARTEMIO CRUZ* AND THE DECLINE OF METANARRATIVE

La muerte de Artemio Cruz is based on the two grand narratives of the West: emancipation and totalization. Its fragmented exposition traces, in a reverse movement, the story of a man's life from his death as a rich and powerful patriarch in the capital to his birth as a destitute and illegitimate child in the jungle. Cruz's social and material progress is always bought at the cost of moral or spiritual corruption, and this ineluctable decadence finds its counterpoint in the history of Mexico in the twentieth century as depicted in the novel: the promise of authentic popular rebellion is betrayed by greed, violence, and colonialism. Artemio Cruz, then, is the anti-hero of the Enlightenment, the man who leads his people not to justice and freedom, but to injustice and enslavement. The narrative of emancipation is turned on its head. What of the narrative of totalization? Fuentes's work, as so often, is encyclopaedic in its ambitions: the action moves from the capital city, to the deserts of Chihuahua in the north, to the western resort of Acapulco, and the eastern forests of Veracruz. The land itself, in its vastness and multiplicity, is perhaps the protagonist of the novel. Likewise, we are offered representatives of all ranks of society: the remnants of *ancien régime* aristocracy; destitute Indian peasants; soldiers, politicians, businessmen. This external totalizing impulse is matched by an internal correlative: the novel seeks to encompass the entirety of a man's consciousness, all of his thoughts, sensations, and (above all) memories. Yet, as in the case of the narrative of emancipation, that of totalization is negative: we are shown that the character is unable to integrate his experience, embrace the world, find meaning for his existence.

The story, then, is one of alienation: Cruz cannot achieve that integrity of being which is assumed to be the individual's goal. In particular he is unable to reconcile public success (the achievement of power and money) with private failure (the scorn of his wife and daughter). What he claims to possess (and rehearses obsessively in the theatre of memory) are moments of authenticity, places or loci of the natural uncompromised by alienation. These interlocking or over-lapping spheres of the natural involve geography (the forests of Veracruz, far from the blandishments of the capital); youth (Adamic innocence untainted by materialism); and, most importantly, woman (the elemental or instinctive being, untouched, initially at least, by the alienation of the male). I shall return to these points in moment. What is important to note here is that (overtly at least) the book does not question the founding myth of liberal humanism: the autonomy of the individual and the sovereignty of his or her experience. Indeed, the very stress on alienation suggests a nostalgic longing for a totality of experience, for the missing content of art and life which Lyotard identifies as typical of the modernist aesthetic (*Postmodern Condition*, p. 81).[10]

The rigorous experimentalism of Fuentes's technique is equally modernist. He offers not one but three narrating subjects: the 'I' who recounts present sensation; the 'you' who warns of future suffering; the 'he' who recollects past (mis)adventures. Like the disruption of chronological linearity to which it is linked, this diffraction of the narrative voice is at first unsettling to the reader. But the fragmentation is not as radical as it first appears: the various shreds of narrative are skilfully, even masterfully orchestrated by the author so that finally they come to form a coherent picture of one man's reality.[11] And if the interpretation of some episodes is problematic, the potential unreliability of the narrative voices

[10] For *Artemio Cruz* as nostalgia for lost totality see Steven Boldy, 'De Fuentes y de Dante y de Gorostiza ¡siempre tres!', *Iberoromania*, 25 (1987), 103–19.

[11] Most critics have been happy to co-operate with the author in discerning order, harmony, or deep structure in a plural text. See Paul B. Dixon, '*La muerte de Artemio Cruz* and Baroque Correlative Poetry', *Hispanófila*, 28 (1985), 93–102; Aida Elsa Ramírez Mattei, *La narrativa de Carlos Fuentes: Afán por la armonía en la multiplicidad antagónica del mundo* (Río Piedras, Puerto Rico, 1983); Steven Boldy, 'Fathers and Sons in Fuentes's *La muerte de Artemio Cruz*', *BHS* 61 (1984), 31–40.

does not make us question whether key actions actually took place within the fictional world, or are simply imagined. Fuentes shows us the mercantilization of knowledge in the novel: Cruz owns his own newspaper and may publish such 'facts' as he pleases. But this is not applicable to the novel itself: in spite of his experimentalism, Fuentes abides by the rules of bourgeois realism and appeals to the metadiscourse of verisimilitude. The narrative voice is thus fragmented or relativized, but not, finally, deprived of the authority conventionally attributed to the individual 'perspective'.

At first reading, then, *Artemio Cruz* presents itself as a 'strong' modernist text in both ideology and technique: it subordinates formal experiment to the analysis of general questions of time, memory, and subjectivity which are themselves legitimized by the metanarratives of emancipation and totalization. It achieves a tricky fusion of Marxist economics and humanist esssentialism by appeal to the notion of alienation: the ravages of capital and colonialism have stripped Man of those (unexamined) qualities held to be essential to him. As Lyotard has suggested, the concept of alienation is based on negativity, on the fixing of the bar of disjunction between North and South, self and other, woman and man, a fixing which proclaims (none the less) the possibility of its own abolition at some time in the past or future.

How can we offer a postmodern reading of this text, one which takes account of changes in the cultural climate since it was written? I would suggest that such a reading should focus not on the grand narratives of emancipation and totalization, but on the little narrative of the body, of its pleasures and displeasures. Fuentes frequently interjects lists of sensations into the book: of the tastes of tropical fruit, the texture of clothing and furniture, the odours of plants in the forest. He offers minute, hyperrealist reconstructions of the rituals of the male body, as in the passage in which the ageing Cruz shaves and carries out his toilette (pp. 148–9). The attention to sense impression and banal action here can be interpreted by the reader in a Proustian way: they can be seen as the keys to involuntary memory, the silent witnesses to the passing of time. But if we refuse this *mise en signe*, this quest for a return on our literary investment, then we are left with the body itself, and the question of its status. For Fuentes it seems likely that the body is the 'real', in the Lacanian sense; that is, the irreducible substance outside language and representation. Thus it is no accident that Cruz's loss of control over his body signals the beginning of the narrative: through its revelation of the absolute, this violent reminder of the primacy of the metabolism serves as a standard against which we may measure the vicissitudes of Cruz's conscious career in the symbolic arena. But if the body is itself relativized or made cultural, then its function as a natural index of limitation (as the bar of disjunction) is precluded. Cruz's name has been read as that of a martyr, wracked on the cross of bodily torment. But it might better be seen as a crossroads, the intersection of a multiplicity of language games in the chaotic cultural city. Thus his words and deeds as a child of nature in the forest, as a soldier in the wars of revolution, as a lover engaged with a number of women, and as a businessman in search of capital, all of these roles are incompatible, or, in Lyotard's favourite word, incommensurable. That is, they share no single common denominator, and can neither be compared nor contrasted with one another. This diversity is of course highlighted by the fragmentary nature of Fuentes's text, in which we come upon each of Cruz's postures with little or no preparation. However, the incommensurability of these various moments or gestures need not imply alienation, the loss of an authentic origin or the failure to attain 'mature' equilibrium. Rather, it suggests (again in Lyotard's terms) the complexification of the social subject. If each of Cruz's roles is a game, then these games may be coherent within themselves while possessing no common factor, other than that of the social contract with other players, which is itself variable; and they need have no legitimation other than the fact of their performance in time. In other words, the reader is not compelled to invoke metanarratives (whether of capital or labour) in order to see Cruz's career as a social or political performance. The very instability of this career warns us of the terror of totalization. The text itself offers images of this multiple constitution of the subject which is neither one nor many: the threads from a ball of yarn, woven in and out of each other (pp. 33, 78, 85); the sponge, with its innumerable strands coursing through its body (p. 88); the links in the chain of male language, tying man to man, and man to nation (p. 147). For Cruz, as for Lyotard, knowledge is narrative, the interweaving of separate threads.

But the most frequent image of incommensurability is, of course, the body itself. In the meditations and speculations of 'I' and 'you' on the body, we return again and again to the skin or membrane in its various forms: the surface or cortex of the brain (p. 61); the folds of the intestine and abdominal walls (p. 90); the peculiar opacity of skin, which is both translucent and reflective (p. 135). Like the Möbius strip, the epidermis (in spite of its twists and turns) is continuous, unbroken, both inside and outside the body. Even when a membrane (such as the eyelid) seems to mark unambiguously the place of exclusion or exteriority, its status is called into question: 'I' wonders if there is a membrane behind the eyes, as well as in front of them (p. 222). The barrier between self and other is dissolved: Cruz's sensations and possessions are as much a part of his libidinal 'skin' as his body itself. Likewise the smooth surface of the audiotape played to him by his aide echoes back to Cruz the sound of his own voice, sometimes forwards, sometimes backwards, in a parody of the fluid, reversible movements of language in the brain (p. 118). The subject thus returns not as presence, but as particularity, a sequence of intensities on the infinite film of libidinal extension. Linked to this question of surface is the problem of theatre, of masks. Cruz's urbane father-in-law is said to be like a mask without a face; and Cruz sees himself on his first visit as the subject of a masquerade, the mere substitute for his future wife's dead brother (p. 38). As Lyotard suggests, the fact that all social and psychic process is skin does not preclude dissimulation: 'where there is no longer anything but surface, plots and secrets reign' (*Economie*, p. 115). Cruz's references to the membrane are often qualified by appeals to a pure or simple origin: the folds of the cerebral cortex are contrasted with the smooth palm of the new-born child (p. 62). Cruz's wife describes him as the man who constructed himself, who began again after the zero-time of revolution (p. 103). But, as we shall see in a moment, we need not take this myth of origin at face value: indeed, the child's palm is not smooth at birth.

Thus we can read Fuentes's stress on the body, not as a reaffirmation of substance but as a rearticulation of surface: as an opening on to the great ephemeral skin. Such a change in emphasis will set the bar of disjunction spinning: when there is no face behind the mask, then the realm of 'authenticity' (of distinction between self and other) is under threat. I have said that Fuentes's grounds of exclusion (loci 'outside' capitalism and alienation) are geography, youth, and woman. The definitive locus of natural innocence is the province of Veracruz, with its forests and ocean. Here Cruz is raised in a shack by a mulatto, and lounges naked under the trees (p. 287). As a child and young adolescent he is at one with the forest, his hair bleached copper by the sun, his limbs and chest assimilated to the unripe fruit of the jungle (p. 283). Many years after the expulsion from this paradise, it is to Veracruz once more that he returns with his young son, whom he has set up as a little lord of the manor. As they commune with Nature, as they test their bodies in horse-races or mock wrestling matches, father and son are mirror images of one another, barely distinguishable in pure, virile intensity (pp. 167–8, 224–8). What Cruz represses (and what the rhetoric of exclusion in the novel cannot accept) is that this is no innocent repetition of childlike pleasure. However much father and son may dally with the picturesque fishermen on the beach, Cruz has bought the land on which they sport, an act of acquisition no different in kind from any of his others. Thus the land itself is not an innocent backdrop or neutral 'ground', but rather a vital player in the theatre of capital. Indeed, Fuentes has Cruz admit this elsewhere, when his reverie on the beauty of fields and plains by the sea drifts seamlessly into an amorous meditation on their profitability (p. 140). The 'rapport' of far-off lands is at once sensuous and economic.

Another peculiarity of Cruz's paradise (and one equally treated without irony by the author) is that it is exclusively male, 'homosexual' in the etymological sense of the word. Cruz himself is brought up by a stepfather who takes him on birth from between his mother's legs. The father–son idyll is based quite explicitly on the exclusion of the mother and daughter abandoned at home and at school. The decisive moments of Cruz's career are marked by similar (if less pleasant) same-sex games or rituals: Cruz's acceptance by a new president is signalled by the stroking and patting of arms, shoulders, and hips: (homo)sexual politics is eroticized (p. 138); the quarrel between Cruz and the brother of his future wife ends in a 'violent embrace' (pp. 197–8), the prelude to yet another betrayal by Cruz. The problem is not that women, elsewhere held to be essential to the male, are excluded from these vital gestures, but that this bar of exclusion cannot be acknowledged in these places, that unless the text offers us a pure, undivided space of authenticity (the forest, the seashore) the fragmented shards of alienation elsewhere can have no meaning.

The question of woman, then, is the greatest threat to the stability of the text's economy.[12] It is also an index to changes in the practice of reading since the early sixties. The episode with Regina, Cruz's first love, is almost unreadable today. She is elemental, compared to the sea and land; she is childlike, her body barely mature; she is animal, compared at one point to a seagull. And most of all she is subordinate, following the young soldier from town to town, cheerfully making the coffee as her lover lies in bed after a bout of ecstatic love-making (pp. 64–9). This sloppy idealism and casual sexism (again, lacking entirely in irony) is supplemented by crudely essentialist descriptions of sex: when they make love the bodies are entirely isolated from the world (p. 63); at the moment of orgasm she exclaims: 'How you fill me up!' (p. 68). Thus sex is the space magically abstracted from history and politics, but based on a conception of woman as absence or hole. Regina serves mainly to define Cruz's sense of self: he says that on seeing her, he sees himself (p. 73). And her death is necessary to make him a man: when she is hanged by Cruz's opponents, the tears he sheds are the first he has wept as a man (p. 81). It

[12] For women in Fuentes see Gloria Durán, *The Archetypes of Carlos Fuentes: From Witch to Androgyne* (Hamden, Conn., 1980); and Wendy B. Faris, '"Without Sin, and with Pleasure": The Erotic Dimensions of Fuentes's Fiction', *Novel* 20. 1 (Fall 1986), 62–77. For women in Latin American literature see Carmelo Virgillo and Naomi Linstrom (eds.), *Woman as Myth and Metaphor in Latin American Literature* (Columbia, Miss., 1985); Sharon Magnarelli, *The Lost Rib: Female Characters in the Spanish American Novel* (Bucknell, 1985).

is not enough to say that this is how people really saw (or see) their lives, or that we cannot blame Fuentes for his character's *machismo*. The fact remains that the logic of the text demands we take such moments as innocent or value-free, if we are to respond to the amorous desolation which follows Cruz's first experience of love. The text, as written, cannot tolerate this supplementary mark of gender difference at its heart.

The question of Cruz's relation to his wife Catalina is more complex. Cruz claims that his love is genuine, although she herself cannot separate it from Cruz's betrayal of her brother and humiliation of her father: she feels she has been bought like her family's estate. This episode could provoke a number of readings: the liberal humanist will tend to see Cruz's protestations of love as genuine: emotions are not necessarily compromised by economic conditions. The Marxist will tend to see Cruz's feelings as distorted: capitalism dehumanizes individual relations, clouds them with false consciousness. The alternative, however, is that desire and economics are inextricable in sentimental narrative: each is implicit in the other, and neither is sovereign. Thus Cruz's lust for commodities, a desire to acquire and conserve, is equal to his lust for women; his look passes equally over Catalina and her father's estate (p. 55). Yet the pleasure of capitalization is highly sensual: the amorous catalogue of treasures in Cruz's mansion and of delicacies on his table suggest a generalized eroticism, unrestricted to women's bodies or hard cash. Once more, we open out on to the libidinal film which permits variations in intensity, but no exclusions.

Often, however, Fuentes sets up oppositions between the sensual female sphere and the political male one. Thus towards the start of the book 'he' drifts between Cruz's momentous negotiations with the gringos, in which he disposes of the nation's economic future, and his wife and daughter's aimless shopping expedition: a desultory trip to the dress-maker's; perusal of make-up (one brand called, significantly, 'Theatrical'); an inconclusive discussion on the correct pronunciation of the name 'Joan Crawford' (pp. 18–23).[13]

---

[13] Fuentes reveals some interest in camp, especially in his theatre. See Eduardo F. Elías, 'Carlos Fuentes and Movie Stars (Intertextuality in a Mexican Drama)', *LATR* 12. 2 (Spring 1986), 67–77. Bernard Fouques reads Fuentes for the camp way he

The play between these two spheres or registers serves to bring out both the differences and similarities between them. Thus the man's work is important, the woman's leisure trivial. But beneath his apparent authority Cruz is as impotent as his wife, his fate ultimately dependent on the gringos' capital. Like woman, Latin America has been colonized. Fuentes seems at first to be hinting at a postmodernist dissolution of value, in which political differences dissolve into an aesthetics of taste: his advisor on the business deals, Padilla, is an ex-Marxist, who has written a thesis on surplus value (p. 27). The grand narratives are evidently in decline. But in fact the division of labour and power we are shown here (South and North; women and men) serves to reinforce the text's faith in metanarrative through its evident injustice: if both Cruz and his wife are condemned to dissatisfaction it is because a genuine and authentic resolution to both economic and libidinal life is indeed possible, or at least should be attempted. The problem is that within the text the only resolutions offered are those of the virgin forest and the child-woman, myths of origin and alterity, respectively.

Hence Fuentes juxtaposes political economy and psycho-analysis but, in spite of numerous moments of indecision in the text, cannot (finally) fuse them, for to do so would be to abandon legitimation through external enquiry ('What is the answer to Mexico's problems?') and metanarrative ('How can humanism or Marxism solve those problems?'). Such questions are highly complex and it seems better to end with the close analysis of a single passage from the opening paragraphs of the novel.

Yo despierto . . . Me despierta el contacto de ese objeto frío con el miembro. . . . Los párpados me pesan: dos plomos, cobres en la lengua, martillos en el oído, una . . . una como plata oxidada en la respiración. Metálico todo esto. Mineral otra vez. Orino sin saberlo. . . . Abro el ojo derecho y lo veo reflejado en las incrustaciones de vidrio de una bolsa de mujer. Soy esto. Soy esto. Soy este viejo con las facciones partidas por los cuadros desiguales del vidrio. . . . Mueca. Mueca. Mueca. Soy esta mueca que nada tiene que ver con la vejez o el dolor. (p. 9).

deprives images of meaning, in the light of the Lacanian imaginary: 'Fuentes et la médiation littéraire: *Una familia lejana*', *Imprévue*, 1 (1986), 85–97.

I awake. . . . I am woken by the contact of that cold object with my penis. . . . My eyelids feel heavy: two pieces of lead, copper on the tongue, hammers in the ear, a . . . a kind of rusty silver in my breathing. All this is metal. Or again, mineral. I urinate without knowing it. . . . I open my right eye and see it reflected in the fragments of glass set into a woman's handbag. I am this. I am this. I am this old man with his features split up by the uneven squares of glass. . . . Grimace. Grimace. Grimace. I am this grimace which has nothing to do with old age or pain.

The text begins with the entry into consciousness: 'I' awakes. This consciousness is immediately gendered by the reference to the member or phallus. The cold object (the bedpan) serves, like the phallus itself, as a bar of disjunction, marking out the rim between self and world. However, the bar is at once set spinning, the division blurred: the subject has lost control of the space within (involuntary urination); and the properties of the other are metonymically transmitted to this newly alienated body, which is as metallic and reified as the object 'outside' itself. The man's eye is reflected in the distorting mirrors encrusted on a woman's handbag: he says 'I am this'. Thus the woman serves as a prop or lure for the male look, essential for his sense of self, yet herself trivial by nature (what object more trivial than a handbag?). The distinct reflections fragment the face (as Fuentes will the body of narrative): eyelids, nostrils, and cheekbones, each are separate, unconnected. Light seems to penetrate the lids even when they are closed: they suggest a narrative 'skin' that has neither inside nor outside. The face twists into a grimace, one which has no connection with age or grief. Like the masks which will recur throughout the book, it refers to nothing outside itself, to no essence hidden within.

The passage thus offers themes and motifs which will recur later: the little narrative of the body; the masquerade of female display; the varied tensions on the surface of the skin. It thus offers the reader a chance to rescue the novel from the metadiscourse, to seek a micro-resistance uncompromised by totality. If we can see ourselves (like Cruz) as resident aliens in our own bodies then we may not fall prey to those who would reintegrate fragmentation in the cause of aesthetic unity or political terror. At the end of the novel, Cruz's body is opened up by the same lancet ('bisturí' 'bistouri') invoked by Lyotard on the first page of *Economie libidinale*. But as I have tried to show, this opening-out on to the surface, need not imply the same extinction for the reader as it does for the character; rather, it suggests a new and more self-conscious awareness of the body politic which is also shared by Manuel Puig.

3. *LA MUJER ARAÑA* AND THE RETURN OF THE BODY

It is very easy to read *El beso de la mujer araña* as a postmodern text in the vulgar sense of the term. The structure of the novel is fragmentary: we are given the words of the two protagonists with no intervention from a third-person narrator to tell us who or where they are. The texture of the novel is eclectic: the fragments of dialogue are supplemented by lengthy footnotes on such psychoanalytic topics as the Oedipus complex and repression, and by the dry, factual reports of the prison authorities and secret police. The tone of the novel is reflexive: as a narrative about the telling of stories, it offers a critique of the reading process within itself. For example, when the humourless Marxist Valentín remarks how involved he has become with one of the characters in a film retold by Molina (a character about whom he knows almost nothing), then the reader of *La mujer araña* is also made to reflect on his or her engagement with the characters which Puig himself has equally deprived of conventional novelistic 'background'. I shall return to the question of narrative and its status in a moment.

The novel's fragmentation, eclecticism, and reflexivity can easily be read as camp: moral and political issues are, initially at least, overwhelmed by an all-pervasive sense of the aesthetic. Thus the second movie plot retold by Molina comes from a Nazi propaganda film. In the first scene handsome, blond soldiers raid a Jewish butcher's shop in occupied Paris, proclaiming that Europe will be free from hunger when the exploiters of the people are eliminated (p. 55). Later, the French night-club singer Leni manages to avoid the clutches of a lame Resistance fighter and falls into the arms of a divinely handsome German officer. Here, as elsewhere, the focus of Molina's narration is on superficial, sensual detail: furniture, clothing, cosmetics; in short, the 'feminine' sensibility. However, as I argued at the beginning of the chapter, the apparent apoliticism of camp can provide the model for a kind of political practice, albeit an oblique one; and the qualities commonly associated with postmodernism cannot be isolated from their function within a particular text.

What, then, is the function of Puig's formal experimentalism and epistemological relativism? Like Fuentes, Puig seems to be pointing to the decline of the two grand narratives of emancipation and totalization.[14] Thus Valentín and Molina might be taken at first as twin, incompatible heroes in the quest for freedom: the Marxist seeks justice in the economic sphere and the homosexual in its libidinal equivalent. But the action of the novel reveals that this is not the case. Valentín is unable to reduce his libido to the 'correct' ideological format: his real love is not the proletarian comrade, but a woman with a touch of class. And Molina has no interest in any project of sexual liberation: he seeks not the political right to freedom of expression as a gay man, but the unattainable fantasy of a woman's experience of love within a male body. If true emancipation seems impossible for either of the characters, then so does totalization: each sees from a conspicuously limited viewpoint, and in spite of the gradual blurring of the difference between the two (which culminates in their love-making) no solution is offered within the text to the political or sexual problems raised by Puig's choice of characters. But although both Fuentes and Puig offer negative versions of the Enlightenment narratives of legitimation, the function of negativity in each seems rather different. For by offering no solution to the predicament of his characters, Puig seems to suggest that there is no space 'outside' alienation, that social justice and personal authenticity may be quite unattainable. While Cruz's career is exemplary and his deathbed the crux of a nation's agony, Valentín and Molina's confinement is particular (even peculiar), and cannot be made to bear the

---

[14] Lori Chamberlain says that Puig's concern for the problem of the master narratives locates one of his novels 'within a postmodernist poetics and politics': 'The Subject in Exile: Puig's *Eternal Curse on the Reader of these Pages*', *Novel*, 20 (1987), 260–75.

weight of all oppression in Argentina. Puig's characters are simply too idiosyncratic to be representative.

However, it could be argued that the very marginality of Puig's characters offers him the chance to smuggle back into the novel (in a more subtle manner than we find in Fuentes) the old ideals of bourgeois realism and liberal humanism. As in *Artemio Cruz*, the interpretation of fact and fantasy in *La mujer araña* does not make us question the status of the action presented to us as real: we must believe in the objective existence of Molina's love for his mother and Valentín's experience of torture if the relation between the two is to have any meaning. As in Fuentes once more, knowledge is relativized and fragmented, but not, finally, deprived of value. Hence it is possible to read the psychoanalytic footnotes as proof of the sovereignty of the self, of the immunity of complex psychic processes to 'scientific' explanation. The easy elision of libidinal sublimation and political repression suggested by Marcuse is made to seem woefully inadequate and inflexible as an 'explanation' of the characters' very particular predicaments. 'Real' life transcends the rigid categories of objective enquiry. Similarly, it is possible to read the practice of sex in the novel in the way we have read it in Fuentes: as an oasis 'outside' history and politics where individuals find intimate, unalienated communion.[15] After they have made love, Molina says that he went to touch his own face thinking it was Valentín's: they are both the same (p. 222); Valentín replies that he is convinced that sex is innocence itself (p. 224). The fact that the relationship is homosexual perhaps makes the reader more willing to accept these words as authentic evidence of a privileged moment than Fuentes's more lyrical effusions on heterosexual love. For where Fuentes's love-scenes are hamstrung by stereotypical notions of femininity, Puig omits the question of woman altogether. In spite of the inadequacy of the characters as ambassadors of sexual emancipation, the love between the two men can be read as a space of authentic subjectivity, all the more authoritative because of its very marginality.

[15] This is how Elías Miguel Muñoz reads sex in 'El discurso utópico de la sexualidad en *El beso de la mujer araña* de Manuel Puig', *RI* 52 (1986), 361–78. For the possibilities of freedom see Juan Manuel García Ramos, *La narrativa de Manuel Puig: Por una crítica de libertad* (La Laguna, 1982).

Struggling free from the grand narratives of political and psychiatric terror, the deviant becomes dominant, for a moment at least, and in tragically reduced circumstances.

One obstacle to this essentialist reading of homosexuality in the novel is that Molina's post-coital words are not entirely reliable: the reader, unlike Valentín, knows that Molina has co-operated to some extent with the authorities in their attempt to make Valentín betray his co-revolutionaries. Love, even between men, is never innocent. Indeed, elsewhere in the book there is much discussion on what it means to be a man (p. 69). Fuentes, as we have seen, is oblivious to the implications of the same-sex idylls he lends his character. Puig, however, is not uncritical of exclusive relations between men. By making explicit the homosexual theme in his book, he makes us look again at such clichés as 'You're as much a man as I am' or 'All men are alike', both of which are addressed by Valentín to Molina (pp. 65, 147). Puig seems to be suggesting (like some feminists) that all men are homosexual, whatever their libidinal preference. But by calling attention to this theme (rather than repressing it as Fuentes does) he reveals that such relations are never uncompromised by power. Thus Valentín fails to convince Molina that it would be more liberating, less exploitative, if he (Molina) took a more active role in love-making. For Molina, pleasure cannot be separated from fear and domination (p. 246). Indeed earlier, when Valentín compares the cell to a desert island in which each may act in perfect freedom towards the other, Molina is unconvinced: he can conceive of no act of love which is disinterested (p. 206). As we shall see, the desert island is just another space on the surface of the earth, as subject as any other to the ravages of desire and capital.

We are moving towards a reading of this text which is postmodern in Lyotard's sense of the word. *La mujer araña* takes the two grand narratives of *Economie libidinale* (political economy and psychoanalysis) and plays them off against each other. And it does so in a much more subtle way than the proponents of sexual politics in the sixties, who are cited and (implicitly) ironized in the footnotes.[16] Valentín is in favour of

[16] For the mutually deconstructing play between body of text and footnotes see Lucille Kerr, *Suspended Fictions: Reading Novels by Manuel Puig* (Urbana and Chicago,

the emancipation of women (p. 23) and preaches that the quest for social justice must take precedence over the pleasures of the body (p. 33). His sub-Freudian 'analyses' of characters in Molina's movies betray the same totalizing dogma as his political prescriptions. But having set up this violent hierarchy of the economic and the libidinal, he is forced to admit its inadequacy: there can be no conscious control over the choice of the desired object. The point is not (or not simply) that desire cannot be contained by political diktat; nor that desire is essentially chaotic or anarchic. Rather, it is that desires shares a structure with political economy, and that structure is narrative. This interpenetration of Marxism, psychoanalysis, and narrative is carefully orchestrated throughout the novel. Thus a technical footnote on the oral and anal stages of sexual development is followed by the scene in which Molina lovingly cleans the faeces from his sick partner's bed and body (pp. 141–5). Or again, in Molina's fourth film, the young playboy hero joins forces with terrorists to murder his capitalist father (p. 149): politics and psychoanalysis invade the space of romance in the form of the oldest of narratives, the story of Oedipus. The retelling of the fifth film (*Return of the Zombie Woman*) is interspersed with italicized fragments of physical disintegration and decay: glass masks and skulls, gangrenous lungs and hearts (pp. 170, 180). When the grand narratives break down, the body intrudes in all its violence and unpredictability.

But, as I said before, the body is not random, for all its violence. The text invites us to construct an economy of narrative based on the psychoanalytic theory and Marxist polemic it itself provides. Thus narrative (like desire, like economics) is based on the possibility of exchange: Molina must check continually that Valentín is listening and is responsive to his stories. The persistence of narrative requires a fluctuation between reserve and expenditure. Like the child with its faeces or the businessman with his capital, Molina surrenders his substance when it is needed, and then withholds it in order to stimulate greater appetite. And of course this libidinal economy is also that of the author, who

1987), 226. This book contains an excellent account of *El beso de la mujer araña* entitled 'The Politics of Seduction' (pp. 184–235).

releases narrative material to the reader in an inconsistent and intermittent manner. When Molina retells the Nazi narrative, Valentín is shocked: he says that this kind of fantasy is a dangerous delusion, an act of wilful alienation (p. 85). But if we take narrative as a form of knowledge, as a language game with specific rules, then we need neither reject fantasy as false consciousness nor evacuate it of all political content. Molina himself is well aware that narrative is conventional: he knows that the Resistance were heroes in real life—it's just that they're not in the film (p. 84). I would suggest that this remark can be taken as acknowledging an awareness of the relativization of knowledge which need not imply the dissolution of all standards of value. Thus the movie plots as retold in the book are not true or false in any absolute sense, neither alienating fantasy nor authentic refuge from the terror of the real. Rather, they provide multiple images of a radically shifting and fragmented surface which is social practice itself.

As in the case of Fuentes, woman plays the largest role in the game of love. Molina's films parade before us the well-worn stereotypes of femininity: the animalesque heroine of *Cat People*; the sentimental Parisienne, Leni; the innocent wife terrorized on the island of the zombies. Woman is natural, emotional, passive. Where Puig differs from Fuentes, of course, is that such images are highly ironized, steeped in camp. They cannot pass for authentic notions of women, as Fuentes's heroines claim to; rather, they stress the artifice of woman under patriarchy, her existence as masquerade: in the fictitious Caribbean set of her Paris night-club, Leni clutches a velvet flower (p. 80), emblematic of the fact that woman may mimic the 'natural' but can offer no authentic refuge from the desolate wastes of male alienation. We are constantly reminded that these images derive from films (Spanish 'película'); like Lyotard's great ephemeral skin ('pellicule'), they are all surface and no essence, a mere play of intensities. And like Lyotard's pagan theatrics, Puig's cinematic fiesta offers no inside or outside, just a number of conflicting and irreconcilable forces. It is no accident that Leni should sing in a mock-up of a tropical lagoon. Like woman, Latin America is colonized from birth, a fictitious entity from its very inception.

The North American heroine of the *Zombie Woman* is greeted
on her husband's Caribbean island by native drumming:
Latin America is always already an exotic other, the perfect
backdrop for the pulsating rhythms of the body. The zombies
themselves can be read as parodies of the Third World
subject, compelled to obey the master's voice, while straining
for an autonomy which will always be denied. Like Artemio
Cruz's wife and daughter, the heroines of Molina's movies are
often confined within their houses, their lives destroyed by
men; but unlike Fuentes's women, Puig's have no chance of
freedom, beyond the mythical realm of romance: they are the
very substance of the narratives they inhabit, of the intertwining
of passion and economics. Indeed, the image of the mad
woman on the tropical island confirms Lyotard's suggestion
that psychiatry and colonialism are intimately linked, each
based on the imposition of exteriority, on the creation of an
object (the woman, the savage) subject to a dominant gaze.
Thus Puig does not simply reject stereotypes of woman and
Latin America; but nor is he content to revel in them. If there
is no 'authentic' face behind the mask, then the stereotype is
at once oppressive and pleasurable, actual and illusory.
Perhaps these points will be made clearer by a close reading of
a text from the opening paragraphs of *La mujer araña*.

—A ella se le ve que algo raro tiene, que no es una mujer como todas
. . . [tiene] una carita un poco de gata . . .
—¿Y los ojos?
—Claros, casi seguro que verdes, los entrecierra para dibujar mejor,
Mira al modelo, la pantera negra del zoológico . . .
—¿Y ella no tiene frío?
—No, no se acuerda del frío, está como en otro mundo, ensimismada
dibujando a la pantera.
—Si está ensimismada, no está en otro mundo. Esa es una
contradicción.
—Sí, es cierto, ella está ensimismada, metida en el mundo que tiene
adentro de ella misma. (pp. 9–10)

'You can see there's something funny about her, that she's not a
woman like all the others . . . her face is a bit like a cat's . . .'
'And what are her eyes like?'
'Light-coloured, almost certainly green, and she screws them up
in order to draw better. She's looking at her model, the black
panther in the zoo . . .'

'And she's not cold?'

'No, she doesn't notice the cold, she's as if in another world, completely absorbed as she draws the panther.'

'If she's absorbed in herself, she's not in another world. That's a contradiction.'

'Yes, that's it, she's all wrapped up in herself, in the world inside herself.'

As in the case of *Artemio Cruz*, we are confronted at once with an unidentified speaking voice: the third-person narrator is conspicuous by his absence. A woman is the object of the voice's attention: the man's gaze roams over her face identifying each feature in turn. If she is feline, it is because, in the world of filmic stereotype, woman's sexuality is animal, and once aroused cannot be sated. The reference to 'a woman like any other' will prove ironic. For the novel's parade of extraordinary women will undermine any received notions of female essence. The second voice interjects to request more detail—but the first is not sure of the colour of the woman's eyes. As we learn later, he is describing a scene from a film, the original *Cat People* of 1943, produced by Val Lewton and directed by Jacques Tourneur. As readers we cannot yet be sure that the novel is referring to a work of art outside itself; but the pervasive, even oppressive, reflexivity of the book is hinted at by the woman's activity. Just as the unnamed Molina 'paints' her in words, so she is drawing, attempting to represent the object of her desire and terror, the male panther in the cage. The question of whether she can be both self-absorbed and in another world as she draws seems trivial at first. But it announces an important theme in the novel. Does art induce authenticity or alienation in the subject? Are we led more deeply into ourselves or distracted from true self-awareness by the seductive lure of fiction? It is typical of Molina that he should claim that there is no distinction. The world within the self is another world: fantasy and authenticity cannot be separated. The close description of shoes, nails, and stockings which follows the passage is typical of Molina's attention to the surface of the woman's body, to her camouflage. It is telling that he is unsure if the pink colour comes from legs or stockings: in the filmic masquerade, the bar between inside and outside is abolished.

The openings of both *Artemio Cruz* and *La mujer araña* inspire uncertainty in the reader by means of a rather similar experiment in form. But it is obvious that the tone of the two passages is very different. It would be naïve, however, to suppose that Puig's camp sensibility makes him less serious a writer than Fuentes. By plunging us immediately into the act of story-telling, Puig hints at the importance of narrative in all its forms. This point is confirmed at the end of the novel. Valentín, horribly tortured, is hallucinating in the prison infirmary. The attention to the suffering body is here rather similar to Fuentes. In his dream Valentín comes to a tropical island, but finds it is made up of the white skin of a woman: desire and economics fuse once more in the fluid surface of his imagination (p. 284). He comes upon the spider woman (the name he has earlier given to Molina). The threads of her web pass through her body: again, the subject is multiple, constituted by its own chains or bonds. He thinks of the death of Molina, who has been killed by the revolutionaries as he waited to pass on information given to him by Valentín. Was Molina martyred for the political cause or did he choose to die romantically like one of the heroines in his films? The question can have no final answer. But I would suggest that it requires none: if we take narrative as a form of knowledge then this story of sacrifice brings its own legitimation—it requires no 'external' enquiry into the supposed facts of the case (no metadiscourse) to justify it. What *La mujer araña* reveals is that narrative is neither fantasy nor truth, but history. As Lyotard says with reference to the Gulag, one way of approaching terror is by displacing the grand narratives of Right and Left by the little narratives ('historiettes') of people's lives.[17] For Lyotard, the people as a collective or monolithic singular is not a subject. But nor, we might add, is the individual, as an absolute or essential entity. The re-evaluation of story-telling, as proposed by both Lyotard's philosophy and Puig's novel, thus points the way to a model of resistance to terror which is neither liberal humanist, nor Marxist; that is, a model which is both particular in its attention to historical circumstance and general in its awareness of communal relations. A story

---

[17] *Instructions païennes*, p. 39.

originates from one person, but must be told to another. In its stress on the primacy of narrative, *La mujer araña* is both a pragmatics and an agonistics of social practice.

4. THE END OF HISTORY?

Lyotard claims that his vision of language games and instabilities is different from the helpless fragmentation and atomization of the subject suggested by other theorists of the postmodern. It is certainly more sophisticated. Whether it is of any value to Latin Americans (as opposed to European readers of Latin American narrative) is quite another question. As one speaker objected to Lyotard at a recent conference on postmodernism in London,[18] the quest for discontinuity and incommensurability may be a luxury which only those already secure of their own sense of cultural identity can enjoy: it holds few attractions for those still striving to attain a sense of self, for the deprived and the dispossessed. In particular, Lyotard's dismissal of 'the people' as an authentic subject and his promotion of a dispersed model of (micro-)resistance seem irrelevant to the collective problems of the Third World, to the suffering of the masses. The closing pages of *Economie libidinale* are particularly disturbing here with their call for 'an invulnerable plot without head, without home, without programme, without project' (p. 311). Like the reference to smoking dope at the beginning of the book (or to Janis Joplin at the end), these words come uncomfortably close to the doomed romantic anti-capitalism of the hippies. We might add that, historically, the *metoikoi* praised by Lyotard paid taxes but were denied the civil liberties granted full Athenian citizens. Taxation without representation: this was the lot of the resident aliens, rather different from the role of barbarous resistance they are made to play by Lyotard. But Lyotard would say (and, indeed, has said, with reference to the struggle against French colonialism in Algeria)[19] that to demand collective action of the peoples of the Third World, to expect them to express their predicament in terms of alienation or class struggle, is itself colonialist: the playing-out

---

[18] The conference was held at the ICA in 1985; the papers pub. in 1986.
[19] In a verbal reply to a question at the above conference.

of domestic problems on the exotic stage of the South. We Europeans demand a return not just on the commodities, but also on the concepts we are so eager to export.

Perhaps a combination of two Lyotardian terms can offer a model of Latin American narrative, valid for European readers at least, who are likely to be disenchanted with state socialism. First, we have the *pellicule*: the ceaseless movement of the libidinal skin or film, defined by the rotating bar. This suggests the instability and volatility of Latin American writing. Second, we have the *tenseur*: the stretching or tightening of this surface, which allows an intricate play of intensities without exclusions. This suggests the elastic political forces endlessly regrouping on the infinite band. In *Artemio Cruz* we moved (in my reading) from the *tenseur* to the *pellicule*: moral and political difference cedes to libidinal play; in *La mujer araña* we moved from the *pellicule* to the *tenseur*: the formless movement of the filmic image cedes to a political purpose, which is no less potent for being unstable. To borrow a term from architecture, both novels point to a 'critical regionalism'[20] for Latin America: an understanding of its culture as neither natural nor exotic (neither desert island nor film set). What we cannot do is claim instability as a goal in itself, as an essential instrument of emancipation.[21] As Frederick Jameson suggests in his introduction to *The Postmodern Condition*, 'the dynamic of perpetual change [advocated by Lyotard] . . . is the very "permanent revolution" of capitalism itself' (p. xx).[22] But once more Lyotard has anticipated this objection. In an appendix to *The Postmodern Condition* he brands the eclecticism of international consumerism (American food, French fashion, Japanese technology) with the name 'the realism of money' (p. 76).[23] And in a very recent text on the

[20] Kenneth Frampton, 'Towards a Critical Regionalism: Six Points for an Architecture of Resistance', in *Postmodern Culture* (pp. 16–30).

[21] One theorist of postmodernism who stresses the challenge to identity posed by cultural discontinuity is Gianni Vattimo. See the early work *Poesia e ontologia* (Milan, 1985), 207.

[22] Jean Franco makes a similar point when she notes how experimental Latin America writers favour 'the very values promoted by a new stage of capitalism'; see 'The Crisis of the Liberal Imagination and the Utopia of Writing', *IL* I. 1 (1976–7), 5–24 (p. 22).

[23] For capitalism and modernity see also Lyotard's essay 'Appendice svelte à la question postmoderne', in *Tombeau de l'intellectuel* (Paris, 1984), 75–87.

sublime[24] he equates the ceaseless novelty of the avant-garde with the productive strategies of capitalism, ever eager to colonize new and more exotic areas. But to say we cannot attribute any essential force to formal experiment is not to deny it all value: the Latin American novel (and the theory of postmodernism) may yet escape the clutches of the grand narratives, which remain more potent than some commentators would have us believe.

If we seek a final distinction between earlier writers such as Fuentes and later ones such as Puig, it cannot be the banal dichotomies of serious versus camp, political versus personal, profound versus superficial. Fuentes is modernist because he still believes, nostalgically, in the missing content of human essence, the unpresentable which can never be revealed. At one point Laura, Artemio Cruz's married lover, asks Cruz what he thinks a woman in a favourite painting is looking at as she directs her gaze beyond the frame (p. 217). Cruz refuses to answer the question, but we may answer it for him: she is looking at the unpresentable, the always-absent term required by Fuentes's characters to cure their alienation.[25] For Puig, on the other hand, the question cannot even be posed: representation has no 'outside', especially for women, and the limits of the cultural image are those of life itself. The problem of the unpresentable thus shifts from content to representation. For Lyotard this is the very definition of postmodernism: 'that which denies itself the solace of good forms, the consensus of a taste which would make it possible to share collectively the nostalgia for the unattainable' (p. 81). The movement from *Artemio Cruz* to *La mujer araña* marks the loss of just this sense of formal and aesthetic certainty. But if, as Lyotard believes, the old certainties have been replaced by new instabilities, this need not mean that history and politics have come to an end.

[24] 'The Sublime and the Avant Garde', *Paragraph*, 6 (1985), 1–18.

[25] In 'The Potential Novel', a paper read in Cambridge in 1987, Fuentes rejects the grand narratives, but puts his faith in the ability of the novel to say the 'unsayable'. For Lyotard such a position would remain modernist in spite of its denial of the master discourses.

CONCLUSION: READING THE SAME

In the Introduction I suggested that, in spite of the diversity of texts to be treated, three motifs would tend to recur. These motifs are woman, resistance, and the body itself. This book was offered, initially, as a contribution to men's studies: its aim was to shift the focus of investigation from an all-too-visible femininity to the darker continent of male sexuality. However, it has proved impossible to prevent the question of woman from returning, however hard it is repressed. This is not simply because of the nature of the texts I have chosen for analysis. Indeed, neither Spanish literature nor (male) French theory is known for its peculiar attention to women. On the contrary, as we have seen, the canon of Hispanic texts is overwhelmingly masculine in orientation, and thinkers such as Barthes and Foucault have been attacked for their lack of concern for femininity. The return of the woman is thus symptomatic of the ubiquity of a mode of thought which specifies woman as *the* sex, the term which must first be excluded and then analysed by male discourse. It is not possible simply to step outside this conundrum. Freud claims that the relation between the sexual instinct and its object is arbitrary, and Lacan that the *objet petit a* is set in motion by the force of the subject's own desire. But it remains the case that subjects are dependent on an object if they are to speak at all. And, in our culture, that object remains massively female. The only pragmatic approach would be to stress that the categories of gender difference are mutually constituting, that each bears within itself a (negative) definition of the other. Such a deconstruction of opposites would, however, itself remain metaphysical unless it acknowledged the violent hierarchy which continues to operate between the two terms, the ability of one to exercise power over the other.

Recent theories of sexuality and culture often seem to lead to impasses of this kind. Thus Irigaray suggests that any model of the subject is always assimilated to the masculine, and Barthes that any attempt to transgress boundaries will always be recuperated. Lacan denies the possibility of a relation between the sexes, and Foucault questions the subject's capacity for self-knowledge. Finally, Althusser claims that there is no space outside ideology, and Lyotard that collective action is impossible when society is so radically fragmented. Desire appears to be insatiable, and power ubiquitous. However, I would suggest that such pronouncements need not imply political quietism. Rather, they serve a strategic function in provoking a radical interrogation of our cultural (and sexual) condition. Indeed, it would be absurd to take these theorists as legislators when they have worked so hard, in their very different ways, to unsettle the very idea of universal Law. And here the role of literature is vital. For the literary text cannot be confined within the safe parameters of denotation, and may be defined by its tendency towards an uncontrollable surplus of meaning, intentionality, and cultural reference. It is for this reason that I have attempted to read the 'great authors' (Góngora, Galdós, Neruda) against the grain, to untangle knots and tease out contradictions in texts often held to be organically structured and aesthetically unified. Hence if I suggest literature be read as theory it is not because it offers authoritative access to the truth, but because it reveals the hesitant and deviant process which links language to a real which must itself remain inaccessible.

Foucault promises at the end of *La volonté de savoir* that resistance is to be found not in the transgression of law but in the body and its pleasures. By now the significance of this remark should be clear. It suggests not that we retreat into the bourgeois asylum of a private sphere, but that we accept the specificity of a position which is neither transcendent nor blindly physiological. The shift from the individual to the body would thus suggest a shift in critical practice from moral duty to pleasure, and from the celebration of the canon to a critique of tradition. A criticism which would be, in the common senses of the word, critical (at once oppositional and transitional). This is not a purely literary concern, although it is of relevance to the way in which 'literature' can be taught. It is also a question which concerns the relation between university and society. In a recent article which treats the state of the (literary) subject Jacqueline Rose claims that in the late 1980s 'the link between the literary institution and its outside . . . [is] even more urgent.' But she goes on to say that this urgency should not express itself 'in the form of a liberal defence of the humanities for their own sake. But as part of a constant need for literary and cultural studies to expose and challenge the realm of dominant identifications and fantasies.'[1] The technical languages to which I have appealed in this volume (and which traditionalists will no doubt continue to denounce as 'jargon') can play a major role in undoing those identifications, undermining those fantasies.

It should come as no surprise, then, that critics working in the field of cultural studies should draw on the same theorists as a literary critic such as myself. One excellent example is Simon Watney's *Policing Desire: Pornography, AIDS, and the Media* (London, 1987). In his approach to one of the latest and most urgent of political problems Watney draws unselfconsciously on Freud, Foucault, and Kristeva. At one point he cites a passage from Foucault's *Discipline and Punish* which can serve as a fitting epilogue to my own study. It reads as follows:

The body is directly involved in a political field; power relations have an immediate hold upon it: they invest it, train it, torture it, force it to carry out tasks, to perform ceremonies, and to emit signs. The political investment of the body is bound up, in accordance with complex, reciprocal relations, with its economic use . . . the body becomes a useful force only if it is both a productive body and a subjugated body.(p. 16)

Productive and subjugated: such will be the role of critics who persist in reproducing the images of a dominant order. But if we refuse the reproductive role, then we must return to a body which is particular, but not individual; arbitrary, but not random; material, but not fixed. As the most uncompromising emblem of difference, the body shows us that we need not read the same.

[1] 'The State of the Subject (ii): The Institution of Feminism', *CQ* 29. 4 (1987), 9–15 (p. 15).

BIBLIOGRAPHY

I. GENERAL AND THEORETICAL

Althusser, Louis, *Lenin and Philosophy* (London, 1971).

Anderson, Benedict, *Imagined Communities: Reflections on the Origin and Spread of Nationalism* (London, 1983).

Barthes, Roland, *Mythologies* (Paris, 1957).

—— *Essais critiques* (Paris, 1964).

—— *Critique et vérité* (Paris, 1966).

—— *L'Empire des signes* (Geneva, 1970).

—— *S/Z* (Paris, 1970).

—— *Sade, Fourier, Loyola* (Paris, 1971).

—— *Le Degré zéro de l'écriture: Nouveaux essais critiques* (Paris, 1972).

—— *Le Plaisir du texte* (Paris, 1973).

—— *Fragments d'un discours amoureux* (Paris, 1977).

—— *Roland Barthes par Roland Barthes* (Paris, 1980).

—— *Incidents* (Paris, 1987).

Benton, Ted, *The Rise and Fall of Structural Marxism* (London, 1984).

Bowie, Malcolm, 'Lacan and Literature', *RS* 5 (1984–5), 1–26.

—— *Freud, Proust, and Lacan: Theory as Fiction* (Cambridge, 1987).

Brod, Harry (ed.), *The Making of Masculinities* (Winchester, Mass., 1987).

Carter, Angela, *The Sadeian Woman* (London, 1979).

Chapman, Rowena, and Rutherford, Jonathan (eds.), *Male Order: Unwrapping Masculinity* (London, 1988).

Coward, Rosalind, *Patriarchal Precedents* (London, 1983).

—— *Female Desire: Woman's Sexuality Today* (London, 1984).

Culler, Jonathan, *The Pursuit of Signs* (London, 1981).

—— *Barthes* (London, 1983).

—— *On Deconstruction: Theory and Criticism after Structuralism* (London, 1983).

Deconstructing 'Difference', special issue of *Screen* 28. 1 (Winter 1987).

Derrida, Jacques, 'Le Facteur de la vérité', in *La Carte postale de Socrate à Freud et au-delà* (Paris, 1980), 441–524.

Difference: On Representation and Sexuality, catalogue of exhibition curated by Kate Linker and Jane Weinstock (New York, 1984).

Dollimore, Jonathan, 'Different Desires: Subjectivity and Transgression in Wilde and Gide', *TP* 1 (1987), 48–67.

During, Simon, 'Postmodernism or Post-colonialism Today', *TP* 1 (1987), 32–47.

Easthope, Antony, *Poetry as Discourse* (London, 1983).

—— *What a Man's Gotta Do: The Masculine Myth in Popular Culture* (London, 1986).

Foreman, Ann, *Femininity as Alienation* (London, 1977).

Foster, Alasdair, 'Exhibitions: Heroes, Fools, and Martyrs', *Ten. 8: International Photography Magazine*, 28 (1988), 54–63.

Foster, Hal (ed.), *Postmodern Culture* (London, 1985).
Foucault, Michel, *Raymond Roussel* (Paris, 1963).
—— *Les Mots et les choses* (Paris, 1966).
—— '*Theatrum philosophicum*', *Critique*, 26 (1970), 885–908.
—— *Histoire de la folie à l'âge classique* (Paris, 1972).
—— *Ceci n'est pas une pipe* (Montpellier, 1973).
—— *Surveiller et punir: Naissance de la prison* (Paris, 1975).
—— *La Volonté de savoir* (Paris, 1976).
—— 'Preface to Transgression', in *Language, Counter-memory, Practice*, ed. F. Bouchard and Sherry Simon (Oxford, 1977), 29–52.
—— *Power/Knowledge*, ed. Colin Gordon (Brighton, 1980).
—— *Le Souci de soi* (Paris, 1984).
—— *L'Usage des plaisirs* (Paris, 1984).
—— *Les Aveux de la chair* (forthcoming).
—— and Farge, Arlette, *Le Désordre des familles* (Paris, 1982).
Frampton, Kenneth, 'Towards a Critical Regionalism: Six Points for an Architecture of Resistance', in *Postmodern Culture*, ed. Hal Foster (London, 1985), 16–30.
Freud, Sigmund, *On Sexuality* (Harmondsworth, 1977).
Gallop, Jane, *Feminism and Psychoanalysis: The Daughter's Seduction* (London, 1982).
—— '*Quand nos lèvres s'écrivent*: Irigaray's Body Politic', *RR* 74 (1983), 77–83.
—— 'The Bodily Enigma', paper read in London, 1987.
—— *Thinking through the Body* (forthcoming).
Genette, Gérard, 'Une poétique structurale?', *TQ* 7 (1961), 13–19.
Gilman, Sander L., *Difference and Pathology* (Ithaca, 1985).
Green, David, 'On Foucault: Disciplinary Power and Photography', *Camerawork*, 32 (Summer 1985), 6–9.
Greer, Germaine, 'The Proper Study of Womankind', *TLS* (3 9 June 1988), 616, 629.
Griffiths, Morwenna, and Whitford, Margaret, *Feminist Perspectives in Philosophy* (London, 1988).
Hamburger, Michael, *The Truth of Poetry* (Harmondsworth, 1972).
Heath, Stephen, *The Sexual Fix* (London, 1982).
Hocquenghem, Guy, *Homosexual Desire* (London, 1978).
Hoy, David Couzens (ed.), *Foucault: A Critical Reader* (Oxford, 1986).
Hutcheon, Linda, 'Beginning to Theorize Postmodernism', *TP* 1 (1987), 10–31.
ICA Documents, 4: Postmodernism (London, 1986).
Irigaray, Luce, *Speculum, de l'autre femme* (Paris, 1974).
—— *Ce sexe qui n'en est pas un* (Paris, 1977).
—— *Et l'une ne bouge pas sans l'autre* (Paris, 1979).
—— *Amante marine: de Friedrich Nietzsche* (Paris, 1980).
—— *Passions élémentaires* (Paris, 1982).
—— *Éthique de la différence sexuelle* (Paris, 1984).
—— 'A Chance of Life: Limits to the Concepts of the Neuter and the Universal in Science and Knowledge', paper read at the ICA in London, 1987.

Jacobus, Mary (ed.), *Women Writing and Writing about Women* (London, 1980).
Jardine, Alice A., *Gynesis: Configurations of Woman and Modernity* (Ithaca and London, 1985).
—— and Smith, Paul (eds.), *Men in Feminism* (New York, 1987).
Kiberd, Declan, *Men and Feminism in Modern Literature* (London, 1985).
Kristeva, Julia, *La Révolution du langage poétique* (Paris, 1974).
—— *About Chinese Women* (London, 1977).
—— *Polylogue* (Paris, 1977).
—— *Histoires d'amour* (Paris, 1983).
—— *Soleil noir: Dépression et mélancholie* (Paris, 1987).
Kuhn, Annette, and Wolpe, Ann Marie (eds.), *Feminism and Materialism* (London, 1978).
Lacan, Jacques, *Écrits*, i (Paris, 1966).
—— *Écrits*, ii (Paris, 1971).
—— *Le Séminaire: Livre xx: Encore* (Paris, 1975).
—— *Écrits: A Selection*, trans. Alan Sheridan (London, 1977).
Laing, David, *The Marxist Theory of Art* (Hassocks, Sussex, 1978).
Livingstone, Rodney (ed.), intro. to Georg Lukács, *Essays on Realism* (London, 1980).
Lukács, Georg, *History and Class Consciousness* (London, 1968).
Lyotard, Jean-François, *Economie libidinale* (Paris, 1974).
—— *Instructions païennes* (Paris, 1977).
—— *Tombeau de l'intellectuel et autres papiers* (Paris, 1984).
—— 'The Sublime and the Avant Garde', *Paragraph*, 6 (1985), 1–18.
—— *The Postmodern Condition*, trans. Geoff Bennington and Brian Massumi (Manchester, 1986).
Maclean, Ian, *The Renaissance Notion of Woman* (Cambridge, 1980).
Marx, Karl, *Capital*, i, intro. Ernest Mandel, trans. Ben Fowkes, ed. Quintin Hoare (Harmondsworth, 1976).
'Men', special issue of *Marxism Today* (April 1988).
Merck, Mandy, 'Difference and its Discontents', *Screen* 28. 1 (Winter 1987), 2–9.
Miller, J. Hillis, 'The Triumph of Theory, the Resistance to Reading, and the Question of Material Base', *PMLA* 102 (1987), 281–91.
Mitchell, Juliet, and Rose, Jacqueline (eds.), *Feminine Sexuality: Jacques Lacan and the école freudienne* (London, 1982).
Moi, Toril, *Sexual/Textual Politics: Feminist Literary Theory* (London, 1985).
Ong, Walter J., *Orality and Literacy: The Technologizing of the Word* (London, 1982).
Plato, *Symposium*, ed. W. R. M. Lamb (London, 1925).
Poster, Mark, 'Foucault and the Tyranny of Greece', in David Couzens Hoy (ed.), *Foucault: A Critical Reader* (Oxford, 1986), 205–20.
Quintilian, *Institutio oratoria*, ed. H. E. Butler (London, 1922).
Rabinow, Paul (ed.), *The Foucault Reader* (Harmondsworth, 1986).
Rose, Jacqueline, *Sexuality in the Field of Vision* (London, 1986).
—— 'The State of the Subject (ii): The Institution of Feminism', *CQ* 29. 4 (1987), 9–15.
Scaliger, Julius Caesar, *Poetices libri septem* (Lyons, 1561).

Segal, Naomi, *The Unintended Reader: Feminism and 'Manon Lescaut'* (Cambridge, 1986).
Sexual Difference, special issue of *OLR* 8. 1–2 (1986).
Sheridan, Alan, *Michel Foucault: The Will to Truth* (London and New York, 1982).
Shiach, Morag, 'Roland Barthes: Some Feminist Fragments', paper read at conference on Barthes in Warwick, 1985.
Sontag, Susan, 'Notes on Camp', in *Against Interpretation* (New York, 1967), 275–92.
Swindells, Julia, 'Falling Short with Marx: Some Glimpses of Nineteenth Century Sexual Ideology', *LTP* 3 (1984), 56–70.
Tasso, Torquato, *Discorsi dell'arte poetica e del poema heroico*, ed. Luigi Poma (Bari, 1964).
Tesauro, Emmanuele, *Il cannocchiale aristotelico* (Bad Homburg, 1968).
Todorov, Tzvetan, *Les Genres du discours* (Paris, 1978).
Vattimo, Gianni, *Poesia e ontologia* (Milan, 1985).
Vogel, Ursula, 'Rationalism and Romanticism: Strategies for Women's Liberation', in *Feminism and Political Theory* (London, 1986).
Watney, Simon, *Policing Desire: Pornography, AIDS, and the Media* (London, 1987).
Weedon, Chris, *Feminist Practice and Post-structuralist Theory* (Oxford, 1987).
Weinberg, Bernard, *A History of Literary Criticism in the Italian Renaissance* (Chicago, 1961).
Whitford, Margaret, 'Luce Irigaray's Critique of Rationality', in *Feminist Perspectives in Philosophy* (London, 1988), 109–30.
Wright, Elizabeth, *Psychoanalytic Criticism: Theory in Practice* (London and New York, 1984).

2. HISPANIC AND LITERARY

Alas, Leopoldo ['Clarín'], *Solos de Clarín* (Madrid, 1891).
Aldacara, Bridget, 'The Revolution of 1868 and the Rebellion of Rosalía Bringas', *AG* 18 (1983), 49–60.
Anderson, David G., 'Pablo Neruda's Non-celebratory Elementary Odes', *RN* 26 (1986), 226–31.
Andradi, Esther, and Portugal, Ana María, *Ser mujer en el Perú* (Lima, 1978).
Andreu, Alicia Graciela, *Galdós y la literatura popular* (Madrid, 1982).
Aricó, José, *Marx y América Latina* (Lima, 1980).
Beverley, John, intro. to Luis de Góngora, *Soledades* (Madrid, 1979).
—— *Aspects of Góngora's 'Soledades'* (Amsterdam, 1980).
—— 'Barroco de estado: Góngora y el gongorismo', in *Del 'Lazarillo' al Sandinismo* (Minneapolis, 1987), 77–99.
Binding, Paul, *Lorca: The Gay Imagination* (London, 1985).
Bly, Peter A., *Galdós's Novel of the Historical Imagination* (Liverpool, 1983).
—— (ed.), *Galdós y la historia* (Ottawa, 1988).
Boldy, Steven, 'Fathers and Sons in Fuentes's *La muerte de Artemio cruz*', *BHS* 61 (1984), 31–40.

—— 'De Fuentes y de Dante y de Gorostiza ¡siempre tres!', *Iberoromania*, 25 (1987), 103–19.

Boudot, Pierre, *La Jouissance de Dieu ou le roman courtois de Thérèse d'Avila* (Paris, 1979).

Britton, R. K., 'The Political Dimension of César Vallejo's *Poemas humanos*', *MLR* 70 (1975), 539–49.

Burrows, Ruth, *Inner Castle Explored* (London, 1981).

Burton, Julianne, 'The Greatest Punishment: Female and Male in Lorca's Tragedies', in *Women in Hispanic Literature* (Berkeley, 1983), 259–79.

Byrd, Suzanne, 'Panerotism: A Progressive Concept in the Final Trilogy of García Lorca', *GLR* 3 (1975), 53–6.

Chamberlain, Lori, 'The Subject in Exile: Puig's *Eternal Curse on the Reader of these Pages*', *Novel*, 20 (1987), 260–75.

Close, Lorna, 'Vallejo, Heidegger, and Language', in *Words of Power: Essays in Honour of Alison Fairlie* (Glasgow, 1987), 163–86.

Colecchia, Francesca, *García Lorca: A Selectively Annotated Bibliography of Criticism* (New York and London, 1979).

Covarrubias, Sebastián de, *Emblemas morales* (Madrid, 1610).

DeCoster, Cyrus, *Juan Valera* (New York, 1974).

Didier, Béatrice, 'Thérèse d'Avila et le désir de Dieu', in *L'Écriture-femme* (Paris, 1981), 51–70.

Dixon, Paul B., '*La muerte de Artemio Cruz* and Baroque Correlative Poetry', *Hispanófila*, 28 (1985), 93–102.

Durán, Gloria, *The Archetypes of Carlos Fuentes: From Witch to Androgyne* (Hamden, Conn., 1980).

Durán, Manuel, intro. to *Lorca: A Collection of Critical Essays* (Englewood Cliffs, NJ, 1963).

Edwards, Gwynne, *Lorca: The Theatre Beneath the Sand* (London and Boston, 1980).

Elías, Eduardo F., 'Carlos Fuentes and Movie Stars (Intertextuality in a Mexican Drama)', *LATR* 12. 2 (Spring 1986), 67–77.

Espinosa, Juan de, *Diálogo en laude de las mujeres* (Madrid, 1946).

Faris, Wendy B., '"Without Sin, and With Pleasure": The Erotic Dimensions of Fuentes's Fiction', *Novel* 20. 1 (Fall 1986), 62–77.

Fernández Cifuentes, Luis, Review of Ian Gibson, *Federico García Lorca*, *NRFH* 34 (1985–6), 224–32.

—— 'Signs for Sale in the City of Galdós', *MLN* 103 (1988), 289–311.

Foa, Sandra M., *Feminismo y forma narrativa: Estudio del tema y las técnicas de María de Zayas y Sotomayor* (Valencia, 1979).

Fouques, Bernard, 'Fuentes et la médiation littéraire: *Una familia lejana*', *Imprévue*, (1986), 85–97.

Fox, Linda C., 'Power in the Family and Beyond: Doña Perfecta and Bernarda Alba as Manipulators of their Destinies', *Hispanófila*, 29 (1985), 57–65.

Franco, Jean, intro. to *Pablo Neruda: Selected Poems* (Harmondsworth, 1975).

—— *César Vallejo: The Dialectics of Poetry and Silence* (Cambridge, 1976).

—— 'The Crisis of the Liberal Imagination and the Utopia of Writing', *IL* 1. 1 (1976–7), 5–24.

—— 'Trends and Priorities for Research in Latin American Literature', *IL* 16 (1983), 107–20.

—— 'Gender, Death, and Resistance: Facing the Ethical Vacuum', paper read in New York, 1985.

Fuentes, Carlos, *La muerte de Artemio Cruz* (Madrid, 1983).

—— 'The Potential Novel', paper read in Cambridge, 1987.

Galerstein, Carolyn, 'The Political Power of Bernarda Alba', in *Drama, Sex, and Politics* (Cambridge, 1985), 183–90.

Gallego Morell, Antonio (ed.), *Garcilaso de la Vega y sus comentaristas* (Madrid, 1972).

García Cruz, Arturo, *Ideología y vivencias en la obra de Juan Valera* (Salamanca, 1978).

García de la Concha, Víctor, *El arte literario de Santa Teresa* (Barcelona, 1978).

García Lorca, Federico, *El público*, ed. Rafael Martínez Nadal (Oxford, 1976).

—— *La casa de Bernarda Alba*, ed. H. Ramsden (Manchester, 1983).

—— *Alocución al pueblo de Fuentevaqueros*, ed. Manuel Fernández Montesinos and Andrés Soria Olmedo (Granada, 1986).

—— *La casa de Bernarda Alba*, ed. Allen Josephs and Juan Caballero (Madrid, 1986).

—— *El público*, ed. María Clementa Millán (Madrid, 1987).

García Ramos, Juan Manuel, *La narrativa de Manuel Puig: Por una crítica de libertad* (La Laguna, 1982).

Gibson, Ian, *Federico García Lorca: De Fuente Vaqueros a Nueva York* (Barcelona, 1985).

Gilman, Stephen, *Galdós and the Art of the European Novel* (Princeton, 1981).

Gold, Hazel, 'Francisco's Folly: Picturing Reality in Galdós's *La de Bringas*', *HR* 54 (1986, 47–66.

Gold, Janet N., 'Reading the Love Myth: Tusquets with the Help of Barthes', *HR* 55 (1987), 337–46.

Góngora, Luis de, *El 'Polifemo'* . . . *comentado*, ed. José García de Salcedo Coronel (Madrid, 1629).

—— *Todas las obras*, ed. Gonzalo de Hoces (Madrid, 1634).

—— *'Soledades'* . . . *comentadas*, ed. José García de Salcedo Coronel (Madrid, 1636).

—— *The Solitudes*, trans. E. M. Wilson (Cambridge, 1965).

—— *Poems*, ed. R. O. Jones (Cambridge, 1966).

—— *Polyphemus and Galatea: A Study in the Interpretation of a Baroque Poem*, ed. Alexander A. Parker, trans. Gilbert F. Cunningham (Edinburgh, 1977).

—— *Antología poética*, ed. Antonio Carreira (Madrid, 1986).

González López, Luis, *Las mujeres de Juan Valera* (Madrid, 1934).

Gornall, J. F. G., 'Góngora's *Soledades*: "Alabanza de aldea" without "Menosprecio de corte"?' *BHS* 59 (1982), 21–5.

Gullón, Ricardo, *Psicologías del autor y lógicas del personaje* (Madrid, 1979).

Hart, Stephen, 'Was César Vallejo a Communist? A Fresh Look at an Old Problem', *Iberoromania*, 22 (1986), 106–33.

—— *Religión, política, y ciencia en la obra de César Vallejo* (London, 1987).

Havard, Robert G., 'The Hidden Parts of Bernarda Alba', *RN* 26 (1985), 102–8.

Jesús, Teresa de, *Su vida* (Madrid, 1978).

Kavanaugh, Kieran, intro. to Teresa de Jesús, *The Interior Castle* (London, 1979).

Kerr, Lucille, *Suspended Fictions: Reading Novels by Manuel Puig* (Urbana and Chicago, 1987).

King, Ursula, 'Mysticism and Feminism or Why Look at Women Mystics?', in *Teresa de Jesús and her World*, ed. Margaret A. Rees (Leeds, 1981).

Kirkpatrick, Susan, 'On the Threshold of the Realist Novel: Gender and Genre in *La gaviota*', *PMLA* 98 (1983), 323–40.

Krynen, Jean, *L'Esthétisme de Juan Valera* (Salamanca, 1946).

Lewis, Thomas E., 'Galdos's Gloria as Ideological *Dispositio*', *MLN* 94 (1979), 258–82.

—— '*Fortunata y Jacinta*: Galdós and the Production of the Literary Referent', *MLN* 96 (1981)316–39.

Liss, Sheldon B., *Marxist Thought in Latin America* (Berkeley, 1984).

McGuirk, B. J., 'Undoing the Romantic Discourse: A Case Study in Post-Structuralist Analysis. Vallejo's *Trilce* i', *RS* 5 (1984–5), 99–111.

McKendrick, Melveena, *Woman and Society in the Spanish Drama of the Golden Age* (Cambridge, 1974).

Magnarelli, Sharon, *The Lost Rib: Female Characters in the Spanish American Novel* (Bucknell, 1985).

Martínez Arancón, Ana (ed.), *La batalla en torno a Góngora* (Madrid, 1978).

'Masculinidad', pull-out dossier in *El País* (5 May 1988).

Miller, Beth (ed.), *Women in Hispanic Literature: Icons and Fallen Idols* (Berkeley, 1983).

Miller, Stephen, '*La de Bringas* as *Bildungsroman*: A Feminist Reading', *RQ* 34 (1987), 189–99.

Ministerio de Cultura: Instituto de la Mujer, *Plan para la igualdad de oportunidades de las mujeres 1988–90* (Madrid, 1987).

Ministerio de Cultura: Instituto Nacional de las Artes Escénicas y de la Música, programme for Lluís Pascual's production of Lorca, *El público* for the Centro Dramático Nacional (Madrid, 1987).

Molho, Maurice, *Semántica y poética (Góngora, Quevedo)* (Barcelona, 1977).

Montesinos, José F., *Valera o la ficción libre* (Madrid, 1957).

—— *Galdós*, ii (Madrid, 1980).

Montoto, Santiago, *Valera al natural* (Madrid, 1962).

Muñoz, Elías Miguel, 'El discurso utópico de la sexualidad en *El beso de la mujer araña* de Manuel Puig', *RI* 52 (1986), 361–78.

Neruda, Pablo, *El libro de las odas* (Buenos Aires, 1972).

—— *Odas elementales* (Barcelona, 1983).

O'Connor, D. J., 'La mujer lectora y protagonista de la novela española del 1870', *Hispanófila*, 84. 3 (1985), 83–92.

Ortega, José, 'Conciencia social en los tres dramas rurales de García Lorca', *GLR* 9 (1981), 64–90.

Ortega, Julio (ed.), *César Vallejo* (Madrid, 1975).

Paoli, Roberto. 'Mapa anatómico de *Poemas humanos*', in *César Vallejo: Actas del Coloquio Internacional Freie Universität Berlin* (Tübingen, 1981), 41–53.

Peixoto, Marta, 'The Absent Body: Female Signature and Poetic Convention in Cecília Meireles', *BHS* 65 (1988), 87–100.

Pérez de Ayala, Ramón, *Amistades y recuerdos* (Barcelona, 1961).

Pérez-Erdelyi, Mireya, *La pícara y la dama: La imagen de las mujeres en las novelas picaresco-cortesanas de María de Zayas y Sotomayor y Alonso del Castillo Solórzano* (Miami, 1979).

Pérez Galdós, Benito, *La de Bringas*, ed. Alda Blanco and Carlos Blanco Aguinaga (Madrid, 1985).

Perriam, Christopher, 'Metaphorical *Machismo*: Neruda's Love Poetry', *FMLS* 24 (1988), 58–77.

Petit, Marie-Claire, *Les Personnages féminins dans les romans de Benito Pérez Galdós* (Lyons, 1972).

Place, Edwin B., *María de Zayas, an Outstanding Woman Short-story Writer of Seventeenth Century Spain* (Boulder, Colorado, 1923).

Porlán, Rafael, *La Andalucía de Valera* (Seville, 1980).

Pring-Mill, Robert, 'La elaboración de la cebolla', in *Actas del iii congreso internacional de hispanistas* (Mexico, 1970), 739–51.

Puig, Manuel, *El beso de la mujer araña* Barcelona, 1986).

Ramírez Mattei, Aida Elsa, *La narrativa de Carlos Fuentes: Afán por la armonía en la multiplicidad antagónica del mundo* (Río Piedras, Puerto Rico, 1983).

Ramond, Michèle, *Psychotextes: La Question de l'Autre dans Federico García Lorca* (Toulouse, 1986).

Reading for Difference: Feminist Perspectives on Women Novelists of Contemporary Spain, special issue of *ALEC* 12. 1–2 (1987).

Rodríguez Monegal, Emir, *El viajero inmóvil: Introducción a Pablo Neruda* (Buenos Aires, 1966).

Sahuquillo, Angel, *Federico García Lorca y la cultura de la homosexualidad: Lorca, Dalí, Cernuda, Gil-Albert, Prados, y la voz silenciada del amor homosexual* (Stockholm, 1986).

Salomon, Noel, 'Algunos aspectos de lo "humano" en *Poemas humanos*', in *César Vallejo*, ed. Julio Ortega (Madrid, 1974), 289–334.

Sánchez Vidal, Agustín, *Buñuel, Lorca, Dalí: El enigma sin fin* (Barcelona, 1988).

Santa Cruz, Lucía (et al.), *Tres ensayos sobre la mujer chilena* (Santiago, 1978).

Santí, Enrico Mario, *Pablo Neruda: The Poetics of Prophesy* (Ithaca and London, 1982).

Scanlon, Geraldine M., *La polémica feminista en la España contemporánea (1868–1974)* (Madrid, 1986).

Sicard, A., 'Pensamiento y poesía en *Poemas humanos* de César Vallejo: La dialéctica como método poético', *Socialismo y participación*, 19 (1982), 97–103.

Smith, Paul, 'Juan Valera and the Illegitimacy Motif', *Hispania*, 51 (1968), 804–11.

Smith, Paul Julian, '*Descriptio pueri*: Praise of the Young Hero in Some Poets of Renaissance Spain and Italy', *SS* 24 (1983), 57–66.

—— *Writing in the Margin: Spanish Literature of the Golden Age* (Oxford, 1988).

Sobejano, Gonzalo, 'Poesía del cuerpo en *Poemas humanos*', in *Aproximaciones a César Vallejo*, ii (New York, 1971), 181–90.

Tierno Galván, Enrique, 'Don Juan Valera o el buen sentido', in *Idealismo y pragmatismo en el siglo xix español* (Madrid, 1977), 95–129.

Urey, Diane, *Galdós and the Irony of Language* (Cambridge, 1982).

—— 'Isabel II and Historical Truth in the Fourth Series of Galdós's *Episodios Nacionales*', *MLN* 98 (1983), 189–207.

Valenzuela, Luisa, 'The Other Side of the Phallus', in *Reinventing the Americas* (Cambridge, 1987), 242–8.

Valera, Juan, *Juanita la Larga*, ed. Enrique Rubio (Madrid, 1986).

Vallejo, César, *The Complete Posthumous Poetry*, trans. Clayton Eshleman and José Rubia Barcia (Berkeley, 1978).

—— *Poemas humanos*, ed. Francisco Martínez García (Madrid, 1987).

Vilanova, Antonio, 'El peregrino de amor en las *Soledades* de Góngora', in *Estudios dedicados a Menéndez Pidal*, iii (Madrid, 1952), 421–60.

—— *Las fuentes y los temas del 'Polifemo' de Góngora* (Madrid, 1957).

Virgillo, Carmelo, and Linstrom, Naomi (eds.), *Woman as Myth and Metaphor in Latin American Literature* (Columbia, Missouri, 1985).

von Buelow, Christiane, 'The Allegorical Gaze of César Vallejo', *MLN* 100 (1985), 298–329.

—— 'Vallejo's Venus de Milo and the Ruins of Language', forthcoming in *PMLA*.

Woods, M. J., *The Poet and the Natural World in the Age of Góngora* (Oxford, 1978).

Zayas, María de, *Novelas amorosas y ejemplares*, ed. Agustín G. de Amezúa (Madrid, 1948).

—— *A Shameful Revenge and Other Stories*, trans. John Sturrock (London, 1963).

—— *Novelas completas*, ed. María Martínez del Portal (Barcelona, 1973).

INDEX

BIND COVER IN

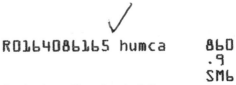